THE
VOYAGEURS

JOSHUA KLOKE

THE
VOYAGEURS

THE CANADIAN MEN'S SOCCER TEAM'S
QUEST TO REACH THE WORLD CUP

DUNDURN
PRESS

Publisher and acquiring editor: Kwame Scott Fraser | Editor: Russell Smith
Cover and interior designer: Laura Boyle
Cover image: Benjamin Steiner
Interior images: Canada Soccer, insert pages i, iii, iv (bottom), v, vi, vii; Canada Soccer/Tony Quinn, insert pages ii, iv (top); Kaj Larsen, insert pages viii, ix, x, xi, xii, xiii, xiv, xv, xvi
Lyrics from "Draw Us Lines" ©The Constantines. Used with permission.

Library and Archives Canada Cataloguing in Publication

Title: The voyageurs : the Canadian Men's Soccer Team's quest to reach the World Cup / Joshua Kloke.
Names: Kloke, Joshua, 1983- author.
Identifiers: Canadiana (print) 20220272530 | Canadiana (ebook) 20220272751 | ISBN 9781459750456 (softcover) | ISBN 9781459750463 (PDF) | ISBN 9781459750470 (EPUB)
Subjects: LCSH: Canada Men's National Soccer Team—Interviews. | LCSH: Canada Men's National Soccer Team—History. | LCSH: World Cup (Soccer)
Classification: LCC GV943.6.C36 K56 2022 | DDC 796.334/6680971—dc23

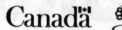

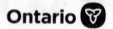

We acknowledge the support of the Canada Council for the Arts and the Ontario Arts Council for our publishing program. We also acknowledge the financial support of the Government of Ontario, through the Ontario Book Publishing Tax Credit and Ontario Creates, and the Government of Canada.

Printed and bound in Canada.

Dundurn Press
1382 Queen Street East
Toronto, Ontario, Canada M4L 1C9
dundurn.com, @dundurnpress 𝕐 f ⊙

For Bastian, who is learning to love the game

Let the hand move its people
And draw us lines from our fiery designs
Unknown unknowns
Let all our gardens grow
And overtake our history
Seeking strength in mystery

Bad weather
Anxiety and fear
Don't give in
Call on her
And live in fascination
Fascination forever

— The Constantines, "Draw Us Lines"

Contents

Author's Note

MY PUBLISHER, FRIENDS, AND COLLEAGUES OFTEN ASKED ME WHAT role the growth of the women's game in Canada, and the women's national team, would have in this book. It's a valid question, and one I struggled with, especially as Bev Priestman's team accomplished one of their final steps in a decade-long rebirth with an Olympic gold medal in the summer of 2021.

Like the other 4.4 million people who watched it in Canada, I was engrossed in the final. That was the highest viewership in the country for any soccer game, female or male, since the 2014 World Cup final.

After I stopped leaping back and forth from my couch to my floor with every final penalty kick, my family peppered me with questions about the team itself, not all of which I could answer.

In the days afterward, I turned to the work of some of the reporters who have continually worked to get the women's national team into the public eye. I shared the stories of this team with my family, and they in turn began reading more about the program and the growth of the women's game.

It's those tremendous reporters who have covered the women's game in Canada far more extensively than I have and have contributed to the growth of the game itself that should be writing a book about the women's team. One of those reporters could do a far more thorough and interesting job than I could.

That this book focuses on the men's national team is not to suggest that the men's national team is more deserving of a book about them than the women's national team is. A book that tried to focus on both programs would be a disservice to the many people, and their stories, who propelled the women's program. Because any talk, say, of Alphonso Davies or Atiba Hutchinson being the best players in Canadian soccer history would be to overlook Christine Sinclair's historic achievements. No player, male or female, has scored more goals for their country than Sinclair has scored for Canada. No soccer player has inspired the country in the way Sinclair has. She was rightly awarded the Lou Marsh Trophy as Canada's top athlete in 2012, the first soccer player to achieve that honour.

Sinclair's achievements are only the tip of the proverbial iceberg, however.

While the Canadian men's national team lay languid for a generation, the women's national team rose to prominence, and did so with fewer resources than the men's team: a silver medal at the 2002 Under-19 world championship, which Canada hosted; a fourth-place finish at the 2003 World Cup; Olympic bronze medals in 2012 and 2016; a quarterfinal finish at the 2015 World Cup, which Canada again hosted and which set a record for highest total attendance in the process.

For an entire generation, soccer success in Canada was properly synonymous with the women's team and not the men's team.

And so, the women's national team and the program itself are deserving of multiple books that analyze and celebrate that success. Combining the growth of the two programs into one book would mean important insight about the women's national team would be lost.

I look forward to reading a book filled with those aforementioned people's stories, and subsequent books about their impact afterward.

The Voyageurs is not an official biography of Canada's men's national soccer team or Canada Soccer. A portion of the royalties from this book will be donated to Grassroots Soccer Hamilton.

Prologue

THE CLOCK HAD NEARLY STRUCK MIDNIGHT WHEN A RELATIVELY short man sat deep inside an empty stadium and made a plea with his towering dreams.

The words came out slowly. The man was exhausted, having led a team through four games in eleven days across North and Central America, sure. But it was also a deliberate effort to ensure his message landed.

"Let your guards down and come with us," said the Canadian men's national team head coach John Herdman, in the distinct Geordie accent that Canadian soccer diehards had come to know and love. "Because this is a special group of people. And that's all I'm going to ask: stick with us now, and we'll get there."

For more than a generation, the men's national team getting "there" — a World Cup — seemed impossible. They remained something between an embarrassment and an afterthought in the country's mainstream consciousness.

But after the team secured their place in the final round of World Cup qualifying for the first time since 1997, Herdman pleaded for more than the diehards to pay attention.

The young and immensely likeable men's national team was the outcome of a generation of growth of the game in Canada. Herdman wasn't alone in his desire to change the narrative and have Canadians see the men's team in a more promising light.

Soccer had enjoyed a wave of popularity at the turn of the century, with participation numbers among Canadian children dwarfing those of every other team sport. Still, soccer was generally thought of in one of three ways.

First, it was usually cast in covert jingoism as a sport played only by people *not* from Canada. There was little doubting the stranglehold the sport had throughout the rest of the world, but, as Canadian soccer journalist John Molinaro often heard, soccer was "that game that they play over there."

Second, as I heard repeatedly growing up playing soccer in suburban Canada, the sport's participation numbers were driven by parents who only wanted a summer activity to keep their hockey-playing children in shape. Hockey's fervent following in Canada meant many Canadians believed no sport could ever ascend to its throne. Soccer might have been enjoyable enough for children, but it was still just a placeholder.

Finally, and perhaps most detrimentally, even if a young Canadian soccer player evolved beyond his or her peers, for many years there hadn't been a wealth of domestic professional opportunities compared to those available in other sports. So, what was the point in continued emotional investment in soccer, if a financial return on that investment would never come?

Yet, every four years, soccer did indeed enjoy widespread emotional investment throughout Canada, much as it did around the world, as the World Cup caused day-to-day life to slow to a crawl.

After Canada's lone appearance at the men's World Cup in 1986, the Canadian men's national team languished on the outside looking in at the world's most hallowed and most popular sporting event.

But by 2022, Canada's transformation as a men's soccer nation saw them ascend to the same stage as the North American soccer powerhouses, the United States and Mexico, and become a prominent part of Canadian sports culture.

When the men's team's goal of qualifying for the 2022 World Cup was realized, the most pressing question became *How did this finally happen?*

I hope this book answers that question. What you're about to read is not a history of soccer in Canada. Tracking a game that has been played in the country nearly from the day it celebrated independence from Great Britain would require multiple historical volumes. This book begins with the Canadian men's national team's first World Cup appearance in 1986 and then simultaneously unpacks the futility they experienced at subsequent World Cup qualifying campaigns and the steps taken by people to help propel the team back to the World Cup and the sport into an unforeseen place.

I've read Raphael Honigstein's book about the rebirth of German soccer, *Das Reboot*, far too many times. *The Voyageurs* is inspired by Honigstein's work, so the stories of the people who dragged the men's national team to the place they found themselves in 2022 are just as important as the events themselves. Interspersed in the thirty-six-year story of the men's team's overhaul between World Cups are profiles of some of the most important figures in Canadian men's soccer and their roles in the program's rebirth.

The story of John Herdman, internationally recognized superstar Alphonso Davies, and the men's national team is far from over. But the story of their success would not exist without the people who paved the way for a long-overlooked team to finally capture the attention both of a country, and, improbably, of the soccer world.

CHAPTER 1

The Rock, the Rooster, and Respectability: Canada's Run to the 1986 World Cup

PAUL DOLAN, STANDING SHOULDER TO SHOULDER WITH THE reigning European champions in a narrow tunnel, wipes a bead of sweat from his brow as he waits to take the pitch at Estadio León deep in central Mexico.

The sweltering midday heat and the raucous crowd are considerably unlike what the lanky twenty-year-old goalkeeper is used to, since he has spent the majority of his professional career playing for a few hundred people here and there with the Edmonton Brick Men, a franchise named after their sponsor, Canadian furniture warehouse store The Brick.

Standing beside France's men's national soccer team moments before starting in goal for Canada's first-ever World Cup match, Dolan is nonplussed.

He peeks behind him to see Bob Lenarduzzi, the more worldly but still wide-eyed Canadian defender, fawning over the players in dark blue jerseys next to him: Michel Platini, the attacking midfielder fresh off winning three straight Ballon d'Or trophies as the best soccer player on the planet. He stands near Jean-Pierre Papin, emerging as one of France's most potent goal scorers. And Papin stands near Dominique Rocheteau, the dynamic winger dominating with Paris Saint-Germain, the reigning French champions.

Outside the tunnel, Canadian forward Dale Mitchell, not named to the starting lineup, is waiting to see his teammates, their white jerseys uncharacteristically emblazoned with the country they call home, emerge.

Oddsmakers confidently placed Canada toward the bottom of the pile of the twenty-four teams likely to win the tournament. Yet as Mitchell's teammates walk out into the sun, he is overcome by emotion.

"That's the moment when you realize it: you're playing in a World Cup, against one of the best teams in the world," said Mitchell. "That moment is more significant than any other."

But Dolan can only shrug and wipe away the sweat that had fallen to his small moustache. Though he, the goalkeeper for the Brick Men, a team many skilled French *pâtissiers* might have been able to play for, is about to take part in the first game in Group C at the 1986 World Cup, he is not succumbing to the moment.

"I didn't feel overhyped," said Dolan, looking back, "because we were such huge underdogs."

If there were ever a sentiment to describe the Canadian men's national team, both up to that point in the program and in the subsequent decades, Dolan has crystallized it. Though this Canadian team had ascended to the highest peak of international soccer, they had done so without the most well-thought-out map.

"We knew we weren't as talented as any of the teams in our group," said Canadian midfielder Mike Sweeney, whose red, curly mop often matched the colour of his national team jersey.

They were a collection of players and coaches who had caught a few breaks and made the most of the opportunities they did have, sure. When considering the growth cycle of the sport in Canada, they were far from a finished product. Despite the fact that they were playing alongside the world's best, soccer remained a fringe sport in their home country.

And it was the lack of a road map that would, in no small part, plague the men's national team for a generation afterward as multiple teams tried, and failed, to reach that same peak. But in reaching the height of international soccer in 1986, those players and coaches blazed a trail for future generations to follow, piece by piece, one mistake and one small victory at a time.

. . .

Before Dolan and his bearded teammates arrived in Estadio León, they had to do what no Canadian side had done before, and what no Canadian side did in the subsequent eight World Cup cycles: actually qualify for the World Cup.

The Confederation of North, Central America, and Caribbean Association Football (Concacaf) was the FIFA governing body that the Canada Soccer Association (CSA) fell under. Mexico, traditional heavy-weights of Concacaf, gained an automatic berth in the 1986 tournament as hosts. The remaining eighteen teams in the region began their journey to the World Cup through the 1985 Concacaf championship, a qualification process that took over a year to unfold. Canada advanced to the final round of the tournament with Costa Rica and Honduras, with the top team to book their ticket to Mexico after each team had played both home and away matches against each of the others.

By playing no-nonsense, kick-and-run soccer, Canada went undefeated in the first three games. Canada's last game in the round would determine its fate. Canada would qualify with either a win or a draw in the final game against Honduras.

Canada's failure to qualify for the 1982 World Cup still lingered. The entire final round of qualification for that tournament had taken place in Honduras, who qualified. Had Canada been able to earn just one more point from the five games they did play, they would have qualified themselves.

With the 1985 match scheduled for mid-September, Canada's head coach Tony Waiters wanted to give his team every advantage possible. His idea of gamesmanship meant hoping some harsh winds, low temperatures, and unfamiliar surroundings would throw the Honduras national team off their game, while making the Canadians feel at home. So, Waiters de-manded that the game be played off the beaten track. The knowledge that qualifying for the World Cup would land the CSA roughly one million in television revenue sharing from FIFA was a factor in his taking extreme measures to qualify.

The CSA agreed in principle but couldn't have imagined just how far Waiters had in mind: the literal edge of the continent, at King George V Park in St. John's, Newfoundland, just a short drive from Cape Spear's historic lighthouse and the easternmost point of North America. Staging the game there would not come cheap, and CSA would be on the hook for it if their team didn't qualify, which only added to the sense of desperation.

There wasn't much dialogue during negotiations for the Honduras match. Waiters, a well-spoken and commanding figure, was adamant. Having played and coached extensively in England, as well as being one of the faces of a surprise North American Soccer League (NASL) Soccer Bowl championship with the Vancouver Whitecaps in 1979, his voice carried weight. His sometimes brash personality did as well.

When the Canadians arrived a full week ahead of the match, however, they found a set-up that didn't exactly remind them of Old Trafford.

"They literally had to put the bleachers up around it [the field] because it [the facility] wasn't really the size of a stadium," said Lenarduzzi. "And if you're worried about crowd access, you would have to be real worried about that one because literally the people that were sitting in the front row could walk onto the field without any real disturbance."

The pitch itself featured large, random squares and triangles of differently coloured grass.

"It wasn't lush green grass," laughs Lenarduzzi.

After a few days, the Canadian side came to adopt the unusual surroundings as their own. As they walked the streets of St. John's in their downtime, locals bombarded the outsiders.

"People would recognize us, and they'd say, 'Oh, you're going to qualify on The Rock!'" said Lenarduzzi. "It was unlike what we would have had in any other city. I think there would have been interest and we probably would have put a good chunk of people in the stadium, but this was almost theirs. And you just got the feeling they were welcoming this opportunity to be a part of it."

The Hondurans were far less enthused, especially given that some of their travelling fans had mistaken St. John's for Saint John, New Brunswick, and had travelled there instead. And the players themselves were equally lacking in enthusiasm.

"I had to look at a map to see where this place was," Honduran midfielder Richardson Smith told the Athletic. "And we're arriving there, and we look down and we see entire patches of these fields covered with ice. They were clearing chunks of ice off the field. It was just shocking, honestly."

The local fans, however, treated the event with typical Newfoundland aplomb, cheering the Canadian side as they trained and waiting for them to sign autographs outside their hotel.

"They wanted us to know that they were behind us and that this would be a real treat for them and a real moment in their sporting history," said Canada midfielder David Norman, who flashed his toothy grin every time he stepped on one of the downtrodden pitches.

Those fans were able to step out of the yellow school buses many had taken to the game and find seats just a few metres away from Canadian forward George Pakos when he smashed home Canada's first goal of the game after a corner kick produced a scramble in front.

Pakos was an outsider on the team, but the trip to Newfoundland was an opportunity for Waiters to reinforce the point that every one of the players he chose deserved to go to a World Cup.

"Some of his selections, you would scratch your head a little bit," said Mitchell.

At thirty-three, Pakos would be the second-oldest player on the eventual World Cup roster, a mostly amateur player who made his living as a water meter reader in Victoria. He had landed on Waiters's radar in the lead-up to the 1984 summer Olympics, before it was announced professionals would be allowed to compete in the tournament.

"[Waiters] saw something in the guy," said Mitchell. "He went in a different direction. He knew what he wanted and that's what he made his selections on."

None of that mattered in the aftermath of the goal, of course.

Minutes after Pakos scored, the commentators were hyping up the broadcast that would come after the soccer game: the national ten-pin bowling championships, to determine who would take part in the 1985 World Cup of Bowling.

After Honduras levelled, Canada relied on a set piece, as they so often would, to score the most important goal in the country's soccer history. Striker Igor Vrablic quickly redirected a corner kick past the Honduran goalkeeper, who bore the brunt of the complaining from teammates in the aftermath.

Waiters's gamble was paying off.

"This is years of preparation, coming to a climax here in St. John's, Newfoundland," said CBC play-by-play announcer Steve Armitage on the broadcast, as the final minutes ticked away, and the home crowd began whistling on their own.

With the referee's whistle securing the 2–1 win for Canada, Waiters ran straight to his team gathering in the centre of the pitch.

The school buses in the parking lot beyond the few thousand fans in attendance were even easier to see once most of those fans stormed the pitch after the final whistle. Those same fans stayed huddled closely around the players as Vrablic was awarded player of the game.

Chants of "Igor, Igor, Igor," only reinforced the feeling that this game was more akin to a high school football game than a continental championship.

CBC colour commentator Graham Leggat read out the names of the entire squad, most of whom would be on their way to Mexico, in succession.

"Heroes," said Leggat, "each and every one of them."

• • •

The more Tony Waiters scratched his thick moustache and pored over the players available to him for the World Cup, the closer he inched to a realization on how his team had to play. Given how much time their more talented group-stage opponents, France, Hungary, and the Soviet Union, would spend in possession of the ball, this Canadian team wasn't going to play sexy football.

So, they had best be able to run the opposition into the ground.

The high altitudes in Mexico would present a challenge. Waiters took his team to Whistler to train before even lengthier stays near mountain peaks in Colorado.

Waiters had to prepare the team for longer runs, given that nearly half the team made their livings solely as indoor soccer players.

After lasting nearly two decades and welcoming some of the game's most prodigious talents for victory laps in North America, including Pelé, Franz Beckenbauer, and Johan Cruyff, the North American Soccer League had folded after the 1984 season, leaving many players to instead ply their trade indoors, with boards surrounding the pitch.

Even with some European opportunities, players like Sweeney had opted to play in the Major Indoor Soccer League, then at the height of its popularity, "because we were making more money."

As a result, those same players were more accustomed to short bursts of speed and a frantic pace of play.

"Playing indoor was crazy," said Sweeney.

And so, the emphasis of Canada's pre–World Cup preparations was on running hills, and running them often. Team runs were not seen as a lackadaisical warm-up for players to have a chinwag. Multiple times a day, Waiters would bark at his players to maintain their stamina through trying runs through rocky landscapes.

So much so that Paul Dolan and fellow goalkeeper Tino Lettieri would let the rest of the team run ahead up the hill before deking behind a tree, waiting for the team to make their way back down, and rejoining them toward the bottom of the hill.

"Tough sledding," said Dolan.

Between runs, Waiters's message to his team was consistent: on the pitch, they should not pretend to be something they were not. One of Waiters's innate strengths as a coach was his understanding of his group, not trying to force his square-peg players into round holes.

Waiters implored his team to lean into their Canadianness to help form their identity in Mexico.

"Canadians are famously boring," said Sweeney. "Put your nose to the grindstone. Work hard."

Becoming a no-nonsense team of worker bees was an idea nearly the entire team got on board with, even if they also knew it limited their chances of outscoring their opponents.

By the time they left Colorado, the anxiety about having to play in Mexico had dissipated.

"[Waiters] made us believe we were physically prepared to play," said Mitchell.

The Canadian team arrived in their base, a leafy, isolated hotel outside of the quiet city of Irapuato, for daily training and video sessions. With Canada's games being scheduled at Estadio Sergio León Chávez in Irapuato and the nearby Estadio Nou Camp, two of the smaller host stadiums in the

World Cup, the Canadian team experience was considerably more sedate than that of many of their counterparts. Waiters had made multiple trips ahead of the World Cup to scout the area for a resort with a field that could be converted into a world-class training pitch.

"No outside influence," said Dolan. "Our gathering spot. Our bubble."

Waiters's accent, softened some after many years spent away from his home county of Merseyside, England, became the commanding voice throughout the camp. He continued to focus in on their strategy in meetings and in training sessions: play compact defensively and sit deeper in their own half when the opposition has the ball, man-mark players in the middle of the pitch, press the opposition with their improved fitness in the opposition half, and if and when Canada might get the ball, send long balls through the channels to one of Canada's lonely forwards at the top of their 4-4-2 formation.

"We had the fitness and the desire to make all that work," said Sweeney.

It wasn't as if Canada didn't have scorers. Mitchell, Carl Valentine, and Branko Segota found the back of the net regularly with their club teams. On a pristine-looking bright green training pitch that made King George V Park feel very distant, Waiters had to put up with his fair share of moaning from some of his forwards about the amount of pressing and defensive work they'd have to do in-game.

But Waiters was insistent: Canada would play to their strengths as a defence-first outfit.

"Everyone bought in, and we had to, because we knew that was part of the DNA. If we had passengers, that wouldn't help the other ten players," said Mitchell.

What mattered to Waiters when determining who would actually line up for Canada in World Cup games, perhaps more than anything, was what players showed of themselves in training.

The split between players based in western Canada, largely British Columbia, and the east of Canada, including Ontario, was nearly equal. To keep travel costs low, Waiters had agreed to hold separate training camps for the two groups whenever possible. In sessions leading up the tournament, Waiters saw an opportunity to ramp up the intensity and would pit players and staff from the west of Canada against those from eastern provinces in training matches.

"Those five-a-side matches were like war," said midfielder David Norman. "It was Tony's way of getting you to play the way you train. And you were not losing those games."

In one game, a staff member from Ontario knocked the ball out of bounds. Despite calls from players, including Dolan, for the play to be whistled dead, he continued to play the ball toward the goal, and put a goal past Dolan.

"I was furious," said Dolan.

Later in the game, with the memory still vivid, the staff member again came in toward goal. This time, Dolan landed a heavy, two-footed tackle on him that in any organized game would have quickly seen Dolan sent off.

"Ass over teakettle," Dolan said of the staff member. It was his goal to put this member of his own team who'd previously embarrassed him "in crutches."

"Guy are playing for places in the starting eleven, and Tony wasn't a guy who stuck to the big names. He stuck to the guys that he thought could execute his game plan," said Dolan.

Which is perhaps why Dolan, to the surprise of many, was named the starting goalkeeper for the first game against France. Dolan had only a handful of professional games at that point, compared to the far more experienced Lettieri.

"Just keep doing what you've been doing, big man," Waiters said to Dolan, after training ahead of the first match.

In the final meeting before the game against France, Waiters wanted to instill that same sense of confidence in the rest of the team.

When he would pause video of France's games to pick apart their tendencies, Waiters would intentionally butcher some of the names of France's more popular players. He wanted some of his younger players to believe that the European champions were just another team and not be intimidated, not unlike the experience many might have had lining up against unfamiliar faces in indoor soccer games.

It worked on some players, even if the more experienced players such as Mitchell had to cover their mouths in laughter at their coach's obvious ploy.

"He had that belief in himself, and he definitely had an effect," said Mitchell.

The Canadian contingent boarded their bus for the ninety-minute drive along a dusty road from their home base into León. Pregame chatter was lacking as players stared out the windows into the middle of Mexico.

"Just thinking about your fate ahead," said Dolan.

As the bus pulled closer to the stadium, groups of local fans tried to bring the fate of the Canadians into focus by holding up their fingers to signify how many goals they thought would be scored in the game.

"They had two hands up: ten, and then zero," said Lenarduzzi. "They were mocking us. You're the bull and you're going to the bullfight."

Still, whatever the local fans tried to do to dampen the spirits of the Canadians had little effect when they finally found themselves in the tunnel.

Sweeney peered at his counterpart, French midfielder Alain Giresse. Giresse had been named French footballer of the year twice and was part of France's "*carré magique*," a narrow midfield foursome that dominated international soccer at the time. But Sweeney's only thoughts were confident ones.

"A tiny little guy," he remembers thinking of the five-foot-four Giresse. "Which obviously made me feel pretty good."

The Canadian spirits were further boosted when they got a reminder of home. Three years earlier, Giresse's teammate, Michel Platini, and famed Italian side Juventus had played a friendly against NASL side the Toronto Blizzard in Toronto's Exhibition Stadium. The over forty-one thousand fans had constituted, at the time, the largest crowd to ever watch a soccer match in Canada.

But, in front of those thousands of fans, Canadian captain Bruce Wilson's bearded face had burned a place in Platini's brain. Platini turned to Wilson and, moments before taking the pitch, smiled, and said, "Toronto Blizzard, right?"

And from the opening kickoff, Wilson and his teammates continued to let that confidence guide them.

France didn't come out with the vigour the Canadians were expecting. Sweeney watched the French team knock the ball around and believed the European champions were intimidated by the altitude.

"They didn't want to burn themselves out, and we weren't worried about it," said Sweeney.

Canada had their chances. Even with his jersey hanging long over his shorts, making him look as if he wasn't wearing shorts at all, Wilson sent a typical long ball in the air. It eventually drew French goalkeeper Joël Bats far out of his goal. Bats misplayed the ball, allowing Igor Vrablic to corral it and put a shot on net, but multiple French defenders took Bats's place in goal. Sweeney then hit a free kick toward the goal. Ian Bridge leapt into the air to head the ball off the post.

"Well, that will cheer them up a bit," said Barry Davies on the broadcast, almost in jest, while Bridge sprinted back into his own half to fulfill his defensive duties.

Where the French ran, the Canadians put their heads down and ran with them. The Canadians continued to earn the vocal respect of the English broadcasters by sending crosses in from wide areas. At halftime, with the score 0–0, Canada's evident confidence seemed to be paying off.

"We weren't afraid of anybody," said scrappy midfielder Gerry Gray. "We didn't give a shit who they were."

Even when Canada had a corner kick against them, Dolan found himself shouting to his nearby teammates: "Let's not let this ball drop. This is too much fun."

The French fans behind the Canada goal got in on the fun in the second half during a goal kick when they threw a live rooster onto the pitch, landing it a few feet from Dolan. (The French Football Federation's logo was a rooster.)

His inexperience meant that sort of banter was lost on Dolan, who tried to keep a calm facade with his hands on his hips, before the linesman expertly corralled the rooster with his offside flag and dragged it off the pitch by the tail.

"Probably in my older years and in a club game, I would have had a laugh," said Dolan.

France eventually grew into the game, picking apart Canada with short, quick passes and forcing Dolan to make diving saves to keep his team's hopes alive. Papin himself missed the net or had his shots saved by Dolan repeatedly, so often that the commentators suggested he change his boots during the match.

With fifteen minutes remaining, optimism reigned for the Canadians.

"In your mind, you're believing you can get a draw and you're comfortably through in your first game," said Sweeney.

"The Gods are clearly on Canada's side," Davies said on the broadcast in the seventy-ninth minute, after Luis Fernandez's shot ricocheted off a goalpost to the right of Dolan.

Seconds later, Fernandez again had the ball near the touch line and sent a cross high into the air that Canadian players swear got caught in the Mexican altitude.

"More of a hidden hope ball that hangs longer," said Lenarduzzi.

As Dolan came off his line and swiped at the ball over his head without any luck, the ball landed on the feet of substitute French forward Yannick Stopyra, who had a few more inches of space between him and Lenarduzzi than he perhaps should have. Dolan shouted for the ball.

"So, I stopped, assuming that he had it and he didn't," said Lenarduzzi. "[Stopyra] got into the far post, did really well because he put the ball back across the line. And then Papin has a tap-in."

"A heartbreaker," said Sweeney.

The French players breathed a collective sigh of relief, knowing they would not have to answer for a draw against a soccer minnow playing its first ever World Cup game. And the Canadians had little choice but to feel lifted, not just about how they had played, but in their hopes, moving forward with the toughest test out of the way.

"We were right there," said Sweeney.

As the final seconds of the game wound down, David Norman quickly began shuffling out of his position. For two weeks, he had been devising a plan. Even though players were under strict instruction from their federations not to exchange jerseys with the opposition postgame, as can be custom, for fear of players being seen topless on the broadcast, if Norman was going to play against France, he was going to get a souvenir from Michel Platini, still one of the world's best.

At the referee's final whistle, he bypassed shaking hands with any nearby French player, sprinted toward Platini, looked one of the world's greatest midfielders in the eye, and mimicked the act of trading jerseys. Platini motioned to the tunnel to complete the swap there, even as multiple Canadian teammates quickly followed Norman to try to obtain Platini's jersey.

"The dream worked out," said Norman.

After the game, Dolan and Lenarduzzi were the two Canadian players pulled aside by FIFA for random drug testing. While Lenarduzzi completed his test quickly, the heat had left Dolan completely dehydrated and unable to produce a urine sample on command.

To expedite the process, officials offered Dolan a few local beers. An hour later, Dolan's teammates had boarded their bus and gone back to their resort when Dolan was finally able to produce an aided sample. He procured his own ride back to the resort and when he finally arrived, he found his teammates sitting poolside, buoyed by the surprise result and a few local beers of their own.

They implored the hero of the day to catch up, without knowing that Dolan himself had probably lapped them by a few *cervezas* by that point.

. . .

Canada's optimism remained ahead of their next game, against Hungary. Multiple Canadians had travelled to Estadio Sergio León Chávez the day after their loss to France and had smiled as the Soviet Union demolished the Hungarians 6–0.

"Hungary looked like they were running in sand," said Lenarduzzi.

The Canadians believed Hungary might very well have felt demoralized following the loss, which could benefit Canada in their hopes of finishing third in their group and, against the odds, moving on to the knockout round.

"We went from being fearful of getting hammered against a team with the stature of France to feeling like, 'You know what, we just have to turn up and we could win this game,'" said Lenarduzzi.

Waiters made just two changes to his lineup, opting for the more experienced Lettieri in goal and the more defensive-minded Gray in for Sweeney in the midfield. All along, Waiters did his best to downplay any enthusiasm, trying to remind his group that the Hungarians' heads would be full of continued flack from their local media.

Just two minutes after kickoff, the Canadians were quickly reminded of what can happen when you underestimate your opponent: while Canada tried to clear a Hungary cross, the ball was instead inadvertently knocked directly toward Lettieri, who had little chance of stopping Márton Esterházy's shot from just outside the six-yard box.

The early goal eventually allowed Canada to attack with a little more freedom than they were used to, highlighted by Valentine and Segota linking up for an admirable give-and-go inside the Hungary box, and Segota putting a powerful free kick on goal from distance.

Canadians watching at home were privy to Steve Armitage's call, which transformed the game for fans unfamiliar with soccer. Segota's free kick being a "blistering drive" was not unlike how Armitage might describe an Al MacInnis slapshot for the Calgary Flames.

With far more back-and-forth in the play, and more sustained pressure in the opposition half compared to the loss against France, fans watching on the CBC might have believed more in Canada's chances than expected.

But those chances diminished in the seventy-fifth minute when Canada was caught pressing forward and were left outmanned after Hungarian midfielder Lajos Détári played a ball over the Canadian defenders. Détári followed the play and eventually buried his own rebound.

As Détári ran around the pitch with his arms extended wide, the Canadians buried their heads, knowing that with France and the Soviet Union having drawn the day before, it would now take a minor miracle in the form of a lopsided win over the Soviet Union to extend their stay in Mexico.

Frustrations boiled over minutes later as Hungarian forward György Bognár tried to find space past Sweeney with a run. Sweeney, feeling out of options, gave Bognár's white jersey a tug. Already sitting on a yellow card, as Bognár toppled to the grass Sweeney knew referee Jamal Al Sharif would have to go back to his pocket for a red card.

"If we're Brazil, France, or Mexico, I don't get that red card," said Sweeney. "If it's Canada, it's easy to give a red card."

Though the mood had soured compared to days earlier, Lettieri tried to boost spirits after the loss by taking over cooking duties in the kitchen. In his post-playing days, he would open an Italian restaurant in Minnesota.

Canadians like Bridge still tried to appreciate how far they'd come as a group in the downtime after training, whether it be playing cards or throwing up a few lawn chairs in the shade by the team's hot tub and indulging in more of those local beers.

"Those are the things that are like postcards in my mind," Bridge told Sportsnet in 2014.

Bridge and his teammates' conclusion at the World Cup was anything but a postcard, though. All but eliminated from contention for the knockout stage, with little but pride at stake, their hopes of getting a result hinged on their ability to run the Soviet Union into the ground.

Yet after three hours of that kind of effort in continued altitude and heat, the Canadians ran out of steam and met their match in a squad who needed a win to ensure their World Cup would continue.

In the fifth minute, Lettieri had to make a save off his goal line, and the Soviet Union didn't let up.

"They were machines. I thought we were fit," said Gray, "but they looked like they could run all day, and I'm breathing out of my ass."

Canada's worst showing of their three games in Mexico nearly turned around in the forty-fourth minute, when a corner kick fell to the feet of Lenarduzzi just outside the six-yard box with no defenders between him and the goal. Lenarduzzi panicked.

The result of the play embodied Canada's three-game run at the World Cup: without the skill that had been ingrained in their opponents through decades of experience, Canada's valiant, workmanlike approach ultimately came up far short.

Lenarduzzi barely connected with the ball, and his missed sitter was followed by two Soviet Union goals in the second half.

After the loss, legendary Soviet goalkeeper Rinat Dasayev added insult to injury when Dolan attempted to swap shirts with him. Dasayev flashed a cheeky grin, elbowed Dolan in the ribs, offered a quick "*Nyet*," and walked away.

Dasayev's ribbing, both literal and figurative, was warranted. Canada was one of two teams to board their flight home from Mexico without a point, and the only team not to score a goal. For all the Canadians' athleticism, the record books did not look kindly on their creativity, buildup, and attack, which after the World Cup Waiters called "frenzied."

In the history of the World Cup, only four teams have played three group stage games without scoring a goal.

The World Cup was becoming the most pivotal showcase for the sport's most creative and dynamic players, but those were attributes the Canadian national team clearly lacked, as did the sport's young players in Canada, and needed to develop.

No matter how much this team ran at the World Cup, they could not run from the truth about the quality of the Canadian player.

"Here, we weren't able to strike on our own terms," Waiters said after the World Cup. Without any idea of what lay ahead for the national team, Waiters added that he wanted Canadian teams in future World Cups to believe that they could produce "technique under pressure."

Without any goals, a true storybook ending eluded the Canadian side. They fulfilled their goal of earning respect among many who doubted their ability to even stay in games against far more sophisticated opponents. But it was still clear that, while they had indeed reached international soccer's summit with their first World Cup appearance, they could not escape how difficult it would be to return to that summit.

"Our ambition as players and as a team was to compete well," Bruce Wilson told Sportsnet in 2014, "to represent our country well."

Years later, the players remain proud of their effort. But the lingering questions about what an upset victory would have done are still there.

"We expected there to be growth in the game in Canada with us in the World Cup. If we had won a game ..." said Gray, as his voice trails off.

In the aftermath of the tournament, Waiters could feel proud.

"If we had been blown out by teams, as everyone was expecting we would, then we would be back to square one in soccer; we would be building from ashes," said Waiters.

He could take pride not only in his players, but in himself for how well his plans had come to fruition. He bet on a far corner of the country to provide the support the team needed to propel them. He bet on a number of players who had no business being at a World Cup delivering results. And he bet on his team to come together and play an industrious yet unspectacular style of soccer their fans two borders north of Mexico would understand and appreciate, a style he thought embodied millions of Canadians themselves.

"We gained respectability," Waiters said at the conclusion of Canada's run, "and have given ourselves something to build on."

CHAPTER 2

"He Had the Ability to Empower People": Tony Waiters Changed the Way Canadian Players Approached the Game

BOB LENARDUZZI WAS SITTING IN A SHABBY, CRAMPED DORM ROOM at Harvard University alongside three of his veteran Canadian national teammates at the 1984 summer Olympics when he heard a surprise knock at the door.

Lenarduzzi answered but didn't find anyone waiting on the other side. Instead, there sat four cases of Molson Canadian beer without a note of any kind. He and his teammates wondered aloud if they were being pranked. Or, with some of their most important games upcoming, were they being set up by their coaching staff to test their wills?

Each of Lenarduzzi, Dale Mitchell, Ian Bridge, and Bruce Wilson grabbed a case and stuffed as many of the stubby beer bottles into their fridge as possible. Maybe after their next game, they thought, they'd have a beer or two. Maybe.

Later that night at a team dinner, Tony Waiters pulled the four players in close to ask if they'd received a delivery.

"We did, but what are we supposed to do with that?" the veterans asked collectively.

"Look," said Waiters, towering over them and raising up his mammoth hands, "I trust you guys. You've all been around the game for long enough. You know when to have a beer or two and when not to. In fact, what I'd like you to do is invite some of the younger guys in for a beer."

Lenarduzzi, himself a future coach, smiled at his teammates, reminded once again of the value Waiters placed on togetherness within his squad.

If Waiters wanted to deliver a message from the side of the pitch, he had to ensure every member of the team was capable of sharing it on the pitch. The former goalkeeper wanted his team thinking and acting as a unit and believing that the sum was greater than the parts. That attitude had become his hallmark since taking over the team in 1982 and ended up having a far greater impact than his players originally anticipated.

"He had the ability to empower people," said Lenarduzzi.

Being appointed the Canadian head coach was Waiters's crowning achievement, not only because the team's two most notable triumphs to date occurred under his watch — a quarterfinal berth in the 1984 Olympics and a berth in the 1986 World Cup — but also because he instilled two things into the men's national team they were lacking: first, a hardened style of play that would remain entrenched within the team for a generation, and, perhaps more importantly, a sense of self-belief that had never existed previously.

"We definitely needed that at that point," said Mike Sweeney. "We were a young team. We didn't have the history of Brazil."

Though it would dip and waver at times, it was that final belief that would become overwhelmingly evident within the psyche of the national team in 1986 and, eventually, in their next World Cup berth in 2022.

Whether or not Waiters's players believed it at first, he wanted his team to compete as if they belonged in international soccer and not be content with just landing an invitation to the dance.

"You just planned each and every game," Sweeney remembers, "to be part of your new history."

. . .

Long-time Plymouth Argyle secretary Graham Little usually encountered some difficulty when he wanted to get in touch with Tony Waiters outside of working hours.

Even in the mid-1970s, when Waiters was serving as the manager of the English side, team business wouldn't necessarily be over when Waiters left the stadium for the day. But if Little called Waiters at his home and asked for him in his ever-patient tone, Waiters's wife Anne would almost always offer the same response: "He's out for a run."

That relentless dedication to fitness was how many in Plymouth came to remember Waiters during his five-year spell managing on the coast of the Celtic Sea from 1972 to 1977, one of the most pivotal stretches in the club's history: a man who didn't just demand plenty from his players but was able to back up those demands with a level of fitness unparalleled among managers in England at the time.

"In my twenty-six years [at Plymouth], there were twelve managers, and I would say he had the strongest character of the lot," said Little. "And he was a very, very fit man."

Waiters was offered the job, his first as manager, after the recommendation of a Plymouth Argyle player who had grown up near Blackpool, where Waiters enjoyed an eight-year career stopping shots. Waiters was capped five times for the English national team and began coaching with England's national youth team almost immediately after his retirement from playing.

Thinking like a player was always at the heart of his decisions. If his team couldn't outplay the opposition, Waiters pushed them to outwork them. Little would peer through thick trees on their training sessions in city parks and find it difficult to differentiate between the players and Waiters, who would eagerly take part in every drill to help players understand his demands, but also to inspire them with his own fitness.

"Every day," said Little.

Waiters's efforts saw Plymouth Argyle, then in the third division, go on a remarkable run to the 1974 League Cup semifinal, upsetting top division sides Burnley, Birmingham City, and Queens Park Rangers along the way, before getting promoted to the second division in 1975.

The club was without a proper training ground. Waiters himself sold the local council on the benefits of building one.

"No one expected that," said Little.

After Waiters fell out with Plymouth Argyle's directors, the Vancouver Whitecaps offered a short-term contract during the 1977 season. Waiters's family thought they were embarking on a brief working holiday and Tony would have some spare time to write books on coaching, nothing more. Yet, British Columbia being one of the more stunning parts of the world, and Waiters finding immediate success with the Whitecaps, he never left.

Waiters maintained his same methods of hardened training built on strong fitness and a rigid defensive approach, later saying that he believed he could have "turned out a team of Canadians without using any import players and been competitive."

After signing a three-year extension, Waiters was named NASL Coach of the Year in 1978 for helping turn the Whitecaps into a force in the league. He brought in notable imports, such as Alan Ball, Carl Valentine, and Trevor Whymark, all of whom were fresh off playing in England's first or second division. In the third year of that contract, he propelled the Whitecaps to one of the most notable seasons in Vancouver sports history with their win in the 1979 NASL Soccer Bowl. Fans clinging high up on street-light poles were among the thousands who gathered for the ensuing championship parade, one of the biggest public gatherings in Vancouver history.

Waiters's increased profile in Canada, combined with his international experience and educational approach to coaching, evidenced by his continued writing on the topic that eventually made its way into a number of books, made him a natural choice to take over the men's national team in 1982.

Immediately, Waiters began to demand more and more funding from the CSA. The organization was a largely amateur outfit, often beset by financial woes, but Waiters saw just enough talent in his players that he thought he could get them to a World Cup. He was relentless in his pursuit of more financial resources for increased training camps and better bonuses for players to help motivate them toward this new chapter in their careers.

His players were reassured by how patiently and thoughtfully he spoke to them, always looking them directly in the eye.

"[Waiters] was a player himself," said Canadian captain Bruce Wilson, "and looked after the players as best he could."

Thinking like a player is part of Waiters's legacy within the men's national team. It carried on well after he stepped down after the 1986 World Cup.

In those years soccer was not ingrained in the Canadian psyche the way it was in, well, more nations than the players could count. What business did Canada have competing against these other countries? Canada had qualified for only one of the previous four Olympic tournaments heading into 1984, and that was as hosts in 1976. Losses then to the Soviet Union and North Korea had made for a short and forgettable tournament. Canada had not even entered a team for qualification in any previous Olympic games, all the way back to 1908.

None of which mattered to Waiters.

"He just had a commanding personality," said Sweeney. Waiters repeatedly told players they'd only succeed if they believed in their own futures. "Many times, when you're in the middle of the war of a game and it's chaotic, he was never flustered."

That happened because he was more prepared than any men's team coach in the program's history to that point. To get the level of organization he required, Waiters presented tactical nuances via endless VHS tapes and data on the opposition in a way that took his players aback.

"Things that now, you just do, but in those days the vast majority of coaches didn't do," said Sweeney. "He just did not want to give up a goal."

After drawing against Iraq and losing against Yugoslavia in the opening round of the 1984 summer Olympics, Canada had one day off before facing Cameroon, who were ahead of them in the group standings. Waiters took that time to show video of specific tactical nuances the Cameroon team would display and provided instructions to each of his players on the tendencies of the opposition player he'd be marking.

What was common practice among the more advanced coaches in soccer's most prominent countries at the time was newfound and inspiring to the Canadians. By covering every element of the game in their preparation, Waiters's own belief that an upset would be possible percolated into his squad.

Canada ended up trouncing Cameroon 3–1 in their final group-stage game to gain a berth in the quarterfinals.

"He understood the Canadian mentality, the Canadian player, and got the best out of them," said midfielder Gerry Gray.

That Canadian side forced eventual silver medallists Brazil, undisputed heavyweights of the soccer world, with future World Cup winner and national team manager Dunga on their team, to penalties in those quarterfinals. It was undeniable evidence that the Canadians' attitude was changing.

As the team regrouped the day after their loss to Brazil, faces were not long, but instead held higher than they ever had been in the program. Nearly the entire group would stay together going into the 1986 World Cup. The confidence they'd gained as a unit was evident, so much of which could be attributed to Waiters himself.

"We used that as a springboard into the qualifying process for the World Cup," said Mitchell. "I think that that story is important to be told."

• • •

After the 1986 World Cup, Waiters believed that for the Canadian soccer ecosystem to grow, and for the momentum to continue, a domestic league was paramount.

"This is only a dead end for us if nothing comes from this World Cup in 1987. If we don't get a professional league in place, our chances of making Italy in 1990 are very slight," he said at the conclusion of Canada's 1986 World Cup run.

To Waiters, the handful of players who were potentially capable of progressing to the next stage of their careers had gotten enough exposure after the World Cup to ensure they could make the jump to Europe.

"But the majority [of Canadian professional soccer players] weren't ready," said Lenarduzzi. "[Waiters] just felt that we needed the base to build from."

Waiters would never have admitted to wanting to create any sort of legacy within the Canadian soccer community. At least, not openly.

But his ability to steer his players toward a decision, all while empowering those same players to believe the decision was theirs alone, was unparalleled in Canadian soccer at the time.

In the weeks leading up to the 1986 World Cup, Waiters pulled Lenarduzzi aside. At thirty-one, Lenarduzzi's career was winding down, but he still possessed the veteran savvy that made him a trusted player among his coaches.

"How do you feel about coaching?" Waiters asked Lenarduzzi.

At first, Lenarduzzi was stunned: he'd never thought much about it, nor did he want to believe that the curtains might be closing on his time as a player.

"Well," Waiters offered, "there's talk of a Canadian soccer league."

Lenarduzzi waved off his suggestion, instead choosing to focus on the World Cup itself.

But when he returned home, out of contract with the Tacoma Stars, he was reminded of the realities of being a Canadian soccer player.

"You get to a World Cup, great, but how do you feed your family when the options are minimal?" said Lenarduzzi.

Waiters was already putting together a group of people who could be involved in creating a Vancouver franchise for the nascent league. He believed in a Canadian league so much that he donated his bonus earned by qualifying for the 1986 World Cup to what would eventually become the Vancouver-based team in the Canadian Soccer League, the 86ers.

The inspiration that Waiters shared with Lenarduzzi was contagious and unavoidable. Waiters signed Lenarduzzi to be the player-coach of the 86ers.

"I need to see it through," Lenarduzzi remembers telling his doubtful wife, Deanne, "and if it doesn't work, then at least we gave it a go."

Knowing that Waiters had put his own money into the project was enough to help Lenarduzzi walk into countless beer-soaked bars throughout Vancouver to meet with pockets of soccer fans, buy them a pint, and try to convince them of the possibilities in this crowd-funded project.

Lenarduzzi and Waiters ended up recruiting eighty-four other people — along with themselves — to make up the eighty-six members of the West Coast Soccer Society who each invested five hundred dollars and became co-owners of the club.

The wallets always opened a little bit quicker when Waiters was the one making the pitch.

"He was a person that had an aura about him," said Mitchell.

His faith in Canadian players never wavered. In 2010, in the middle of some of the darkest times for the men's national team, he still championed them, thoughtfully telling OSA TV that "the Canadian youth soccer player is as good as anywhere in the world, quite frankly, if given the opportunity."

Waiters's November 2020 death brought an insistence that his legacy become far more wide-reaching than perhaps the humble Waiters ever would have wanted.

Paul Dolan was one of his players who remembered how he had changed their fortunes in a way few other Canadian coaches made the effort to do.

After the 1986 World Cup, Waiters acted as Dolan's agent and mentor, helping him get a training spell at Sheffield Wednesday in England.

"I didn't have a lot of games under my belt before that first World Cup qualifier at such a young age," said Dolan, "but he had faith in me."

For his belief in the future of Canadian players, he was remembered for changing what the men's national team were capable of.

"I don't think it's a stretch," Dolan told the *Vancouver Sun* after Waiters's death, "when people say he was the single biggest influence on Canadian soccer."

CHAPTER 3

Getting a New League, Getting Lost in a Spy Movie, and Getting Concacafed: 1987–1998

NICK DASOVIC WOULD EARN SIXTY-THREE CAPS FOR THE MEN'S NAtional team and play in some of the team's most pivotal matches through the 1990s, but throughout the start of the decade friends would always lead with the same question: "How's the construction work going?"

He would politely nod his head, tuck his shoulder-length hair behind his ear and share a detail or two about his work before sneaking in a vital piece of information: he was also playing professional soccer in Canada.

What Dasovic usually heard next was not unfamiliar to professional Canadian players: There's professional soccer in Canada?

Dasovic's friends, though, couldn't be blamed for the question. Throughout the 1980s and 1990s, across North America, professional soccer leagues provided little stability for the country's best players to ply their trade. It meant players like Dasovic literally had to ply other trades to supplement their income. And that took away from the hours they could spend training and improving.

Tony Waiters hoped players could avoid Dasovic's situation. With consistent playing time and coaching, he and other optimists believed that the raw but promising talent that existed throughout the country could be honed.

Yet hesitation in starting a Canadian-based full-time professional league was justified. In 1983, the Canadian Professional Soccer League had lasted just one summer before folding. The North American Soccer League (NASL) enjoyed wild success in the 1970s, with five Canadian cities being represented at different points, before flaming out in 1984, thanks, in part, to overspending on player salaries.

The Major Indoor Soccer League was at the height of its popularity at the time of the NASL's decline. Many top Canadians were playing in the American-based indoor league, with more goals and a more frantic pace than the outdoor game. Could a Canadian outdoor soccer league generate the same kind of interest?

Other short-lived leagues dotted the soccer landscape too, but none of that mattered to people like Waiters and founding Canadian Soccer League commissioner Dale Barnes. The league's founders spotted a problem that would continue to haunt Canadian players for more than a generation: the inherent difficulty in getting work visas that would allow them to play in U.S.-based leagues.

So, their ostensible goals ahead of the CSL's inaugural season in 1987 were noble enough: bring veteran Canadian players from the World Cup team home and provide a breeding ground for younger Canadian players in need of regular playing time.

"There were talented players littered throughout Canada," said Gerry Gray, "but they just needed experience."

The first season of the new Canadian Soccer League featured the Vancouver 86ers, the Calgary Kickers, the Edmonton Brick Men, the Winnipeg Fury, the Hamilton Steelers, the North York Rockets, the Toronto Blizzard, and the National Capital Pioneers in Ottawa.

Making good on the first goal was easy enough. In total, eighteen members of Canada's 1986 World Cup squad ended up logging time in the CSL. Finally, being able to, say, attend a barbecue with friends on short notice carried weight for some of those players. *If we aren't going to live a glamorous lifestyle anyway*, they asked themselves, *why not do our jobs with the comforts of home around us?*

In the late 1980s, Gray was earning most of his salary from playing in the MISL. The CSL wanted to avoid the lavish spending that became the NASL's downfall and instituted a tight salary cap for team wages. Gray was offered a place on Lenarduzzi's Vancouver 86ers, but turned his former teammate down, instead slogging his way through yearly contracts and summer jobs with Ontario-based teams.

"[My parents] got to see my kids, and I got to see them," Gray explained.

His experience certainly didn't line up with the league founders' grand aspirations. Even with a salary cap, experienced players knew how quickly travel bills would add up and were skeptical about how long the league could sustain itself financially. The league stretched as far as from England to Syria.

"Question: If God had wanted a Canadian Soccer League why did he make the country so big?" was how famed *Vancouver Sun* sports writer Archie McDonald opened his February 26, 1987, column after then CSL commissioner Dale Barnes had addressed the media for the first time ahead of the 1987 season. "Answer: Because he owns shares in an airline."

. . .

Few people embodied the general instability throughout Canadian professional soccer in the 1980s and 1990s better than the square-jawed and well-built goalkeeper Pat Onstad.

The Vancouver-born Onstad had become a player of repute at the University of British Columbia while pursuing degrees in both human kinetics and education.

His first professional season with the CSL's 86ers, in 1987, brought a salary of $4,500.

"Just a way to plug the gap until the university season," said Onstad.

After one season in his hometown, he'd log as many kilometres chasing the next paycheque as some VIA Rail conductors at the time, bouncing back and forth playing between Winnipeg and Toronto.

Onstad's experience suggested the league wasn't exactly a beacon of professionalism. Players would only train in the afternoons because coaches had full-time jobs. Tired players could only muster up so much effort after days working their own jobs. Onstad never had a specific goalkeeper coach. And then, there were the late nights.

"We'd go out too often," said Onstad. "But [these were] still the best players playing in Canada."

The short seasons meant Onstad was forced to find recreational men's teams to train with in the off-season.

"You had to figure things out yourself," said Onstad. "It was a mosaic, trying to figure out how you'd keep playing this game you loved."

That love was tested even after he started playing for the national team late in the 1980s and into the 1990s. He had a job interview at a Vancouver school the day after one of his seasons ended. A few days later, he was offered a full-time job with the career stability he'd long desired.

But his mind would drift back to the pitch in the middle of delivering lessons, and so when the Edmonton Drillers offered him a contract to play indoor soccer in the National Professional Soccer League (NPSL), he walked out of the classroom for good after just one year.

Two years later, Onstad was standing in a crowded bar with his team-mates, on a road trip with the A-League's Rochester Raging Rhinos, then in the middle of back-to-back championship seasons. There he first met his future wife Becky, who asked him, as people do in bars, what he did for a living.

By this point, Onstad had been a professional soccer player for eleven years.

"But when people asked me what I did, I never said I was a professional soccer player," said Onstad. Instead, he would opt to talk about his teaching.

Yet this time, standing beside Becky, the national team goalkeeper was in the middle of one of the best seasons of his life and felt strangely confident. His jaw relaxed with a smile as he told her he was a professional soccer player.

"No," said Becky, shaking her head, "what do you really do?"

Onstad reverted to his standard line about being a school teacher. Becky perked up. Athletic, intelligent, well-spoken, and with a stable career to boot? Onstad was a catch.

But as important as that conversation was to Onstad's future, it also reminded him of the dreary reality of that time in his life.

"Soccer was just a way to make a bit of money," he said.

• • •

There were promising early returns in the CSL, including sponsorship deals with brands such as Molson, and a broadcast deal with TSN (The Sports Network). With limited salaries, teams had little choice but to rely heavily on young, unproven Canadians along with the veterans who had returned to Canada.

"It was so crucial for my development," said Paul Peschisolido, a smallish forward who would end up earning fifty-three caps for the Canadian national team. Before finishing high school in Ajax, Ontario, Peschisolido began darting through back lines for the Toronto Blizzard as an eighteen-year-old and would earn rookie of the year honours.

"Where else are you going to get competitive football? Where you can progress?" asked Peschisolido, who would go on to play regularly in England's second division.

Yet just four years into the league's existence, cracks were threatening to bring the entire house crumbling down. With player salaries that would be more appropriate for semi-professional players and with training standards that varied throughout the league, the product wasn't strong enough to keep Canadians who had previously been exposed to the game in Europe continually interested. And the majority of ownership groups struggled to remain committed to funding the league as difficult-to-stomach bank statements continually arrived in the mail.

"The financial wherewithal just wasn't there," said Lenarduzzi, whose 86ers won four successive CSL championships from 1988 to 1991. "If you were reliant on sponsorship dollars, that was going to be tough. If you're reliant on gates, then that was going to be tough, because all you need is a bad run of performances and you're struggling to make the next payroll."

He recalls being on the right side of the ledger in the 86ers' first season by, in his estimation, "a thousand bucks," before losing tens of thousands of dollars the year afterward. Being funded by a non-profit group was not sustainable for a growing league.

And while the league expanded into Montreal in 1988, Victoria in 1989, and Kitchener and London in 1990, the league's first team to fold, the Calgary Kickers, did so after the 1989 season.

The team in London, notably, was funded for one season by the other owners in the league. In 1992, the *Vancouver Sun* reported that Richmond, B.C.-based contractor and eventual owner of the 86ers Milan Ilich was the only team owner to have paid his sixty-five-thousand-dollar annual league dues in full, which helped keep the London team alive for that season. He also paid the travel and accommodation costs for the Toronto Blizzard when they came to Vancouver for a game.

After the 1991 season, teams in Hamilton, Kitchener, and Nova Scotia folded. The league's founders had overestimated the interest in the sport that qualifying for the 1986 World Cup would bring. Travel costs were insurmountable, and strong early crowds of a few thousand in each city sharply dwindled to a few hundred for each game once the novelty had worn off.

Soccer was still an oddity in the mainstream Canadian sports consciousness.

At the end of the 1992 season, which featured just six teams, the 86ers, who had become one of the league's most reliable teams, jumped ship and joined the American Professional Soccer League. They believed there was more financial stability in the American league, despite that league having only five teams. Teams from Toronto and Montreal soon joined them.

After just six seasons, Tony Waiters's dream was dead, and the CSL became one of the many extinct leagues that had struggled to make a cultural impact but ended up dotting the North American soccer landscape.

• • •

Whatever luck the Canadian team might have had in qualifying for the 1986 World Cup ran out for the next one.

They received a bye to the second round of qualifying for the 1989 Concacaf Championship, along with the four other highest-ranked teams in the region. A home-and-away series against Guatemala meant that if they could beat Guatemala on aggregate, they'd be through to the Concacaf Championship, in which the top two teams in the five-team tournament would qualify for the 1990 World Cup.

They were handed other advantages, too: Mexico's national team was disqualified from the Concacaf Championship after the "Cachirules" scandal, which saw the Mexican Football Federation knowingly send at least four over-age players to the 1988 Concacaf U-20 tournament.

But that wouldn't even matter if Canada couldn't overcome the 1–0 loss in Guatemala City in their opening away leg.

Six days later, in Swangard Stadium in Burnaby, B.C., two first-half away goals put Guatemala in the driver's seat. Canada applied pressure only after it was far too late, scoring two goals in the final ten minutes for a 3–2 win, but, even with the 3–3 aggregate draw, goals scored on the road were the tiebreaker. Those two crucial away goals sent Guatemala through.

The quick and unceremonious end to Canada's 1990 World Cup hopes was in stark contrast to their almost fairy-tale run to the previous World Cup, leading to an alarmingly silent dressing room postgame.

Mike Sweeney sat with a beer, scratched his mess of red hair, and put a bow on his national team career.

"As far as the World Cup or Olympic competition, I think this is definitely the last time around because of the age and the amount of time it takes to play these tournaments," he told reporters.

Sweeney's placid frustration can be forgiven, given that what he remembers from that brief qualifying campaign was consistent questions from players about the pool of money for countries that do qualify for the World Cup: What percentage of that money would go to the players? And would every player earn the same amount, or would players who started more games earn more than the players who were used as substitutes?

They were the kind of questions that only serve as a distraction for a team trying to qualify for the most prominent sporting event on the planet.

But they were also the kind of questions that Sweeney had no trouble asking of the CSA himself: "Why would you guys get to this point, where we're two weeks away from a huge qualifying game," he remembers asking, "and you don't have this wrapped up?"

Sweeney, eventually named to the Canadian men's all-time Best XI as part of Canada Soccer's centennial celebrations in 2012, does understand the predicament the association was in at the time, with soccer not part of the mainstream sporting consciousness.

"They don't have a lot of money, they don't have a lot of resources," said Sweeney. "They were always, always in a tough spot."

• • •

In 2017, Michael Findlay, then assistant coach of the men's national team, said Canadians "probably have the most unattractive passports in football," a notion that had been built up over generations.

Take the case of Alex Bunbury, whose sixteen goals for Canada remain among the most in the program. His career suggests the short-lived CSL wasn't a total loss and that certain players just travel different paths to success.

After starting as a twenty-year-old with the Steelers, the soft-eyed Bunbury bet on himself and left the comforts of Hamilton, travelling east on the 401, in the hopes of heading even further east, and joining the Montreal Supra.

His gamble paid off when someone watching him in the stands of the Complexe sportif Claude-Robillard looked past the running track that circled the field and picked out his goal-scoring prowess. This vague figure claimed to be from France and sold Bunbury on his connections with Le Havre, one of the oldest clubs in France. He insisted Bunbury was talented enough to play in France.

"And I can arrange something for you," Bunbury was told.

It was if he'd stepped into a strange film that intertwined French soccer with international espionage. Yet the randomness of the event was unfortunately emblematic of how Canadian players moved abroad.

Despite making a decent impression at Le Havre, Bunbury's Canadian passport made attaining the proper paperwork difficult. But he did forge a connection with former English international Graham Rix, rounding out his career at Le Havre. Rix sold Bunbury on the idea that if his trial in France did not work out, Rix had a club for him.

Rix had connections with Liam Brady, a former teammate early in his managerial days at Celtic FC in Scotland. Bunbury drove to Glasgow but, six weeks into his trial, with the number of foreign spots limited and Canadian players still largely unproven, he was unable to attain a work permit. Short spells at Aston Villa and Wimbledon ended with the same result.

"A crazy, round-the-world adventure," said Bunbury, with his laugh undermining just how monumental a problem this was for Canadian players.

Despite making his debut for Canada as an eighteen-year-old in 1986, he wasn't called into the qualifying campaign for the 1990 World Cup. He played in ten sporadic friendlies before the 1994 World Cup qualifying campaign and, to his detriment as a centre-forward, did not find the back of the net once.

Whether or not Bunbury had proven he could score in international soccer, Bob Lenarduzzi, named national team head coach in 1992, eventually called Bunbury into the squad ahead of qualifiers for the 1994 World Cup as Canada's scoring threats from the 1986 World Cup looked past their prime.

The rest of the core of the squad was sound enough: Randy Samuel, Carl Valentine, and Dale Mitchell helped provide the veteran leadership, and Lenarduzzi had convinced Sweeney to rejoin the fold, as well. Lenarduzzi's goal was to empower players and add an injection of offensive talent, helped by Peschisolido and Bunbury.

Given the interest Bunbury had attracted in Europe, and what Bunbury had gained from those training stints, Lenarduzzi started him in all six of Canada's matches in the second round of World Cup qualifying, in a group with El Salvador, Jamaica, and Bermuda.

Lenarduzzi's decision looked like a poor one as Bunbury failed to get consistently meaningful touches on the ball in the penalty area. Instead, thirty-four-year-old Mitchell shouldered the load, scoring in a 1–1 opening-day away draw against Jamaica and again in a 1–0 home win against the same team.

After four of six matches, Canada sat level with Jamaica for second place. They needed to gain crucial points against Bermuda. That's when Bunbury announced himself as a national team player. He netted a hat trick in the space of the opening thirty-five minutes to seal a 4–2 win in Burnaby. A road draw in Bermuda then sent Canada to the final round of home-and-away matches with El Salvador, Honduras, and Mexico.

With Bunbury's hat trick having raised eyebrows, he again received a call out of the blue from someone who believed he could land Bunbury on an English side.

Bunbury rolled his eyes. He had heard this kind of sell job before. But, as in all spy movies, a plot twist was coming.

"I'm not going to tell you the club," Bunbury remembers being told by Jerome Anderson, who was beginning to make a name for himself as an agent. "You just need to fly here."

There was a ticket to London waiting for him at the Vancouver International Airport. With no club side to return to and his bags already packed, Bunbury's options were limited.

When Bunbury landed in London, Anderson told him they were heading straight to a training session to "do a John Wayne" and strongarm the still-unnamed club into giving him a contract.

The plan was simple. Bunbury, though too exhausted to string a sentence together, would make an immediate impression and then, so Anderson hoped, they would seal a contract within a matter of days.

As the pair circled around the city proper into east London, Anderson casually mentioned they were en route to West Ham United, one of the most prominent clubs in England.

After one day of training, Bunbury scored in an exhibition match, which gave Anderson the confidence to storm into the club's offices to demand that the club give the mysterious Canadian player a contract.

While Anderson was with the team officials, Bunbury rubbed his hands together anxiously as he waited in the car. The twenty-two-year-old thought of his wife and two children back in Canada.

"I've got good news and bad news," Anderson told Bunbury, when he returned a few hours later. "You've just signed a five-year contract with West Ham United."

Bunbury smiled a child-like smile.

"The bad news is, we have to wait for your work permit to be approved," said Anderson.

Bunbury felt the blood rush out of his face: he had seen this movie before. He returned to Canada for national team duty. But, eventually, he was told his work permit had actually arrived and he had to return to England for his physical. It was, he hoped, the start of a promising career in Europe.

Bunbury had logged time for West Ham's reserve side and was pushing for a role in the starting eleven when Canada's national team sent a letter to the club informing them of the upcoming games Bunbury was being called into the national team to play.

Bunbury was summoned into the offices of West Ham managers Billy Bonds and Harry Redknapp. They skipped the formalities: "Club or country?"

"I thought they were just testing me," said Bunbury.

He answered "country."

"Billy Bonds almost fell off of his chair when I said that," said Bunbury.

The two read the letter aloud with a healthy dose of expletives thrown in. They placed an ultimatum on the young forward: after West Ham had shown faith in him, he needed to choose between missing time from Premier League games to play for Canada or telling his national federation he was unavailable.

Bunbury had been born in Guyana, and his mind quickly filled with thoughts about the life he and his family enjoyed because the Canadian borders had been opened to him.

"I can't turn my back on my country," Bunbury remembers saying.

As he prepared to fly back to North America, he was told his decision would make it virtually impossible for him to land a spot on the West Ham first team.

But there was another opportunity in North America. The United States gained automatic qualification as hosts of the 1994 World Cup and would not play in the qualification tournament. One guaranteed spot was available to Concacaf teams, with the second-place team in final Concacaf qualification going on to play games against teams in other regions, with a World Cup berth still on the line.

Bunbury's maddening last few years fuelled him as he continued his international hot streak, scoring in the team's opening two matches in the final round. He'd formed a synergetic attack with John Catliff, who added three goals of his own through the first three matches. Midway through the first three matches, Canada was, improbably, at the top of the table.

Yet even as he was propelling Canada along offensively, his mind would wander back to England.

"One can only imagine what it could have been like had I stayed there," he said. Bunbury never played a Premier League game for West Ham.

Bunbury was freed of regret, however, not long afterward, when he was transferred to Portuguese first-division side Maritimo, where he would go on to become the team's all-time leading scorer after six years.

"I don't think any [other] North American player could say that they're the all-time leading scorer for a [European] first-division club," he said.

• • •

Concacafed: adjective (informal) or past-tense verb (informal).

In 2015, Sportsnet senior editor Jamie Doyle admitted, in a story, that many casual Canadian soccer fans might not be fully aware what *Concacaf* means.

"As a noun, it's the clumsy acronym for the Confederation of North and Central American and Caribbean Association Football, the regional FIFA affiliate in which Canada is a member. As a verb, though, it means something else entirely," wrote Doyle.

Doyle was describing Mexico's "scandalous" 2015 Gold Cup win over Panama. The Gold Cup had evolved from the Concacaf Championship into a mostly biennial meeting of the region's top teams and other invitees.

Panama, down to ten men after a questionable red card, were outplaying Mexico. But they became the victim of another highly questionable call in which a penalty was immediately awarded after a Panama defender fell on the ball in the box but did not inhibit any Mexican players from playing that ball.

Mexico would go on to win in extra time, giving every Panamanian player on the pitch the right to tell the kind of story that hundreds of others across the region could nod along to.

"Essentially to be CONCACAFed is to be screwed — hugely, obviously and inevitably — generally by shocking refereeing that tilts a key match in the favour of a bigger team, more often than not Mexico," wrote Doyle.

Twenty-two years before this article was written, Canada were lifted in confidence by their results in the first three World Cup qualifying match-days and quietly liked their chances as they prepared to play Mexico in one of the sport's cathedrals, Estadio Azteca.

They were quickly awoken from their fever dream on that fourth match-day by the sound of over a hundred thousand Mexican fans, seemingly standing on top of each other, row after row, growing louder and more vociferous with every one of Mexico's four goals in a rout of the Canadians.

Even if Canada could handle their Central American counterparts, it was clear that their road to the World Cup in the United States would go through Mexico.

A crucial win in El Salvador had set up that final matchday against Mexico, who had eight points to Canada's seven. The winner would go through to the World Cup.

Canada was under no illusions about how they would have to play to pull off an upset.

"In talking to Mexican players years later, they hated playing us," said Dasovic. "We'd fight tooth and nail, and we wouldn't give up. Every tackle, they felt it."

The CSA missed the brazenness Waiters had employed years earlier when getting the 1985 Mexico game set in frigid Newfoundland. Before that final stage started, there was some concern within Canadian soccer circles that if Canada were eliminated by the final matchday, attendance would be paltry. Then owner of the Toronto Blizzard, Karsten von Wersebe, offered to host the game at downtown Varsity Stadium, the Blizzard's home venue, to start the season.

Von Wersebe argued that if Canada were still alive and kicking by that point, the CSA would have no problem making money from ticket sales. If they weren't, von Wersebe would cover whatever costs there were, just to show off the stadium the Blizzard played out of.

"It wasn't the wrong thing to do, but at the same time we're thinking ahead that we probably aren't going to be in a meaningful game by the time we play Mexico," said Lenarduzzi. "Sure enough, it *was* a meaningful game."

And so, Canada scrambled to garner whatever advantage they could. As hosts, Canada could draw up the dimensions of the field, within certain limits. They asked for the pitch to be drawn up narrow to allow for a more physical game, which would favour them.

"And then we show up for the game and the lines are taken off and [the field was] actually widened," said goalkeeper Craig Forrest, one of the most imposing yet convivial players in national team history.

It was around this point that concerns emerged throughout the team about whether Canada would even be on a level playing field.

"We knew [FIFA] wanted Mexico to go through," said Forrest.

He, like many, asked why a full set of referees from Germany were flown in to officiate the match, instead of referees from other countries nearby. Players wondered: Had these referees been given collective instructions?

"An absolute travesty," said Peschisolido of the referee situation.

The Canadian players knew what they were up against: because the World Cup was being hosted in the United States, and because a lot of Mexicans lived in the United States, and because of the intense following the national team enjoyed from home, some players believed it was financially better for FIFA that Mexico advance.

Leading up to the game, Canadian soccer officials continually bragged to players and coaches that the match had sold out. But those players and coaches could only shake their heads. They knew how fervent a following the Mexican national team had, especially in cities like Toronto, where there was already a large Mexican contingent.

These same players' fears were proven correct when a sea of green Mexico jerseys greeted them in the stands, coupled with relentless taunting of the home crowd in Spanish.

"It was almost demoralizing," said Lenarduzzi.

Yet Canada relied on their veterans with impressive aggressiveness. They continually tried to send balls high over the Mexican midfield and into the box to utilize Bunbury and the hot streak he was on.

When Mexico was in possession, Canadian defenders swarmed them. Pudgy-cheeked Frank Yallop came in with a swift yet forceful tackle from behind to dispossess Mexican attacker David Patiño early in the first half. The opening frame was fairly even until Canada gained the advantage from one of their oldest allies on the pitch: a set piece.

From well over twenty-five yards away from the Mexican goal, an in-swinging and floating free kick took a single bounce off the fray near Mexican goalkeeper Jorge Campos. Bunbury leapt in the air, headed the ball down past Campos for a goal that immediately joined George Pakos's goal nearly eight years earlier as one of Canada's most important, ever.

As Lenarduzzi paced around the side of the pitch in the seconds afterward, his baggy red track pants flapping in the wind, he pumped his fist in the belief that Canada was returning to the World Cup.

For the next fifteen minutes or so, Canada looked like it could beat the best team in the region when it mattered. That is, until the Mexicans pressed forward, sent a quick pass in front of Forrest, and found a gaping hole in the Canadian defence that Hugo Sanchez capitalized on with a bullet of a shot past Forrest.

Sanchez somersaulted through the air in jubilation and the thousands of waving Mexican flags blocked the view of the University of Toronto in the background of the stadium.

"I think if we came away from the first half with a lead, things might have been different," Lenarduzzi said after the game.

To try and tilt the pitch in their direction, Lenarduzzi brought on Peschisolido to help beat down the Mexican defence.

In the fifty-third minute, he did just that: a free kick in Canada's own half led to Peschisolido being sprung, by the slimmest of margins, with his Mexican defender nearby, into the Mexico box. Canadian midfielder Lyndon Hooper made a precise run in front of his defender to find himself clear in on goal. Peschisolido, likely correct in his belief that he was onside, played a pass that fell right to Hooper's feet. Hooper shovelled the ball past Campos and began running to his teammates with his right arm in the air. It was the kind of swift attack Canada was not known for.

Behind the goal, photographers abandoned their posts and leapt in joy. Canada now needed to bunker for just over thirty minutes to reach a World Cup.

But with Hooper's arm still in the air, he slowed to a crawl. The linesman had called the goal offside and Campos, wisely, quickly put the ball back in play to turn the disallowed goal into an ancient memory.

The chatter between the Canadians on the field reached a fever pitch.

"Without a shadow of a doubt," according to Peschisolido, the team believed they were in the middle of a game being called against them.

"[Players] were convinced that [Hooper's goal] wasn't offside," said Lenarduzzi. "And they weren't guys that were looking for conspiracy theories."

The rest of the match played out in the kind of predictable manner that made Doyle's article easy to believe. Throw-ins that should have been awarded to Canada were not. Whenever the Canadians got within a few feet of Campos, the offside flag was raised.

Crucially, when Forrest came out to challenge Mexican forward Francisco Javier Cruz on a breakaway, Cruz lost control of the ball and put his studs up while colliding with Forrest, a punishable offence that drew no card from the referee.

Forrest could only hobble when he arose after several minutes on the ground. After the collision, Mexico quickly attacked the Canadian goal and, after some calamitous Canadian defending, Cruz, nicknamed "*El Abuelo*" (Grandpa) by the Mexican broadcast team, sealed Canada's fate with a tap-in goal.

Forrest punched the back of his goal in disgust.

Mexico would qualify directly to the World Cup, and Canada would lose a home-and-away playoff against Australia to end their own World Cup dreams.

Decades after the loss to Mexico, many who were in Varsity Stadium that day still wonder: Were Canada victim of the Soccer Gods waving their hands and shifting fate one way? Or was there something more nefarious at play, with Canada being part of a conspiracy embedded in the region's soccer history?

Whether the former or the latter, they are among the growing pains of any organization that doesn't have *Mexico* written at the top of that day's team sheet but is looking to emerge as a bona fide soccer nation.

And those pains sting all the more considering, as Peschisolido said, the players put in one of their better performances of the qualifying campaign.

"As Canadian players, what we always wanted to do was, instead of playing a qualifying fixture in lovely Vancouver, let's take them to Newfoundland and have them freeze their balls off in minus-twenty-five weather. As an organization, these are things that anyone who has a winning mentality would go for. Whereas we seemed to miss out on all these things," said Peschisolido.

Perhaps if the organization had thought less about the bottom line and more about the long-term success that a win in a more uncomfortable situation would have brought, the resentment throughout the lineup would not have lasted more than a generation afterward.

"As little old Canada, sometimes when you want things to go your way, they don't," said Peschisolido. "We allowed these things to happen."

· · ·

Canada missed out on a World Cup that was a near complete success for the host country and propelled the tournament to a wider audience.

Yes, the notion of the United States hosting the fabled tournament initially drew the ire of many media members and traditional thinkers throughout the soccer world.

Guimaraes Octavio Pinto, Brazilian Football Confederation president from 1986 to 1989, told reporters as the hosting rights were confirmed in 1988 that "taking the World Cup to the United States is like taking the World Series to Brazil."

Nevertheless, the reasons for the United States being awarded the hosting rights to the 1994 World Cup were obvious.

"The United States is the only unconquered continent in the soccer set," said Peter Pullen, a member of the Brazilian bid delegation, in the *New York Times* when the United States were awarded the hosting rights. "There is a great potential for economic power, and a lot of people can make a lot of money if the games take off."

The tournament drew the highest total and average per game attendance figures in its history, a number which remained uncontested until the 2018 World Cup.

The exposure players get from playing in the World Cup is almost unquantifiable. Had Canada qualified, would Bunbury not have had to take chances on strangers to get playing time in Europe? Would Domenic Mobilio, seen in retrospect as one of the great undiscovered Canadian talents and the all-time leading scorer for the pre-MLS Vancouver Whitecaps, been able to play more than just two games outside of North America?

In short, would Canadian players have had to worry less about their professional futures?

An important condition to the United States being awarded the World Cup was FIFA's instruction for the United States Soccer Federation to develop a top-flight domestic league, which eventually became Major League Soccer. The NASL had folded in 1984.

Eighteen of the twenty-two players on Canada's 1986 World Cup team had logged time in the NASL, but, in the wake of failing to qualify for the 1994 World Cup, Canadian players desperately needed exposure and playing opportunities. They would not get those opportunities in U.S.-based Major

League Soccer. Domestic players were prioritized in the top-flight American league, which kicked off in April 1996. Teams were allowed only five foreign players on each roster. According to Soccer America, only four Canadians played in MLS in 1996.

Among them was Frank Yallop, who left Ipswich Town in England after an illustrious thirteen-year career to finish off with the Tampa Bay Mutiny.

"MLS was very smart," Yallop says. "They made sure that every American who was playing abroad, they got them home. Whether they were overpaid or not, it didn't matter. They got them back."

The immediate quality of the play on the pitch was secondary to the long-term vision.

MLS opted to act as a single entity, with each team being owned by the league. But the league's wealthy investors would individually operate each team. The financial clout of the investors in MLS far outweighed what the CSL operated with.

When initial interest and attendance waned and MLS lost hundreds of millions of dollars in its first five years of existence, relying on billionaires to bankroll multiple teams when the losses piled up allowed MLS to weather the financial storm; among them were Robert Kraft, who operated the Kraft Group, which owned the NFL's New England Patriots and MLS's New England Revolution, and long-time soccer and football executive Lamar Hunt, who began by owning two MLS teams, the Kansas City Wizards and the Columbus Crew.

And with the majority of top American players having returned home, their national team benefitted.

"All of a sudden, you look at their qualifying campaigns afterward, you've got American coaches, all the players are at home, it's easier to get players to camps, and it's easier to train," said Yallop.

By contrast, the Canadian players were scattered across the planet, including some in contention for the national team who were logging time playing college soccer.

"We were trying players out during that time by flying guys in to try out, they were not quite there, so they'd fly home, we'd bring another guy in," said Dasovic. "It was almost like American Idol. It was a time of frustration, but it was the reality."

• • •

For some Concacaf nations, The Hex can be about as fearful as the name conjures up.

The informally named final stage of Concacaf World Cup qualifying, featuring six teams, or The Hexagonal, is home to the sport's dark arts: perilous away trips into unfamiliar scenarios, gamesmanship that verges on illegality, gruelling physicality in matches and, for many players and teams, crushed dreams.

But qualifying for The Hex has been considered the absolute bare minimum for the region's top teams, from its first iteration in 1997 as teams hoped to qualify for the 1998 World Cup.

Through the six iterations of the tournament so far, only ten nations have ever played in The Hex.

In the first run of The Hex, Canada qualified with the region's elite with a surprisingly ruthless run through the third round of qualifying, becoming the only team in the region to go without a loss through six games while allowing just one goal against. Bunbury was at the height of his powers with Maritimo and scored five goals in those six games.

The World Cup had expanded to thirty-two teams for the first time ever, and the top three finishers in The Hex would qualify for the World Cup. Come the beginning of March 1997, when the Canadians boarded a flight to Mexico City to begin their campaign against Mexico at the Azteca, it was reasonable to expect that Canada would be one of them. They were ranked forty-sixth in the world according to FIFA's rankings, a position that would remain their highest until 2021.

"We should have qualified," said Bunbury.

Instead, Canada's run was already threatened in just the first half. Playing at altitude and in front of a typically intimidating Mexican crowd was proving to be a tall task. In the second half, Mexico knocked four goals past Craig Forrest in a 4–0 Canada loss.

"There are no preparations you can do for that," said Peschisolido of playing in the Azteca.

The next half they played in The Hex was nearly as discouraging. The United States scored two goals, then a third in the second half, leaving Canada the only team to have suffered two losses in their first two games.

Canada's goal scoring dried up, with two 0–0 draws afterward. By the time they registered their only win, a 1–0 result over Costa Rica in Edmonton, the likelihood of their flying to France the following summer had all but vanished.

And when Canada travelled to Estadio Cuscatlán in San Salvador to play El Salvador, the difference between playing games at the placid Swangard Stadium in picturesque Burnaby and playing in Central America was evident.

"Did we have organization? Were we prepared? Sometimes you'd go to these places to play, and it was difficult," said Peschisolido.

As the Canadian team warmed up, and as the game itself continued, Peschisolido describes it as "mental torture" that his teammates were put through. In countries where poverty can be, unfortunately, rampant, soccer stokes nationalistic fervour, visitors are unwelcome, players are consistently aware of the military presence around the stadium, and many visiting teams are subject to the kind of hostility that gets passed down over the years through barroom conversations.

Peschisolido will never forget the first time he was hit with a bag of urine, launched at his Canadian side from the crowd.

"In professional sports, we talk about it being a game of inches," said Peschisolido. "But we're talking about acres of things that go against you. How can you really stay focused through that?"

Canada would lose 4–1, putting them and their World Cup hopes on the ropes.

The mood was low among the Canadian team, and predictably so. And it was only exacerbated by a growing sense of resentment from players toward the sport's governing body in Canada.

"Every time there was a World Cup cycle you always knew there was going be a fight for compensation for players," said Onstad.

Yet compensation, slight as it might have been for players who were determined to play for their country and qualify for a World Cup, was secondary to their concerns about how their needs as athletes were being addressed, or, more specifically, were not being addressed. Canadians would see how players from other nearby nations travelled. They would shake their heads when they were put up in hotels that didn't offer amenities necessary for athletes to maintain peak condition, were booked onto the earliest possible flights, and stuck in middle seats for trans-Atlantic flights a few days before vital qualification games, to save a few dollars.

If the federation they were playing for wanted optimal results from their players, then the expectation was that they should be treated as such. But players felt the CSA's preparations for tournaments usually lacked detailed plans for proper accommodation, training schedules, and recovery options.

While Terry Quinn would eventually become a respected figure in Canadian soccer, that he moved from the CSA's finance committee to its treasurer before finally becoming the association's president during the 1994 and 1998 World Cup qualification cycles suggests the organization was more concerned with balancing the books than with setting up players for optimal success.

"It just felt like wherever they could cut corners, they would cut corners," said Onstad of the CSA. "And in the end, that's a cultural thing. When you do that from the top, that message filters down pretty quickly. If they're willing to cut corners, why shouldn't we cut corners?"

Canada finished dead last in their first run of The Hex. They were officially eliminated by the United States after a 3–0 loss at Swangard. It was this loss that allowed the United States to themselves qualify. They'd be going to three World Cups in a row for the first time. The gap between the two nations had widened almost irrevocably.

"The loss once again magnified Bobby Lenarduzzi's shortcomings as national coach of Canada," *Toronto Star* sports reporter Norman Da Costa wrote, while also taking issue with Lenarduzzi's "outdated game plans and loyalty to has-beens."

After two failed World Cup qualifying runs, Lenarduzzi was sure his time was done. But he wanted to impart a controversial message to the Canadian soccer community.

Asked after the loss how it felt for the United States to have qualified on Canada's turf, Lenarduzzi waved off the question at first, before essentially telling the assembled media that despite Canada's not qualifying, the next most important thing was that the Americans qualified.

"Our fortunes are directly tied to how well they do," Lenarduzzi remembers telling his players.

In the aftermath of the loss and his comments, Lenarduzzi received a stern dressing-down from the CSA board for what they believed was an endorsement of their rivals.

But Lenarduzzi was adamant: with the American MLS now two seasons into its existence, if Canada weren't going to the World Cup, the United States needed to go to give MLS "a shot in the arm."

"I'm not that patriotic that I can't see the bigger picture," said Lenarduzzi.

At the time, there were only ten MLS teams. But Lenarduzzi looked at how MLS's counterparts, MLB and the NBA, also eventually expanded to Canada as their leagues grew.

Without a serious domestic league in Canada, any exposure the Americans garnered for their national team would, hopefully, lead to more growth for MLS and eventually, fingers crossed, more professional opportunities close to home for Canadian players.

"They're going to come into Canada," Lenarduzzi remembers telling the CSA board of MLS before he resigned. "They had to."

An optimist might fall back to the very nickname of the tournament and insist that the men's team were cursed. But those on the ground saw the alarming truth: until the Canadian soccer infrastructure was fixed, the World Cup would remain a fever dream.

Sixteen of the twenty-one players on the United States roster for the 1998 World Cup were playing in MLS.

That the United States finished dead last among the thirty-two teams in the tournament was, to some, an indictment of the league's quality. But it also represented potential for evolution in the American soccer system, with players using the league as a springboard to future success. By the 2002 World Cup, eleven of the USA's twenty-three players were playing in MLS, and five other players in Europe's top leagues had previously played in MLS.

Meanwhile, without a professional league of their own and without opportunities to play in MLS, Canada would fail to even reach the next five iterations of The Hex.

"It's the reality of soccer in Canada," said Sweeney. "It's just not the same game compared to these other countries."

CHAPTER 4

"He's Got Red in His Veins, but It's Canadian Red": Craig Forrest's Desire to Play for Canada Changed the Course of His Career

AS A TEENAGER, CRAIG FORREST KNEW CANADA WAS NOT A SOC-
cer hotbed.

Like his friends in the Vancouver suburb of Coquitlam, he followed the Vancouver Canucks closely. Such was custom in the Greater Vancouver Area, and for many teenagers across Canada, where the NHL's place atop the sports pyramid in major Canadian cities was uncontested.

But as his skills as an athletic, shot-stopping goalkeeper grew, and as Forrest himself grew into a lanky teenager who could utilize his reach, his interest in soccer also grew. At twelve, he might have been late to start playing the game. But he caught up quickly as his brash laugh became a constant around his local minor soccer club in Coquitlam, but also in the British Columbia U-16 and U-18 provincial teams.

The Vancouver Whitecaps had captured the imagination of their city in 1979 with their improbable win in the North American Soccer League (NASL)'s Soccer Bowl. But by the time Forrest would even be able to consider playing for his local club, they, along with the rest of the NASL, folded in 1984.

He learned that the heartbeat of the global game emanated from Europe. But what he did not know, and what other Canadian players as talented as Forrest were also wondering, was how anyone from outside of Europe would ever be able to make their way across the Atlantic Ocean to play soccer for a career.

The path to becoming a Vancouver Canuck, after all, was well-trodden: the sport's best players from junior hockey leagues were selected in the annual NHL draft.

Forrest wanted to leave Canada and wanted to leave fast. But the draft was a foreign concept to European soccer, making the path to European leagues for talented, curious outsiders like Forrest an unknown.

"There wasn't a road map," said Forrest.

When Phil Trenter, a local firefighter who had been a reserve player for English side Ipswich Town, saw Forrest play and invited the young goaltender to join him in a Vancouver recreational men's league side, Forrest could not have believed how that would help propel him toward Europe.

Trenter was able to use his connections at his old club to get sixteen-year-old Forrest a trial at Ipswich Town as a trainee. For Forrest that meant leaving school, his friends, and, much to the chagrin of his mother, his family, in Canada as he boarded a flight to England. He would not return to Canada to live for over twenty years.

"It still affects her to this day," said Forrest.

Forrest went to Ipswich Town on his own, and like other Canadian players at the time, was left to his own devices without the aforementioned road map.

"Craig's had a path that a lot of us followed: leaving home at a young age and pursuing a career in very difficult times," said former teammate Nick Dasovic. "As much as people think it sounds lovely, you're leaving your family behind, there's no internet, you don't call your parents on a regular basis: it's too damn expensive to call. There's no texting. When you leave, you're on your own."

When Forrest arrived in England and was met by players with far more potential and talent than him, he realized very quickly that if he wanted to make a career out of soccer, he would have to forge his own path.

But what he didn't have to do was continually make arduous and career-threatening journeys to represent the country he left at sixteen.

That, he did on his own.

. . .

It was easy for Forrest to be swept up by the almost alien soccer universe he now found himself in as his career as an Ipswich Town trainee began. Training sessions unfolded on pitches far better manicured than anything he'd played on in Canada, and the sessions themselves were far more rigorous. The veterans were more hardened and enjoyed a level of celebrity in their small town that few soccer players in Canada could.

And yet it was his observations of the upper tier of European soccer that instilled in him something he'd never truly understood before: the importance of and pride in playing for one's national team.

In Canada, the opportunities for players like Forrest to suit up for the national team were rare. Even rarer was national team success, which could diminish any sense of pride.

By the time Forrest arrived in Ipswich in 1985, the reverence surrounding Ipswich players who had represented their national team in the recent past, or were still playing for their national team, grew like wildflowers around the club.

Under the tutelage of legendary manager Sir Bobby Robson, Ipswich had experienced success utilizing foreign players in a way many English sides did not at the time.

"The perception of foreigners was different," said Forrest.

That had likely helped pave the way for the club to take a chance on a young Canadian goalkeeper. Canadian defender Frank Yallop was already playing there.

"It was a perfect storm for a Canadian," said Forrest.

And so, a wide-eyed Forrest lapped up the tales of Arnold Mühren and Frans Thijssen, two Dutch players Robson had brought into the side. They had suited up for the Netherlands while playing for Ipswich not long before Forrest arrived.

In a cramped dressing room, the clatter of boot studs hitting the floor couldn't drown out the stories from Ipswich centre-back Terry Butcher, who played for the English national team against Germany and France in the 1982 World Cup. Those stories helped Forrest's mind to wander and imagine himself playing in front of packed stadiums in Canada in a national team shirt.

Kevin Wilson joined Ipswich around the same time as Forrest and would soon be relied upon to score goals for Northern Ireland in World Cup and Euro qualifiers.

In the corner of the dressing room, a belief became hardened in his mind: to truly have an impactful career, there would be no greater honour for a player in football than pulling on your national team's shirt.

That belief was strengthened in the summer of 1986 when Forrest watched his compatriots compete at their first and only World Cup.

He wanted to play a role the next time Canada had a chance to qualify for the World Cup and believed he could. The CSA believed it too, as they invited him to play a few friendlies for the national team in the summer of 1988, during his club's off-season.

Forrest shut out a decent Chile side, and then made a key save to help Canada beat Greece in penalties. This increased his profile ahead of qualification for the 1989 Concacaf championship, which would determine which teams would qualify for the 1990 World Cup.

By the time Canada's qualification campaign began in October 1988, Forrest had graduated to Ipswich's first team. He knew at the time that clubs did not have to release players to represent their national team. So, when he was called into the Canada team for a home-and-away series against Guatemala, he made the first of many awkward entrances into his club manager's office to discuss a possible release to his national team. The winner of this series would gain an entrance into the final qualification tournament.

Then Ipswich Town manager John Duncan swept his grey hair out of his brow as he heard the tension in Forrest's voice.

"I know it's special playing for your country," Forrest remembers Duncan telling him. "I want you to do it. I'm sure you want to do it. But you have to realize that if you leave and another goalkeeper comes in and does well, you're not going to get your spot back. And you just got in, you're pretty young."

The harsh reality of choosing club or country hit the still-green twenty-one-year-old.

Duncan told Forrest that if he wanted to go he was free to do so. But he added that if Forrest decided he did not want to join his national team out of a justifiable fear of losing his spot, Duncan would take the fall for his young goalkeeper and publicly state that he had refused to release Forrest.

Forrest thought about who was paying his wages and opted for the latter.

"I figured 'Guatemala home and away, they should be OK,'" Forrest said of his national team at the time, perhaps rationalizing his decision. "And they weren't."

Forrest watched in shock as Canada allowed two goals in the home leg in Burnaby, not far from Forrest's hometown, no less, to lose the series and their World Cup hopes on away goals.

He started asking himself the kinds of questions that inevitably pop up in the "regret" stage of grief: why hadn't he joined his national team? Could he have stopped Guatemalan winger Byron Perez's penalty in the first leg, which would have given Canada a better chance to qualify? When would his next chance come?

By the time he answered the questions to himself, he had quietly made a decision: he would do everything in his power never to turn down another call from Canada.

• • •

Though it was still early in Forrest's career, turning down the call from Canada in 1988, at least at first, did indeed hurt the national team.

Because, as singularly talented as Forrest was, often using his reach to stretch wide and make highlight-reel stops, that the country's most prominent player was one who spent the majority of his time off the ball was indicative of Canadian player development.

Being able to rely on the players' natural athleticism was a boon for Canadian soccer coaches. But the lack of creative coaching and further lack of exposure to the most technically advanced players in Europe and South America meant the best Canadian players were rarely dynamic, attacking midfielders, wingers, and forwards.

Hockey was the most popular game in the country, and a game which, especially in the 1980s, rewarded physicality. The best Canadian soccer players were often ones who used their athleticism to defend. So, it holds that the best Canadian players toward the turn of the century were reliable veteran defenders like Frank Yallop, Colin Miller, and Randy Samuel, and emerging defenders like Jason de Vos and Paul Stalteri, who would go on to become some of the country's most celebrated players.

"We basically tried to play in a very simplistic 4-4-2, because most guys are playing in systems that were like that in England or Scotland or wherever they were based in the world. Put your best four defenders, of which we had a lot, and then put your next best four defenders that have a little bit of more technical capacity ahead of that group. So, you had a block of eight that were very defensively oriented, very strong-minded, and understanding of their roles and responsibilities," said Canadian midfielder Nick Dasovic.

When Forrest began taking over starting goalkeeper duties for Canada early in the decade, he became the all-important last line of defence.

"We're the water carriers, we'll do the mess, but you guys go score," said Dasovic of the team's defence-first approach.

Their 1986 World Cup opener against France in the World Cup notwithstanding, the group could often look out at the team warming up at the other end of the pitch and feel overwhelmed by their talent.

But behind them was someone who, even by that point, appeared unfazed. Being exposed to stronger players and more rigorous talent from an early age in England only fed into Forrest's robust confidence.

If his six-foot-four frame didn't make him the natural centre of attention in any room he walked into, his brave cackle of a laugh most certainly would.

And his teammates fed off that self-assurance.

"It obviously gives you a tremendous boost of confidence because here's a very athletic, quality guy behind you. And you have to have that, right? You need to be thinking 'I can go get this ball. But on the chance I get beat, I've got a great goalie behind me that's going to be able to stop it,'" said midfielder Mike Sweeney.

As much as the Canadian national team needed to have a strong final defender, what they perhaps needed more was the shot in the arm that Forrest's swaggering presence provided.

The 1986 World Cup team emanated the egalitarianism Tony Waiters desired. What they lacked was an alpha dog who lapped up every stressful moment.

Forrest's remarkable shot-stopping ability was one thing to Pat Onstad, Forrest's goalkeeper partner for nearly a generation. But it was how Forrest would walk out onto the pitch with his toothy smile beaming, not treating every game like the end of the world, that ultimately stood out. Somewhere deep in Forrest's lanky frame was the belief that he could rescue his national team from whatever mess they got into.

"Paul Dolan and I talked about this a lot: we used to put so much pressure on ourselves playing for Canada; if we make mistakes, that's it, we'll lose the game. We've got to be perfect," said Onstad. "And Craig just had a mindset: just go out and play. It just put [teammates] in a really good place when he was playing the game. He wasn't worried about what anybody else was going to do. He was just going to enjoy the game and play well, which he always did."

• • •

As international tournaments grew in prestige and the World Cup became the most popular sports tournament on the planet, playing for their national team became something soccer players would include at the top of their CV, in plain sight for club contract negotiations.

The modernization and eventual globalization of the game meant that when players made their debuts for their respective national teams, their club teams could also count on being mentioned throughout broadcasts. That kind of free advertising, especially for clubs outside of Europe's elite upper echelon, couldn't have a price tag put on it.

Unfortunately for Forrest, these changes hadn't yet quite begun during his prime.

"Playing for the national team didn't help you," said Forrest. "If anything, it hindered you."

Accepting an invitation to play for the national team would often lead to a scene like the one he had had with John Duncan. He'd knock on his current manager's office door and enter with his head hung low as he'd say he was being asked to play for Canada against the kind of countries his managers would openly deride and would need to fly across an ocean to do so.

Forrest's travels would make athletic therapists interested in maintaining a player's high performance levels shudder.

He remembers playing with the Canadian national team in El Salvador, after camps in Los Angeles and Houston. He still winces recalling his return journey back to England: from El Salvador to Belize, Belize to Houston, Houston to Los Angeles, Los Angeles to Toronto, and then Toronto to London.

"The CSA wanted to save a few bucks," said Forrest.

When Forrest stretched his legs once finally off the plane in London, he was told that one of the other goalkeepers on his English team was hurt, and that he would have to play that same evening.

For European players based in Europe, representing their country meant short-haul flights without seriously differing time zones. The risk to these players' health was lower than it would be for Canadians like Forrest: club managers could rest easy knowing trusted national associations would not keep European players away for long. They also knew these players would often be playing against technically competent countries that played a style of soccer not likely to injure the opposition.

But this was not the case for Forrest, to the point that few Canadian national team players put their own career advancement at risk the way he did.

The Premier League began in 1992. The new top division of English football, it was made up of twenty-two teams that broke off from the Football League and did so knowing there was £305 million in a historic new TV rights deal waiting for them. From being a haven for English players to play rough-and-tumble soccer, the Premier League's teams utilized the influx of financial resources from the rights deal and ensuing sponsorship deals to eventually dip into international markets for high-profile player acquisitions.

The Premier League was symbolic of the globalization of the game, and the inaugural season was the beginning of the league's ascent to unquestioned dominance over other European leagues.

By the early 1990s, Forrest was a regular starter for Ipswich Town, putting him on the ground floor of the nascent league, at least for the time being. Having worked his way up from an outsider, he'd backstopped the club to promotion into the first tier of English football in the 1991–92 season and entrance into the much-hyped Premier League.

On the opening weekend, he was one of only a small group of foreign nationals plying his trade in the league. He stood tall in a 1–1 draw against Aston Villa, who would end up finishing in second place on the league table.

His early stint in the Premier League was remarkable. He started all of the club's first eleven matches in goal, losing only one. Forrest and Ipswich Town drew with top sides Liverpool, Tottenham, and eventual title winners Manchester United in their own famed home ground, Old Trafford.

There was cause for optimism in the smallish town on the banks of River Orwell, and cause for optimism with Forrest, whose stock was rising.

That is, until he was called into the national team for an October 1992 friendly against the United States to prepare for a Concacaf World Cup qualifying match scheduled for a week later.

Forrest hadn't been called into Canada's team for 1990 World Cup qualifying and in 1986 he had seen what his goalkeeping brother Paul Dolan was capable of on the sport's grandest stage.

So, he wasn't going to miss the beginning of Canada's World Cup qualifiers this time, even if that meant missing out on games for the team paying his bills.

"I wanted to be part of the building process," said Forrest.

Those close to him saw that.

"He's got red in his veins, but it's Canadian red," said Yallop. "If you had to paint a picture of Canadian soccer and passion, there's a few guys that would live and breathe for playing for Canada. A lot of those guys that were away from home plying their trade had to absolutely beg their managers to forgive them, and to go and play for Canada."

Yallop had joined the Canadian team ahead of Forrest, but they had to endure those conversations with Ipswich boss John Lyall together.

"There's me and him looking at the manager, 'We can't play in three weeks' time, but we're assuming you're still going to pay us,'" said Yallop. "It was just so awkward."

But after beating Leeds United 4–2, the relationship between Forrest and his club would soon go from awkward to almost detrimental.

Forrest did his part for Canada in the 0–0 friendly draw against the United States, and nine days later, started for Canada in a 1–1 draw against Jamaica to open World Cup qualifying.

It was a decision that irrevocably changed the course of his first Premier League season. Back in England, Lyall had no choice but to start the veteran Clive Baker in goal. Baker was eight years Forrest's senior. After joining

Ipswich from Barnsley FC on a transfer months earlier, Baker wasn't going to let the starter's role go without a fight.

And starting October 17, the day before Canada's match against Jamaica, that's exactly what Baker did. Though Ipswich lost to Chelsea 2–1 that day, they would not lose again with Baker in goal for their next ten matches. Ipswich vaulted high enough up the Premier League table that earning a spot in European competition looked possible.

Lyall, like most managers, didn't want to mess with a good thing. After Forrest returned, he would not take the pitch again that season.

After the end of that Premier League season, the Canadian team were reminded of the importance of Forrest's desire to play for his country as they touched down in Sydney, Australia, after nearly an entire day's worth of flying in August 1993.

Canada was up 2–1 after the first leg of the Concacaf–OFC play-off against Australia after their loss to Mexico months prior. The winner of the two-leg aggregate game would get one last chance to qualify for the World Cup by playing another aggregate series against a team from South America.

The Australian national team at the time were at a similar stage as Canada: they had qualified for just one World Cup previously, in 1974. Their domestic league, the National Soccer League (NSL), had not reached the heights that other sports leagues in the country had and the squad was made up of players playing in local teams and lower-level teams in Europe.

But, like Canada, Australia had an ace in the hole in goal: then twenty-one-year-old Mark Bosnich had broken through with Aston Villa at the end of the 1992–93 season, helping backstop them to their second-place finish. Impressive as it was, the Socceroos would not stand to benefit.

Bosnich was not named to either of the lineups against Canada, and the Canadian contingent began asking around in Sydney: Why wasn't this rising star part of the game-day squad?

"They're making huge sacrifices in order to qualify for the World Cup, which would be huge for them," Sweeney remembers thinking of the Australian side.

Canadian players heard rumblings of frustration from the Australian national team: some said Bosnich had quit the national team to focus on playing for Aston Villa, which had a game the day before the second leg in

Sydney. Others understood that if Bosnich willingly gave up the spot he'd earned the previous season, he might not get it back.

In 2007, Bosnich would clarify, saying it was "wrongly understood" that he had quit the national team. He had opted to stay with his club side as the 1993–94 Premier League season began, but he ended up not playing for Aston Villa.

"I just sat there doing nothing while two huge games went on without me," Bosnich told the *Sun-Herald*. "I tried to do the right thing by everybody but got burned. That will never be allowed to happen again."

What became clear to the Canadian side, with a chance to qualify for the World Cup on the line, was that Forrest was making efforts his peers were not.

Australia came at Canada relentlessly in attack as the Canadians were outshot 10–1 in the first half in Sydney. Forrest was standing on his head to keep Canada's World Cup hopes alive.

Canada would end up losing in a shootout, in part because Sweeney and Alex Bunbury did not convert their penalties.

The Australians were quick to credit Forrest's efforts after the game, which wasn't lost on the Canadian side as they made the long journey back to Canada. They'd gotten as far as they had in part because of Forrest's belief in putting his country before his club.

"That was the biggest thing for him: to make that sacrifice," said Sweeney of Forrest.

Forrest believes that sacrifice may have hindered high-profile moves for him.

In 1997, Forrest's profile and performances saw him outgrow Ipswich Town, which had since been relegated out of the Premier League. He secured a loan to Chelsea, then emerging as one of England's top clubs.

His shutout over Wimbledon, a team battling Chelsea for a place toward the top of the table, improved his standing within the club.

Not long afterward, Forrest's patriotic resolve was again tested as Canada was in the middle of the final round of 1998 World Cup qualification. He accepted a call into the team's camp on the other side of the Atlantic Ocean, making him unavailable for selection for the remainder of the season, including Chelsea's appearance in the FA Cup final. Chelsea's eventual win would seal their first major trophy in twenty-six years.

"If I stayed, I think I could have played in the FA Cup final," said Forrest.

His frustration was coupled with the news from Chelsea that they were interested in extending his loan period. Ipswich, however, "held up the ransom," according to Forrest, and didn't fulfill his wishes for the move.

All along, he was overcome with helplessness. Being with the national team left him unable to have the kind of face-to-face discussions that would have kept him in the loop on the loan deal.

"And I didn't sign for Chelsea …" he said, his voice trailing off.

Not every one of his teammates followed his example. Matches against lower-ranked teams that offered little in the way of exposure were very often skipped by Canadian players.

While it would take a generation, eventually more and more Canadian players learned about the sacrifices players like Forrest had made and would adopt his attitude. The advent of FIFA's international windows, during which few club games were played, made it easier. But even once those windows became commonplace, there were always talented Canadian players who turned down the invitation to play for their national team out of a lack of interest, or a belief that the games on offer weren't winnable.

But Canada's run through 1993 was the closest the national team would get to the World Cup between 1986 and 2022.

That team remains under-discussed in Canadian sports history, much like Forrest's sacrifices for the national team. He, and his 1993 teammates who made similar sacrifices, never received mainstream attention throughout the country.

"[Forrest] is a patriot," said Bob Lenarduzzi, "there's no question."

In 1997, Forrest secured a move to West Ham United and would spend the next five seasons with the London side. A bout with testicular cancer, which Forrest eventually beat, forced his early retirement in 2002. His 107 appearances in the top domestic league on the planet are third among all Canadian players.

More than ten years after his retirement, as the game was evolving in Canada in a way Forrest likely could not have predicted, he finally got the recognition that had eluded him.

When it came time for the CSA to name their all-time Best XI as part of their centennial celebrations in 2012, Forrest was an easy choice in goal.

"He's the best goalkeeper (Canada) has produced so far," said Pat Onstad.

Three years later, he was inducted into the Canadian Sports Hall of Fame.

"My hope is that in some small way my induction will lead to more soccer players' being inducted down the road," said Forrest at the time, "and inspire more boys and girls to take up the sport."

CHAPTER 5

A Coin Flip, a Golden Goal, and an Unbelievable Champion: Canada's 2000 Gold Cup Win

EVEN THE MOST PATRIOTIC CANADIAN, SUCH AS FORREST, wouldn't have fancied the national team's chances before the 2000 Gold Cup.

Canada's trophy cupboard from men's international tournaments wasn't exactly full to the brim. Their 1985 Concacaf Championship was paired with their gold medal in the 1904 summer Olympics, won by Ontario side Galt FC in a three-team tournament. Those were the team's only championships.

The 2000 Gold Cup was to be held in February, and Canada's recent poor results in the region meant they didn't automatically qualify.

They hadn't gotten out of the group stage in the five previous Gold Cups, either.

"We went into [the Gold Cup] thinking [for us] it was going to be a ten-day tournament, five of those days being prepping. The likelihood of us getting out of our group was low," balding midfielder Jeff Clarke told the Athletic.

Yes, there was more European pedigree on the team than on other Canadian teams since 1986. By 2000, of the eighteen-man squad, only four players were plying their trade in North America, and two of those did not see the field. A twenty-one-year-old Dwayne de Rosario, known for his piercing blue eyes and his trickery on the ball, had yet to hit the heights he would in MLS, where his shimmying dance known as the "shake 'n bake" would accompany his 104 MLS goals. Though it would end up being the most of any Canadian MLS player, even he played only twenty-seven minutes.

That said, the European pedigree still deserves qualification: Paul Stalteri was emerging with Werder Bremen in Germany and Garret Kusch was doing the same with Belgium's Mechelen, but otherwise, eleven of the team's eighteen players were playing in England or Scotland at the time of the tournament.

The tournament itself not being held in the summer, when most club leagues would be idle, was a boon for head coach Holger Osieck: if the constantly scowling German head coach could convince those playing in Europe to join the national team in California for a few weeks, and if those players could convince their club teams to let them do it, he'd be getting players in mid-season form.

So Osieck didn't overthink how to deploy his team full of players from the physically intimidating English and Scottish leagues: like the 1986 World Cup team, Canada would be comfortable staying off the ball, outmuscling opposition, and hoping to capitalize on set pieces.

"Maybe when push comes to shove [players from English and Scottish leagues] can really bring it. And it's not only about being physical. It's just about being disciplined more than anything," said Richard Hastings, who was playing for Scottish side Inverness Caledonian Thistle.

And, in Osieck, Canada had the man to ensure this team stayed disciplined.

After a brief playing career in the German lower divisions, he finished his career with the Whitecaps. He spent the majority of his early coaching career with West German youth teams and earned a highlight on his resume by serving as an assistant to Franz Beckenbauer during West Germany's 1990 World Cup win. Time coaching club soccer in Germany, Turkey, and Japan followed. The connections he'd made in Vancouver came in handy when Canada failed to get out of The Hex in 1997 and the men's team job became available.

At the time, it was Osieck's stern approach that many throughout the CSA believed could steer the men's team, even if his approach rubbed some players the wrong way.

"He didn't want guys playing music on the bus," said Forrest. "He was only focused on the game. He wasn't a loose figure, let's put it that way."

Osieck's tactical footprint was simple, but he believed it played to the team's strengths: traditional 4-4-2 or 3-5-2 formations, without allowing much space behind them.

Or, as Forrest more succinctly put it: "Junk it up and keep possession."

So, while this Canadian team was deployed the way many Canadian teams had been, they were doing so with a stronger technical background thanks to exposure to better coaching in established leagues. As the tournament grew closer, there was buy-in to playing unglamorous, defensive soccer, knowing their last line of defence was as formidable as any in the tournament.

"When you had Craig Forrest in net, you always had a puncher's chance. And that was one of the things we hung on," said Clarke.

Forrest was the only player on the squad playing in the Premier League and remained one of the most imposing goalkeepers in the tournament.

Canada would need Forrest, as Costa Rica came at Canada early in the tournament opener, scoring eleven minutes in. It looked as if the team should start booking flights back immediately after the group stage ended, until forward Carlo Corazzin showcased the kind of resolve and discipline Osieck desired and equalized just eight minutes later. Costa Rica scored again in the fifty-fourth minute, but Corazzin knotted the game at two three minutes later. All along, the Central American squad were relentless in attack, but Canada stood firm for a surprising draw against a pre-tournament favourite. With only two group stage games, a draw put Canada in a favourable position to move into the knockout stage.

"It was the most unbelievable goalkeeping display many of us had ever seen," said Clarke. "We came out of that game feeling like we stole something. Your presentation doesn't mean much. It's about the results."

That same attitude was evident in their final group-stage game against tournament invitees South Korea, who were preparing to host the World Cup in two years.

With the game just two days later and the team in need of some rest and regeneration, there was no time for a proper training session. The top two teams would advance out of the group, and in response, Osieck took the team's defensive approach to another gear.

"[Osieck] dumbed down our tactics and just matched up a couple players. I had to mark [aggressive defender Kim Tae-young]. Holger told me he was going to run everywhere, and I just had to follow him. That was my job for the game," said Clarke.

Even if it wasn't going to win Academy Award for Best Visual Effect, Osieck's plan came to fruition as a tried Canadian team managed a 0–0 draw.

Now level with South Korea, which also was on two points from two matches, the fatigued Canadian squad took to the stands two days later in a sparse Los Angeles Memorial Coliseum crowd to watch Costa Rica and South Korea determine their fate. A win by either team would send Canada through to the knockout round for the first time since their tournament officially began in 1991.

In the stands, opinions on their future were largely split.

Some, like Clarke, felt "like kids."

"Deep down, we had hopes," he said.

Others were far more skeptical. Forrest had seen firsthand how Canada had been "Concacafed" almost seven years earlier by Mexico. They'd heard and nodded along to the whispers that those who made decisions in Concacaf didn't have a reputation as being the most scrupulous.

Then president of Concacaf, Jack Warner, would later be implicated in corruption allegations and eventually charged in the United States with wire fraud, racketeering, and money laundering. Perhaps the skeptics were right to not want to put their fate in the football gods that day.

"All the stuff that came out with Jack Warner, we knew it then," said Forrest.

South Korea took a 2–1 lead in the seventy-fifth minute, which only increased the enthusiasm of players like Clarke. But Costa Rica levelled in the eighty-fifth minute, and the group stage ended with all three teams tied on points. Canada and South Korea were tied on both goal differential and goals for.

Players scrambled, with many unsure what their future held.

As fate would have it, a coin toss was the official method to determine the tiebreaker and to see who would advance through the group, perhaps only underlining the doubts many in the team had about the tournament organizers.

"Half the guys went on the bus. They kept saying 'Nothing ever goes our way with Concacaf. We don't ever get the luck,'" said Nash.

"You could imagine Holger, this staunch German, wondering 'What's wrong with these people? They're doing a coin toss?'" said Davide Xausa.

Yet the paranoia from his team had seeped into that staunch German's line of thinking. Many Concacaf officials wanted the coin toss to take place behind closed doors, but Osieck was adamant that the rules not only be followed but followed in plain sight of every reporter and video camera available. In a forgettable tent with cheap plastic tarps, better suited for boring press conferences, the Canadian and South Korean contingents gathered in their track suits to watch then Concacaf general secretary Chuck Blazer, who himself would later admit to conspiring with FIFA Executive Committee members to take bribes, haphazardly toss a quarter in the air.

Osieck quietly called heads.

Never breaking character, Osieck's furrowed brow and scrunched lips remained in place as the heads he called was revealed. He raised his right thumb up, to the elated screams of his team sitting nearby. Even the skeptics were converted, if only for a moment.

"Craig Forrest looked like he was fifteen years old again," said Clarke.

After the cheers died down, a new reality sank in: Canada's quarterfinal opponent would be Mexico, then ranked tenth in the world by FIFA. Twenty-five previous matches against Mexico had led to only two Canadian wins.

Once again, Osieck opted to have Canada sit deep, try to throw Mexico's talented attackers off their game with their physical approach, and pray to those same soccer gods that had smiled on them before for a chance or two on the counterattack.

Costa Rica and Trinidad and Tobago played one quarterfinal immediately ahead of Canada and Mexico and went into extra time. The schedules being what they were, Canada and Mexico were forced to take to the pitch to play without warm-ups. Forrest stood in a hollow tunnel, bouncing a ball off the wall, hardly representing the peak of athletic preparation.

"I wasn't going to have any depth perception out there, get any crosses in beforehand and get a feel for the conditions," said Forrest. "So, we just had to roll with it."

It's perhaps no surprise then that Mexican midfielder Ramon Ramirez opened the score in the first half, to the delight of a nearly entirely Mexican crowd. But, as Kusch explained, the Canadian team "never stopped working [their] asses off" and a heavy challenge to dispossess the Mexicans of the ball in their own half led to two quick passes from the Canadians in the middle of the park and a wild, high cross from Nash in the eighty-third minute into the box. Corazzin connected on a header despite being outmanned, continuing his white-hot scoring streak that would eventually see him score more goals than any other player in the tournament and gain him a well-earned spot in the tournament's Best XI.

The child-like shriek on the Canadian broadcast from Bob Lenarduzzi, doing colour commentating, was undoubtedly shared by any Canadians watching at home.

"It was such a sucker punch," said Forrest.

FIFA was still in the middle of an ultimately failed experiment with the "golden goal," awarding a win to whoever scored first in extra time, which only heightened the sense of dramatics between Canada and Mexico.

The pitch was still wet from an earlier storm, which meant in the ninety-second minute Clarke slipped with the ball and Mexico gained a corner kick. Forrest screamed furiously at his teammates to mark their men.

"I was so nervous; I couldn't see straight," said Clarke.

Canada mercifully cleared the cross and, as was their habit, deliriously broke on the counter-attack. Nash had plenty of space in the Mexican half, and beside him, Kusch waved Hastings, the left back, out of his position and into the attack.

To Nash's right was Paul Stalteri, more of a natural finisher than Hastings, who was pleading with Nash for the ball.

"Richie had an engine like a marathon runner. It didn't surprise me, him making a box-to-box run. Probably what surprised me was that he finished it," said Xausa.

Xausa wasn't alone.

As Hastings corralled the ball with one touch on the bounce and roofed a shot past Mexican goalkeeper Oscar Perez, Lenarduzzi began laughing on the broadcast.

"Oscar Perez is stupefied," said Dobson on the broadcast.

"And so he should be," added Lenarduzzi, still chuckling.

And as stupefied as Perez might have been, it was nothing compared to how the Canadians themselves felt.

Up until a few years previously, in the Concacaf pyramid there was Mexico, and then every other nation. They'd won the previous three Gold Cups and their upset legitimately felt like the most shocking win for nearly every player on the roster, sitting drenched in sweat in the midday San Diego heat after their third game in eight days.

"Guys were asking each other, 'Did we just beat Mexico?'" said Clarke.

On the bus to make their way back to the hotel, the delirium had not worn off.

"There was a group of us senior players sitting at the back of the bus, and we started saying, 'Holy crap, we could go win this whole tournament,'" said Jason de Vos.

Word of the team's surprise run had finally spread north to Canada. Though Sportsnet owned the broadcast rights, they were hesitant to send a full crew down to the tournament, assuming that Canada's tournament would end after two games. But they now had to send Dobson and crew south.

And they weren't alone.

"All of a sudden, the phone starts ringing," said then men's national team manager and director of communications, Morgan Quarry. "People were asking, 'Hey, what's going on down there?'"

The CSA were caught off guard by the team's success.

"We did not have nearly enough marketing campaigns," admitted Quarry.

With three days off and a date with Trinidad and Tobago in the semifinal awaiting Canada, Canadian players had their first chance to recharge and get to know each other. Their hotel pool was the gathering place for a team whose bond and sense of optimism were growing, with the only interruption coming when players had to nip out to the pay phone to call their families and club managers to let them know their Southern California stay was going to be extended.

Forrest's calls with then West Ham United manager Harry Redknapp were almost daily.

Talk about being stupefied.

"He was just fuming," said Forrest. "He was telling me to get back there. 'What do you mean you beat Mexico? You never beat Mexico. What the hell is going on over there?'"

Forrest could have told Redknapp that he was emerging as the star of this tournament, though it would undermine his trademark Canadian modesty.

In the semifinal, Canada's attacking tendencies would be as muted as they had been the entire tournament.

The entire team wanted to maintain strict positional awareness on the pitch, in part because that formula had proven effective so far, and also because there was a lingering suspicion that against Trinidad and Tobago, where Warner hailed from, they could be susceptible to forces beyond their control.

With Mexico and the United States eliminated, the crowds that had been filling the stadiums dwindled to a mere fraction for the game between the two improbable semifinalists.

"We knew we were costing people some money, because there weren't any bums in the seats. So, Trinidad was a worry for us because of Jack Warner more than anything else," said Forrest.

So, Canada, again, sat deep. And in their least glamorous performance of the tournament, Canada ground out a 1–0 win on the strength, again, of some otherworldly goalkeeping from eventual tournament MVP, Craig Forrest.

"[Forrest] was literally a superhero," said Xausa.

His performance helped do two things for Canada: it set up a final with tournament invitees Colombia, then one of the giants of South American soccer, and as the only Concacaf nation still standing in the tournament, ensured they'd represent the region in the following year's Confederations Cup, a World Cup warm-up tournament for the champions of each respective soccer region.

For the players themselves, the house money they were playing with was practically falling out of their pockets. Getting into the knockout round thanks to a coin toss made them feel like a team of destiny, and beating the most highly regarded team in the tournament made them feel like they belonged. Whereas the typical Canadian attitude over the past few years saw teams enter tournaments wondering if they'd get played off the pitch, Forrest's play and his attitude helped teammates ditch the ominous sense of fear, and act liberated off the pitch while still playing controlled football on it. A Canadian side had never been as chatty and upbeat in the final days of a tournament.

"I felt like the stars were aligning and I could get my fingertips on everything," said Forrest. "I didn't feel like I was going to concede a goal."

And against Colombia, he didn't.

Rain ahead of the game meant the Colombians were playing on the kind of slick pitch they typically weren't used to. But it was one that favoured the Canadians: they went in heavy on tackles once again, hoping to knock a ball forward with a little more speed and surprise the South Americans.

Sure enough, when de Vos headed down a Martin Nash corner kick late in the first half toward Colombian goalkeeper Diego Gomez, Gomez was unable to control the ball with his hands as it hit the ground and it just slipped over the goal line.

"One of the ugliest goals," said Dobson, who took a second longer than he probably should have to make the call on the broadcast, due to the surprise of Gomez not handling a routine header.

Colombia emerged from halftime not looking like a team terribly interested in going forward and truly picking apart the Canadian side.

"You could see it meant more to us than it did to them. That's a big factor in football success: What is the social and emotional attachment within the group?" said de Vos.

By the sixty-seventh minute, it was clear what this final meant for the Canadian team's emotions. When Clarke was brought down by Gomez inside the box, his teammates swarmed him as if they'd already put the game to bed.

"It was premature, for sure," said Kusch.

Corrazin converted the penalty and threw a bit of salt in the wounds of the Colombians by sliding chest-first on the wet pitch in celebration. Even a late penalty attempt from Faustino Asprilla met Forrest's chest. Their bewildering, fairy-tale Gold Cup run finished with their being crowned champions.

If they felt like children when they won the coin toss, the shocked laughter throughout the team as they got a look at the trophy, aggressively oversized at more than three feet tall, was even more abundant.

Warner's frown only intensified as he presented the trophy to team captain de Vos, whose defensive stability also saw him named to the tournament's Best XI alongside Forrest and Corazzin.

The trophy was too heavy for de Vos to lift alone. In a moment of perfect symbolism, Forrest lifted his right hand directly over Warner's head to grab the trophy and support his teammate.

As Forrest concluded his postgame interview with Sportsnet, the weight of countless missed opportunities with his club sides due to national team commitments fell off his shoulders. Vindication gave way to tears.

"Unlike anything I'd felt in football," said Forrest.

In a wide locker room better suited for a college football team, players cut short the distance between each other, gathered in clusters, and shared rhetorical thoughts: *See what's possible, when players get released from their teams, buy in to a style of play, and we get a few bounces?*

But as remarkable as the win was, it did not give way to wild celebrations among the team. The players' soccer commitments saw many board flights back to Europe just hours after the win.

Hastings, one of the tournament heroes, could celebrate with only a single beer at Los Angeles International Airport before boarding a red-eye flight back to Scotland.

"It was all very abrupt," he said.

What was equally abrupt was the impact of Canada's achievement. Though the fairy-tale win should have turned enough heads toward the team, the organization, and the sport itself, that the players had to hastily return to their club commitments meant little could be done to amplify their success.

"There was no victory tour, no rolling out of players and making them available to media. It was a major missed opportunity," said long-time Canadian soccer reporter John Molinaro.

And so, even with a fairy-tale win under their belts, the Canadian men's national team remained outsiders, not just at international tournaments, but within the country they called home. Consider that after the women's national team won the bronze medal at the 2012 Olympics, players held clinics for young players, to promote the game and encourage participation, that sold out in short order.

"I've been here twenty-five years, the longest-serving CEO in Canada for soccer, and my eyes have seen a lot, but this was it," George Athanasiou, chief executive of Soccer Nova Scotia, told the *National Post* of the clinic in Halifax. "The enthusiasm of parents trying to get the kids into the camp, I don't know how to describe it to you. Plenty of people were begging for us to put them into the camp."

"That was the time to make Carlo Corazzin or Paul Stalteri someone that kids could aspire to be," said Xausa.

To many observers, the improbable Gold Cup win actually made them realize just how many improvements were needed to modernize and legitimize the Canadian men's national team, and how far away they were from mainstream appeal.

"A complete lack of vision," said Molinaro.

Getting Osieck interviewed on a national hockey game broadcast was about the pinnacle of mainstream media attention, and even that fell alarmingly short of the exposure the women's national team experienced years later.

"We didn't live the lives we should have after 2000, to take our program to that different level," said de Vos.

Dobson was consistently in the ears of people like Quarry, trying to get the players to take part in more media availabilities.

"There was a lot of 'Who is this team? What did they just win? And who's Craig Forrest?'" said Dobson.

But the fact that Forrest, the star of the tournament, who had the kind of easily marketable personality that the program needed, suited up for West Ham United a week after winning the Gold Cup was indicative of the fleeting opportunity.

"Nothing really changed from that point," Forrest said of the men's national team program. "Which is disappointing."

Canada went winless at the ensuing Confederations Cup. While the FIFA rankings do not always present the most complete snapshot of a team's performance, that the men's team ranked as high as fifty-fifth in the world in 2000 before falling as low as ninety-second in 2001, thanks to a series of disappointing losses, speaks to their inability to build off their Gold Cup win.

So, while the men's national team's lone tournament win since their 1985 Concacaf Championship might have been cause for celebration in the minutes after the final whistle, the enduring feeling was one of regret.

"I thought, now we're going to crack on," de Vos told the Athletic in 2019. "Now we're going to build a program, a structure, and have a chance to qualify for the World Cup. The greatest regret of my career is that we didn't do that. We very quickly went back to the culture that was common in the national team program in that era. It was a me-first culture, and it wasn't about us as a group of players, as Canadians working together toward a common goal. We didn't build a legacy. We didn't put the shirt down in a better position than when we picked it up. That's a regret that has lived with me ever since 2000."

. . .

The following is a completely true story, about something that occurred in my high school library in Oshawa, Ontario, on the morning of February 28, 2000, and variations of it likely occurred around Canada that morning.

Dozens of places across Canada could call themselves "hockey towns" at the turn of the century but few could match the stranglehold it had on my hometown. The people who worked in the General Motors plant there or had an association with it played hockey in house leagues, in church leagues, or in the multitude of Oshawa Minor Hockey Association competitive teams. People closely followed the likes of Bobby Orr, Eric Lindros, and John Tavares with the Oshawa Generals, a longstanding Ontario Hockey League (OHL) team and local institution, but even more closely followed the Maple Leafs, who played an hour west, in Toronto.

On a Monday morning spare that day, I sat in my oversized Whitby Iroquois Soccer Club track jacket while aggressively not completing homework, chatting about whoever had passed out from drinking a beer and a half over the weekend.

Students turned their heads when Mr. Skinner arrived: our unfortunately named vice principal, who could barely fit his grin through the library doors. Mr. Skinner had a predilection for chuckling his way through days and getting excited with students about the most inane topics. He didn't score highly in discipline, either. Students tended to look at the floor if they met him in the hall, to avoid an awkward interaction.

But on this Monday morning, Mr. Skinner had the entire library cornered.

"Hey!" he said, breaking the library's noise rules. "Did anyone see that soccer game on the weekend?"

The quiet murmurs turned to audible groans as Mr. Skinner went into detail.

"We beat Colombia!" he said, feigning incredulity.

"Who did?" asked a voice from a back table.

I lowered my head. *Please don't ask me.*

Mr. Skinner raised his arms in the air.

"Canada did! Our men's soccer team!" said Mr. Skinner, guffawing. I'd never known someone so eager to set up the bowling pins for a sardonic reply.

"Canada has a soccer team?" said the faceless teenager, as the groans turned to laughter.

I remain thankful that Mr. Skinner didn't turn to me for support. Because of course I'd watched the Gold Cup final, sitting beside my father in our living room as we, too, watched in astonishment.

We followed the German national team with far more fervour, since forty-six years earlier my grandparents had journeyed from Bad Wildungen in central Germany to Canada as immigrants.

We'd watched Canada's national team together only once before, at the SkyDome Cup in 1995, a strange friendly tournament when Canada played teams of alternates from Portugal and Denmark. That we sat in the nosebleeds probably only made "our" national team feel more like mirage than reality.

But I knew what Mr. Skinner was talking about that Monday morning, because Gerry Dobson's call at the final whistle was still lingering in my brain: "Canada, 2000 Gold Cup Champions. How does that sound?"

I couldn't answer how it "sounded," because I had no idea what it meant. And, on that Monday morning, I'm sure thousands of other Canadians probably didn't know, either.

Canada's improbable Gold Cup win did not inspire a generation of young players. But to our most passionate soccer compatriots, the country's lone tournament win in a generation did reinforce another belief: Canada could be a soccer nation.

And those people were ready to put in the time and effort to make sure it happened.

CHAPTER 6

"This Is Not Life or Death, It's Sport": How a Collection of Passionate Fans Tried to Bring Soccer into the Canadian Mainstream Media Landscape

GERRY DOBSON HAD EVERY RIGHT TO SOUND SURPRISED AS HE delivered his impassioned words at the end of Canada's Gold Cup win, surprised both by the national team's success, and that he found himself making the call.

Twenty years earlier, with little understanding of soccer, Dobson was a junior reporter at Global Television Network in Toronto assigned to cover the North American Soccer League (NASL)'s Blizzard, who at the time were owned by Global.

He'd try to fire up his enthusiasm to sell the game's legends taking their victory lap in NASL, but he knew in his heart that players such as George Best were "well past their best-before date."

As the stink of those best-before dates began wafting through stadiums, Dobson wondered about the prospects of the NASL, and of soccer itself in North America.

"It was a bit of an oddity," Dobson says of the league, with typical diplomacy. "It wasn't universal by any stretch."

The cessation of the NASL after the 1984 season brought the end of Dobson's career as a soccer reporter, or so he thought.

And he can be forgiven for thinking, as well, that he would never call a seminal moment in Canadian soccer, given how rarely the men's national team had broken through to mainstream media appeal. Part of the reason so many players felt frustration with the CSA after their 2000 Gold Cup win was that they had heard this song before: another chance for soccer to be looked at differently by people watching televisions or reading newspapers that would never come.

"Canada has a rich history in the game. Certainly not as rich as hockey or some other sports, but there is a history and I just think they're stuck in that sort of mentality that 'This isn't our game. We're just visitors, so to speak, in the soccer world,'" said John Molinaro.

Coverage of the sport needed to take massive leaps in the sport's growing ecosystem. In the 2000s, it was the task of a few people to deliver the news, insights, and stories of the sport — and to challenge mainstream sports media norms throughout the country.

• • •

In 1998, the Canadian sports broadcasting landscape shifted with the establishment of CTV Sportsnet. The Sports Network (TSN) had dominated the field for over a decade, but Sportsnet challenged that, acquiring cable rights to NHL games from TSN themselves.

Scott Moore had produced successful Olympics broadcasts for TSN, so Sportsnet tapped the well-established and sometimes bullish producer to help launch its network. Moore would end up becoming as influential a Canadian media figure as any other throughout the next decade, particularly because of his ability to avoid traditional lines of thinking.

"[Moore] would try ten crazy ideas," said Dobson. "And if two of them worked, it would be successful."

From Sportsnet's launch, Moore believed soccer could be a vital piece of the programming. He had noticed how the evolving demographics in Canada responded positively to TSN's broadcasts of the 1994 World Cup.

"If you were paying attention, you could see this coming," said Moore.

Moore secured the purchase of the Canadian broadcast rights to England's still-growing Premier League without incurring a huge financial burden. Given Dobson's experience and professionalism, Moore pitched him on hosting Sportsnet's Premier League games.

"Sure," Dobson recalls telling him, "Why not?"

Dobson became the face many Canadian soccer fans would begin their weekend mornings with. Not long after Sportsnet began investing time and resources into those broadcasts, "it started to truly move the needle," according to Moore.

The early success with the Premier League gave Sportsnet the confidence to broadcast the 2002 Women's Under-19 World Championship, hosted in Canada.

"Some of my colleagues at the time made fun of me that we were broadcasting teenage girls' soccer," remembers Moore.

Moore had the last laugh as Canada stormed to the final and Christine Sinclair, who would go on to become one of Canada's best athletes of the century, as well as the top goal scorer in international soccer, had her coming-out party as the tournament's best player.

Canada lost a tightly contested final to the United States, which Moore says earned Sportsnet the biggest rating in the history of the network up to that time.

"You could feel that something special was happening," Moore said, of soccer in Canada.

Sportsnet had the early rights to the Canadian men's national team games, yet their programming of the games spoke to just how high a mountain the sport still had to climb to achieve mainstream recognition. Even with access to the men's national team, Dobson sometimes called games remotely from the Sportsnet studio, as some executives struggled to see the value in shelling out for broadcasters' and reporters' travel, given the men's team's lack of popular recognition throughout the country. Dobson would repeatedly be told that the resources weren't available to send him and a crew on the road, even though covering games remotely, off a live feed, dramatically reduced his ability to give life to the events and the storylines.

"It's a sign of how little respect soccer was given," said Dobson.

That puzzled others, besides Dobson.

In 2000, an insightful blond-haired and fresh-faced recent university graduate, Kristian Jack, moved to Canada from England. From the moment he arrived, he found it "mind-blowing" how many children were playing soccer. And the divide between children playing the game and the way the game was covered in the professional media landscape was equally as mind-blowing for Jack as he tried to insinuate himself into Canada's soccer media.

"[Canadian soccer media] just didn't exist," said Jack. "Covering 'Canadian soccer' just meant covering European leagues. A lot of it comes down to the fact that anybody who was falling in love with soccer in Canada was probably an immigrant [from] somewhere else. They could go and look elsewhere. So why wouldn't they? It's not snobbery, it's just a natural tendency to look to something that's better."

At this time, basketball was gaining in popularity after the Toronto Raptors were founded in 1995, and football and baseball had strong holds, too, given that Canadian franchises in those games had existed for decades.

But of course, the attention paid to those three sports paled in comparison to that paid to hockey. Calling hockey a religion in Canada had become a cliché, but to flip through newspaper sports sections in the country or tune into late-night highlight shows generally proved it was true.

"The people who are running newsrooms, they're old white guys," said Molinaro. "I don't think they're nuanced or sophisticated enough in their thinking that they can get out of their silo."

Perhaps ironically, it was an abandonment of sophistication that led to one of the more ground-breaking attempts to introduce soccer to the Canadian public.

James Sharman had moved from Liverpool to complete a journalism degree at Ryerson University, and, with his charm and proclivity for a quick-witted reply, quickly landed a job as a producer with The Score, a network that began in 1994 but had taken until 2000 to obtain a licence to broadcast live events. The Score sometimes struggled for a piece of the Canadian sports broadcasting pie that other networks were feasting on.

The Score had a once-a-day segment called Sports World that covered international sports, including rugby, cricket, Formula 1 racing, and, of course, soccer.

"And they figured I've got an accent, so let's give it to Sharman," said Sharman.

As the segment Sharman produced began to receive positive feedback, it was developed into a longer package of highlights broadcasted more frequently.

Sharman thought it would be advantageous to lean into soccer highlights and programming, given the worldwide popularity of the game and the evident interest in Canada during the World Cup and the Euros. An important element of The Score's pitch to the CRTC to land their licence to broadcast live sports was their intent to bring soccer to a Canadian audience.

Their fearless attitude empowered them to take risks with their programming. This would continue into 2007, when they landed the Premier League broadcast rights. The Score would also sublicence games back to Sportsnet, but more programming was needed to complement these rights.

Along with other like-minded producers and broadcasters, including Kristian Jack, who joined the network as an intern and eventually began writing scripts, Sharman pushed to make that new programming different from the norm. Sharman's idea was that if the viewer was relaxing at home on the couch watching, why shouldn't the hosts try to emulate that same attitude?

Scripts were written in a way that never tried to talk down to the audience and tried to inject humour wherever possible. As the host, Sharman wanted to converse with the audience as if they were in a bar.

Sharman's vision came to life in the form of *The Footy Show*, a thirty-minute program he hosted alongside Jack dedicated to soccer news, highlights, analysis, and features. The duo's sneakers and open-buttoned shirts helped free the show of the stuffiness that had become commonplace in English soccer programming and some of the more popular sports shows in Canada, which broadcasters believed was necessary to mimic the increasing professionalism in sports.

This is not life or death: it's sport, Sharman remembers thinking.

They sat on couches and worked through sometimes unscripted segments.

"We just shot the shit," said Sharman.

The show caught on with younger audiences because of that approach. Landing Carlsberg as a sponsor not only helped legitimize the show, but also provided much-needed financial resources.

The game of soccer presented another option to more mainstream sports in Canada, and *The Footy Show* epitomized that attitude: they were an alternative, but one that still garnered eyeballs and had plenty of room to grow.

"[Audiences] related to it because we didn't take ourselves too seriously. We wanted the audience to be part of the show," said Jack.

The Footy Show embraced Twitter in the social media platform's early days, reading and reacting to tweets on air. They also created podcasts, before that medium's widescale popularity.

"The Score just tried anything, right?" said Sharman.

One common thread linking every broadcaster and reporter who made up Canada's growing soccer media contingent was a refusal to dumb down their approach to the game, even though they were explaining it to a new crop of fans, viewers, and readers.

"[Canadian fans] know their shit and they will call you out if you try and con them," said Sharman.

Early on in *The Footy Show*'s tenure, Sharman and Jack used language specific to the world of soccer without pause, and assumed their viewers understood that language. Jack's deep dives into the world of soccer tactics were thoughtful, but not for the uninitiated.

Even while some in both The Score's and Sportsnet's marketing, advertising, and management departments wished their talent would try to introduce the game to a wider, naive audience with an educational bent to their scripts, Sharman, Jack, and Dobson were resolute: if they treated the country's soccer fans as intelligent ones, coverage would catch on.

"I never once told myself I was talking to somebody who didn't know anything about the sport," said Jack. "That was my mandate from day one: if we belittle the audience, and make it a soccer broadcast for dummies, then we will never go anywhere."

"From a production point of view, we felt that the game could sell itself enough to the new fans, and they would learn it as they go," said Dobson. "I'll be honest, there were some fans when we first went on the air, I'm not ashamed to admit it, who knew more about the game and about some of the teams than I did."

By the time the 2010 World Cup rolled around, Moore was working at

CBC, who had the tournament's Canadian broadcast rights. By now, the tune of the people around him had changed.

"People really wanted to push to keep the ball rolling after 2010 to see soccer continue to grow in Canada," said Moore. He returned to Sportsnet that year, and again made soccer programming a priority, with more leagues being added.

"We saw the ratings continue to get better and better," said Moore.

And *The Footy Show* had expanded with a bright, dedicated producer in Thomas Dobby, and additional sharp hosts, including Brendan Dunlop and Sid Seixeiro.

As the Score broadcasted from downtown Toronto, fans of various teams in the tournament would stop by the studio's large outdoor screens to watch the show, complemented by 2010 World Cup highlights. Even though it was still challenging for soccer's small, but growing, media membership to convince their bosses that soccer would eventually catch on as a main-stream sport in Canada, seeing the impassioned soccer fans that summer in Canada's largest city only added fuel to that fire.

"There was an element to us knowing that [soccer's rise in Canada] was coming more than anybody else," said Jack. "It was us versus everybody else, really."

. . .

The increase in coverage of the sport in Canada, including the men's nation-al team, was sometimes done without the help of the CSA, whose lack of resources overall meant they lacked the marketing tools to increase aware-ness of their product.

"There was no infrastructure in place to take advantage of winning the Gold Cup," admits Morgan Quarry.

And so properly broadcasting, and therefore publicizing, the men's na-tional team remained a challenge.

When Canada's 2002 World Cup qualification journey got under way with an early match against Cuba in Havana, Dobson convinced Sportsnet that they should broadcast from Havana's dilapidated Estadio Nacional de Fútbol Pedro Marrero. Built in 1929, it turned out to have seen better days. Palm trees were poking in close to the field where stands should have been.

Dobson arrived at the stadium to see the pitch in less-than-desirable condition, with far-too-lengthy grass being cut with rudimentary tools.

He shook his head, but then nearly threw his neck out from shaking his head when he saw where he would be working on game day: not the kind of press box that the Sportsnet team were used to, but an old yellow school bus with doors that had trouble closing completely. That, for the purposes of this game and this game alone, had been repurposed into a mobile, pitch-side production unit.

With Lenarduzzi alongside as his colour commentator, Dobson called the lone goal from Jason de Vos off a set piece in the thirty-ninth minute, which was standard enough procedure.

But being joined in the bus by Canadian head coach Holger Osieck?

Is this real? Dobson remembers thinking to himself as Osieck took a seat beside him. *Is this game really happening this way?*

After being sent off in Canada's Gold Cup final win for barking in the ear of the referee when Colombia was awarded a penalty kick, Osieck was not allowed on Canada's bench for the team's next game, which turned out to be this World Cup qualifier. With other options to watch the rest of the game virtually non-existent, he made his way around the pitch to the bus, where he could watch alongside the broadcasters.

Broadcasting an international game out of a bus? Those on the ground with a keen interest in pushing the sport forward still lacked some degree of whole-hearted support.

"Those things were always a battle, because not everybody in broadcast-ing knew about soccer or cared about soccer," said Dobson. "Everybody had blinders on, seeing baseball, hockey, and football. And soccer was the poor little cousin."

Yet with three Canadian teams having joined a revived MLS by 2012, those in Canadian soccer media began to feel some validation.

"We knew this was going to be gangbusters, because we knew that there was just this grassroots groundswell of soccer support that was just waiting to get a team. We knew what was out there. We felt now we've got something that that we're taking ownership of," said Dobson.

Sportsnet, along with CBC and GolTV, a broadcasting arm of Toronto FC owners Maple Leaf Sports & Entertainment, broadcasted early TFC games.

Dobson wanted to use even more soccer-specific language and to embed themselves within a team — TFC — in a way the network never could have by broadcasting the Premier League only.

"It really gave us a chance to dig our feet into it and come up with ways to hone our skills and make the production as good as it can be," said Dobson.

In 2012, Sportsnet acquired The Score in a transaction valued at $167 million and rebranded it as Sportsnet 360. *The Footy Show* was cancelled in 2013, to the surprise of the hosts. Jack was laid off, while the other hosts remained with the network in various roles. Sharman became one of the network's, and one of the country's, most trusted soccer voices.

Jack landed with TSN not long afterward and became a centrepiece of their soccer programming alongside Luke Wileman.

Sportsnet and TSN would share broadcast rights to TFC, but TSN would soon become the sole broadcaster. Jack would once again hear from executive producers who were worried the approach he was taking was too highbrow, but he remained steadfast.

On November 30, 2016, rivals Toronto FC and the Montreal Impact met in the second leg of the MLS Eastern Conference Final. In front of a packed BMO Field, a downtown-Toronto soccer-specific stadium, in the pouring rain, the two teams played to a 5–2 extra-time thriller that instantly became one of the most memorable games in league history.

An average audience of 1.4 million viewers in Canada watched the game, breaking the record for the country's most-watched MLS game in history.

Ten days later, that record was again broken as Toronto FC played in its first ever MLS Cup final.

The BMO Field press box literally could not contain all the accredited members of the press, with additional journalists being housed in makeshift tents outside, requiring thick gloves to file their copy.

The Canadian soccer media members who were continually driven by their own passion toward the game of soccer were now surrounded by other journalists who had little choice but to cover it, as it became more popular than ever in Canada.

Journalists who had stuck with the job of covering the team included the likes of Neil Davidson, who in his more than twenty years writing about

Canadian soccer for the Canadian Press had travelled across the planet — and dealt with questionable public relations units while doing so — now keeping readers more informed than any of his peers. Molinaro of CBC and Sportsnet, known for his frequent balanced assessments, was another. And, of course, Sharman and Jack were there. Dobson, having retired months earlier, watched from his home.

Like so many of the journalists who had fought to get soccer more coverage in Canada, they were all driven by their own love for the game itself.

"It's not a career. It's a life," said Jack. "It's the passion for the sport, and the need to try and make things better."

Even with the demise of *The Footy Show*, the show's successful run proved there was room for another sport in Canadian sports broadcasting.

"When you take that atmosphere, and put it on a live broadcast, people go, 'This is happening in Canada? These sounds? This roar?' There was so much at stake, but that's exactly what was dreamed up when MLS came into Canada. To be quite frank, it didn't even happen in the United States a lot of the time," said Jack. "And it was happening in our country."

• • •

So, where does the men's national team fit in all of this?

Even with the increased interest in soccer and the changes in the sport's journalism landscape, Dobson and others at Sportsnet still had to "oversell" the team's chances to generate interest within the network when World Cup qualification campaigns came around. With every game in every step of the qualification process, they tried to reinforce just how much qualifying for a World Cup would mean from a broadcast revenue perspective.

"It wasn't a ratings success, the men's national team," said Moore.

Yet by 2019, the outlook of the men's national team had changed drastically, with many young players, such as Alphonso Davies and Jonathan David, showcasing the kind of talent never before seen in Canada. Canada Soccer had lumped all of its commercial properties into one entity called Canadian Soccer Business to increase the opportunity for their teams to be invested in for years ahead.

MediaPro, a multi-billion-dollar Spanish communications company with experience broadcasting UEFA Champions League games in Europe, saw the opportunity to broadcast the men's national team, a new domestic league, and the women's national team.

They bought the rights with the clear intention of including the 2026 World Cup, hosted by Canada, the United States, and Mexico, in the length of the deal. The commercial opportunities for the upcoming World Cup were viewed as endless.

"It starts to become more of the fabric when you're doing MLS and suddenly [Canadian midfielder Jonathan Osorio] is playing for TFC and you're producing players. And now there's a pathway for the men's national team to become part of the discussion," said Jack.

MediaPro unveiled OneSoccer, a soccer-only streaming service to be the exclusive broadcaster of Canadian Soccer Business. Even though OneSoccer faced a fundamental challenge existing alongside the duopoly of Bell and Rogers, which respectively own TSN and Sportsnet, that a network would focus its content solely on soccer in Canada speaks to the evident interest MediaPro saw. Interest in the domestic television rights to Canadian men's national team matches had previously been so low that the CSA had been forced to give them away for free on occasion, or even paid broadcasters. But interest had since grown. MediaPro looked at the strong participation numbers among young Canadian soccer players, coupled with the fact that so many Canadians owned smartphones and were capable of streaming content anywhere, and saw a natural fit.

The reach of, and interest in, the men's national team had clearly changed in the lead-up to the 2022 World Cup, when OneSoccer was able to sub-licence its broadcasts of the qualifying games to Sportsnet.

And that continued interest reached newfound levels after Davies took off with otherworldly speed and ran by multiple Panamanian defenders along the edge of BMO Field, deftly kept a ball from going out of bounds, and then darted by another Panama defender before, almost callously, firing a shot into the back of the net. Though Panama had taken a lead against Canada in the fifth minute of their 2022 World Cup qualifying match, it was Davies's sixty-sixth-minute goal that put Canada up 2–1 before an eventual 4–1 win to keep their World Cup hopes alive.

Davies's goal made for one of Canada's most convincing and important wins since the 2000 Gold Cup and led the highlight shows on Sportsnet and TSN, the very networks OneSoccer was trying to compete against. Laura Armstrong, another journalist who had tirelessly written about Canadian soccer for one of Canada's largest newspapers, the *Toronto Star*, wrote a detailed, second-by-second breakdown of the goal.

Davies's goal caused many people in soccer broadcasting to consider how far they had come. It was the kind of viral moment the men's national team had long been lacking.

And with bravado and an unorthodox approach, it was the perfect encapsulation of what the men's national team represented and their arrival within Canada's mainstream cultural landscape, as well as that of the backers of people like Davies who had worked to promote the sport he was thriving in.

"Soccer is at that point in the growth curve where its growth has been incredible to this point," said Moore, "and it's about to become exponential."

CHAPTER 7

From Parliament to Frankfurt to Brampton: 2000–2011

IN APRIL 2000, THE INTERNATIONAL MONETARY FUND PUBLISHED A significant report that attempted to home in on the key aspects of globalization, a catch-all term that would in many ways define a decade, including movement of people and spread of knowledge.

Though most prominent members of Canada's soccer community probably didn't clamour to read the report, those aspects would end up providing the blueprint for a dramatic shift in Canada's sports landscape at the turn of the century.

Not that you would know it by the men's national team's performances, however.

Their storybook run at the Gold Cup months earlier didn't carry over into qualifying for the 2002 World Cup. A lack of attacking quality was exposed as Canada scored a paltry lone goal in six matches in the second-to-last round of Concacaf World Cup qualifying. This lifeless campaign and stunning drop-off in their performance represented arguably their most forgettable World Cup qualifying campaign.

"It has been some kind of ugly," wrote then *Globe and Mail* columnist Stephen Brunt after the team was eliminated with a 4–0 loss to Trinidad and Tobago, and head coach Holger Osieck offered little explanation for his team's poor performances.

Players who had advanced to Europe were frustrated by the lack of structure in his training sessions: possession drills without proper borders of play, and not enough attention to maintaining a proper shape on the pitch. They'd grown equally weary of his brittle approach.

"He made you feel like you were the worst footballer ever," said Paul Peschisolido.

Turnover was desperately needed as so many of the veteran holdovers from the 1994 World Cup qualifying run were past their best-before date. Six players of the starting eleven in Canada's first game in the final round of qualifying were twenty-six or older.

Even though his team slowed to a crawl for him in their efforts to qualify for the World Cup, Osieck was permitted to stay on as head coach, but the need for a jolt of energy throughout the program was evident.

Because just after the turn of the century, the rise of soccer among Canadian youth was impossible to ignore.

A 2008 report by Statistics Canada on Canadian social trends did make the rounds in the Canadian soccer community in a way the IMF report did not: utilizing data from the 1992 and 2005 Canada general social surveys, the report determined that in 1992 soccer, swimming, hockey, and baseball enjoyed a fairly equal percentage share of the sports children between the ages of five and fourteen were playing.

Yet by 2005 there had been a monumental change: more children were participating in soccer than any other team sport, at a rate almost double that of the next-most-popular sport, swimming. And while participation in soccer had nearly doubled from 1992 to 2005, hockey, long established as one of Canada's national sports and a cultural touchstone, saw a slight decline.

As soccer's popularity grew beyond its fringe roots in the country, the conversations about the sport on the sidelines, in Canadian homes, and in sports-network studios grew louder and louder, leading to one unavoidable question: how had soccer become the most popular youth sport in a country that had long considered hockey an essential part of its cultural fabric?

And two prominent professors were examining that very question.

Peter Donnelly is a professor emeritus of *Sport Policy and Politics* at the University of Toronto, with research interests in sport subcultures and children in high-performance sport. Simon Darnell is an associate professor of *Sport for Development and Peace* at the University of Toronto, with research interests in the sociology of sport and physical activity.

In interviews for this book, they shared their theories on the rise of soccer in Canada.

First, globalization and the spread of information about the most popular game in the world eventually broke down the hardened barriers hockey had put up around the Canadian borders.

"[Soccer] is probably the preeminent globalized sport, one in which the stars are known around the world and where the sport reaches around the world in a way that hockey doesn't," said Darnell.

During his three years working in the United Kingdom, Darnell would commonly reference hockey in discussions with his colleagues.

"But people would say, 'Aren't there, like, ten countries that care about hockey?' The popularity doesn't line up and it isn't as diffused around the world like soccer is," said Darnell. "So, if we put Canada into its international context, and then put this sport into its global context, both of those contribute to soccer becoming a really popular sport for Canadian kids."

Next, even if costs within minor hockey associations vary, they will almost always exceed the cost of registering a child in soccer: indoor ice time is more expensive than time in public parks, and the cost of multiple pieces of expensive equipment easily outweighs the cost of a pair of shinpads, boots, and a ball.

A 2016 three-part *Hamilton Spectator* report combed data from the Ontario Hockey League's players and outlined how "a highly significant number of the league's Ontario-raised players are from suburban neighbourhoods where most people are well-educated, earn high incomes, and live in expensive homes."

"If you think about the difference between soccer and hockey culturally in Canada, hockey still represents that elite exclusiveness and soccer doesn't have those same connotations associated with it. Then that's backed up by how much it costs," said Darnell.

And with eleven players on the field compared to six in hockey, Donnelly believes, soccer presents an option for children to be far more active than they are in hockey, where they can spend large stretches of play sitting on the bench.

"Soccer became really attractive for parents who wanted their kids to be involved and to be active," said Donnelly. "The push-back against hockey just grows through the decade."

A 2009 CBC story cited the CSA's 2007 report that 867,869 soccer players were registered across the country, which was "nearly 310,000 more participants than were in minor hockey."

Emile Therien, former president of the Canada Safety Council, wrote in a 2012 *Toronto Star* editorial that enrolment in Hockey Canada, the sport's governing body, was then at 572,000 players, down more than 200,000 from the sport's peak.

"And the prospects are grim," wrote Therien.

Combined with the rising cost of housing in major urban centres, a reduction in disposable income means soccer's lower cost compared to that of hockey can look more attractive to parents.

"Soccer is the only sport where boys' participation has increased significantly, while hockey — formerly the number-one organized sport for boys — has seen a dip in participation, especially among boys from households in the lowest adjusted income quintile," said the original Statistics Canada report.

"Community soccer leagues were starting to do well and running more and more teams. And it was an opportunity to get your kid playing a sport," said Donnelly.

Donnelly saw more middle-class white parents, traditional proponents of enrolling their children in hockey, "taking a long hard look at the cost and opportunities associated with hockey."

"Unless they have really painted a professional track for their kid, [hockey] becomes less and less attractive as a participation sport," he said.

Then there's the increased research regarding concussion. An understanding among the mainstream sports-viewing public of the harms of concussion increased throughout the decade. Boston University diagnosed former NHL player Reggie Fleming with chronic traumatic encephalopathy, a neurodegenerative brain disease caused in contact sports such as hockey, six months after his death in 2009. While he became the first hockey player known to have the disease, other deceased hockey players would soon follow, including popular enforcer Bob Probert.

"Parents wanted safer opportunities for their children to participate," said Donnelly. "Parenting is changing. You're supposed to know where your kids are and what they're doing twenty-four hours a day by the 1990s. And you also are very protective of your kids' health and integrity in that way."

Finally, Darnell said, the experiences of immigrants bringing their own connections to soccer from abroad has inevitably led to an increase in the number of children who play soccer.

On October 8, 1971, then Canadian prime minister Pierre Trudeau delivered a speech in the country's federal parliament that would shape the country's future: "There is no official culture, nor does any ethnic group take precedence over any other. No citizen or group of citizens is other than Canadian, and all should be treated fairly."

Official policies of multiculturalism and bilingualism would be implemented, and for those seeking to leave their lives abroad and continue them in Canada, Trudeau avowed that the cultures people would bring, or would have already brought, would rightly be treated equally.

According to Statistics Canada, the number and proportion of the foreign-born population in Canada had essentially stayed level from 1911 to 1951 but continued to rise every decade afterward.

Trudeau's vision of a country in which newcomers would not feel pressure to assimilate to a predetermined way of life encouraged a wave of immigration and multiculturalism such as the country had never experienced.

Immigrants infusing their love of the world's most popular sport into popular Canadian culture was an unavoidable and welcome change. Hubs for immigrants such as Brampton, a suburb of Toronto, would eventually produce some of the country's best soccer players, like Atiba Hutchinson and Tajon Buchanan.

"Especially in a city like Toronto, one of the arrival cities of the world, with a huge immigrant population, [the increase of children of immigrants playing soccer] makes sense," said Darnell.

These findings aligned later in the century with the rise of Canada's men's soccer players such as Alphonso Davies, a refugee to Canada, and Jonathan David, an immigrant from Haiti.

The shift toward soccer as a predominant sport among children in Canada is evidence of "glocalization": a hybrid culture in which immigrant parents see their identification as Canadian grow stronger, and popular culture becomes hybridized.

"Over time, people take their global perspective, but they turn it into a local cultural form. And that fits what we're seeing in soccer. People want to be Canadian, but they're going to flex their more traditional cultural tastes," said Darnell.

The increase in children participating in soccer meant the CSA needed both to promote the game to mainstream audiences in a way that mirrored the interest among children in playing soccer, and to establish the national team as a respectable vehicle for change.

• • •

It was inevitable that, with the growth of the game at the grassroots level, exceptionally talented players would eventually emerge.

After his wife had accepted a job in Calgary in 1992, Thomas Niendorf arrived from Germany in his new home with the kind of soccer resume the most aspiring Canadian coaches could only dream of having. The athletically built coach held a UEFA Pro Licence and had worked within the youth academy at legendary German side Bayern Munich as well as with Dynamo Berlin. Yet in Canada he was routinely told by local soccer organizations he was overqualified and that with few paid coaching positions in the sport, it would be better for him to find employment outside of soccer.

"There was not really any professional environment at the time," said Niendorf.

As he began watching young players run through thick grass pitches, he could still see the serious talent, even if a lack of funding and professionals who could dedicate their time and resources into coaching players was evident. Niendorf asked himself what might happen to this talent if proper coaching was in place. His entrepreneurial spirit took hold and he started to run independent coaching clinics, relying on parental support and his own investments rather than government funding or grants, or even club or national team support.

"It was a private initiative to create better environments for players and to give players exposure," said Niendorf.

His training sessions featured more structure than local organizations'. He placed an emphasis on error correction and on instructing players how to learn from their mistakes, instead of simply pointing out those mistakes, as he saw many volunteer coaches doing. He wanted to arm young players with decision-making tools to use in games, and he felt that could be achieved by building age-appropriate training sessions.

"That was a big, big problem in the country. Coaches saw things in the professional game and did these things with eleven- and twelve-year-olds because they have no education," said Niendorf.

Parents across Alberta began asking Niendorf if their children could join his private sessions, or if he could take over entire teams on his own.

And that's how Niendorf first caught a glimpse of fourteen-year-old Owen Hargreaves training in Calgary. He'd been asked to work with Hargreaves's club team, which eventually became part of his academy. Born to an English father and a Welsh mother, who emigrated from the United Kingdom, Hargreaves's qualities on the ball were unparalleled among his peers, as were his work rate, his defensive qualities as a midfielder, and his ability to make every one of his teammates better with pinpoint passing and vision.

A friend working as a youth coach for Bayern Munich was equally impressed when he laid eyes on Hargreaves during a summer vacation in Canada, enough that he suggested they introduce Hargreaves to the Bayern Munich youth set-up. Niendorf was skeptical, but eventually called Wolfgang Dremmler, a scout at Bayern Munich, and asked if Hargreaves could be considered for a trial in Bavaria.

"Thomas, are you sure this is a Canadian kid?" Dremmler asked Niendorf.

Niendorf mentioned Hargreaves's family's roots, and eventually a deal was struck to send the player for a trial in Munich. Generally, when European clubs identify a player of interest, they will pay for a trial. But in this case, Hargreaves would travel to Munich only if Niendorf himself paid Hargreaves's way.

"No one was actively looking at Canadian kids at the time," said Niendorf. "In the end, it was luck that players like Owen Hargreaves came along."

Niendorf accompanied Hargreaves and his parents to the airport for what would be the start of a life-altering journey.

After two years with Bayern's youth and reserve sides, Hargreaves graduated to Bayern's senior side. As a twenty-year-old rookie, Hargreaves was on the team that won the Bundesliga, and he started in the 2001 Champions League final, which Bayern also won. After six more successful seasons, a high-profile transfer to Manchester United followed, where Hargreaves would again win the Champions League, though injuries ultimately limited his time with the club.

Early in his professional career, Hargreaves opted to play for Wales's youth national teams before England swooped in and began a brazen courtship. The prospect of playing for Wales, never mind the Canadian national team, quickly vaporized when he agreed to play for the English national team. That he was the only player to have played for England without having ever lived in the country didn't draw nearly the kind of ire from English fans as it did from Canadian fans, who flooded nascent message boards with vitriol. They were furious that the most talented Canadian player would spurn Canada so easily.

Hargreaves's appearances in the 2002 World Cup, the 2004 Euros, and the 2006 World Cup for England served as cruel reminders for the Canadian soccer community that the men's national team needed to improve the infrastructure to support players of his elite quality. That he aspired to play for the team that offered him the greatest chance for international success also shouldn't be surprising, given Canada's track record up to that point. For years afterward, bringing up Hargreaves's name in debates about the greatest Canadian soccer player elicited responses that were equal parts scorn and longing.

Yet, Hargreaves's emerging from Canada was proof that elite talent existed throughout minor soccer associations in Canada, just needing to be fostered.

Lethbridge-born Nik Ledgerwood also used Niendorf's connections to secure a trial at Bayern Munich. While the chipper young midfielder's trial was unsuccessful, Bayern did reach out to local rivals 1860 Munich to inform them about Ledgerwood's talent. He graduated from 1860 Munich's reserve side to their first side, playing in Germany's second division, then a rare feat for a Canadian.

"It was always about being better than their domestic players, or you wouldn't get a chance," said Ledgerwood.

He was an industrious, all-round player who could shuffle from defensive to offensive responsibilities with ease. His dedication to putting his head down and taking in information from every available coach helped him stick in European leagues and continually log heavy minutes, particularly in Germany, from 2003 to 2016.

Even with Ledgerwood's success, he would face constant derision from his teammates and others around him in Germany about Canada's lack of soccer success and infrastructure. The stigma of being from a country without a soccer history was impossible to escape. Progress since the days of Alex Bunbury and Craig Forrest was slow.

"'You come from Canada?' Ledgerwood remembers being asked. "'Do you even have a league?'"

Hargreaves's success, unfortunately, didn't change the perception of Canadian players in Europe.

"They didn't really look at him as a Canadian player because of his English background," said Niendorf.

But what had changed, domestically, was the belief that Canadian players could compete with their global counterparts.

• • •

Across the country, the rise in participation numbers led to a growing concern: organizations would not be able to harness players' potential if they were being coached by volunteers without expertise and age-specific coaching methods.

Infighting within the CSA regarding best practices, fuelled by the divergent beliefs held by different provincial heads and the amount of power these provinces enjoyed in decision-making, threatened continued growth. It led to people going out on their own in the hopes of developing players.

People like Michael Findlay, who from 2003 to 2011 was director of football development at British Columbia Soccer. With a pair of piercing eyes and a manner that tried to cut through the surrounding bullshit, Findlay believed the tallest barrier between soccer the fringe sport, enjoyed by thousands of children in the summer, and mainstream success in Canada, in which those same children provided the eventual foundation for successful national teams, was coaching education.

"Aside from the complete outliers, the talent of a thirteen-to-fifteen-year-old in Canada, whether they're in Victoria or Newfoundland, is not much different in Holland, Germany, Italy, England, anywhere in the world," said Findlay. "It's the opportunity they have to then take that talent and have the appropriate environment to then go to the next level."

Findlay wanted province-wide high-performance goals, organizational standards-based coach development, and he wanted to learn from successful organizations how to get them. Osieck connected Findlay and another British Columbia–based coach, Markus Reinkens, with former coaching trainer Erich Rutemöller and Ulf Schott, then head of talent development at the German soccer association (Deutsche Fussball Bund) in the hopes of gleaning insight from one of the world's most astute and advanced soccer federations.

The doors of the federation were literally opened for Findlay and Reinkens in Frankfurt. In a sleek office adorned with photos of the German national team's many world-class players, the group spoke at length about the DFB's newly established Talent Development Program, a federation-wide overhaul of their coaching and programming that was a response to the national team's continued poor performances at major tournaments. The focus of the program was regional centres with unified standards across Germany that would focus on player development. These standards would also be in line with professional clubs and their own academies.

Eventually, this Talent Development Program was seen as a major influence on Germany's 2014 World Cup–winning team.

And over continued cups of espresso, Rutemöller and Schott did not treat the standards they'd implemented and the insight they'd gleaned as state secrets.

"I got more material out of the DFB at that time than I'd ever got from [the CSA]," said Findlay. "They just handed it to me and said 'Go ahead.'"

Midway through their conversation, Rutemöller became less interested in pumping his own federation's tires and began inquiring about Canadian soccer. To better understand the challenges Findlay and Reinkens faced,

Rutemöller pulled out a multi-layered map of North America. Findlay homed in on British Columbia, discussing how the provincial organization served as the governing body for such a sizable land mass.

He turned to Rutemöller, who crossed his arms.

"He literally looked over at me and said 'You're fucked,'" said Findlay.

Findlay sat in stunned silence.

"'It's impossible. Look at the size of you,'" Findlay remembers Rutemöller saying, as he then pulled out a map of Germany and explained how the small size of Germany, compared to British Columbia, made travel throughout the various regional development centres easier, which helped to identify players in need of development.

He stressed an idea that Findlay would try to implement in British Columbia: by creating smaller soccer communities, players would benefit by having more access to skills development programs and proper coaching.

"We came back to British Columbia and said, 'Look, let's just think about British Columbia like Germany,'" said Findlay. "Which then forced, in my opinion, the districts to get their shit together."

Regionalized development programs were born to ensure that the quality of the coaching a player in a large city centre such as Vancouver would receive was the same as a player would get in smaller cities.

Findlay says Adam Straith, who moved from Victoria into the Vancouver Whitecaps residency program, and eventually to Germany, where he played for various professional clubs for over a decade and made forty-three appearances for the national team, was one player who specifically benefitted from the implementation of the program.

"At that time, they had nowhere else to go," said Findlay.

Changes weren't isolated to British Columbia, either. Reinkens eventually moved to the Saskatchewan Soccer Association and worked to apply that same idea of regionalization in talent development to that province.

"If you continue to try and just randomly go around and provide some information or do a workshop in a location, if we don't provide structure, regionalize, and connect the communities that are in those areas together, we're not going to be as successful as we'd hoped it would be," said Reinkens.

But Findlay's findings still highlighted another problem in Canadian soccer.

"What we don't have," Findlay said sternly, "is compliance."

Findlay's new connections at the DFB were essentially alluding to how in a country Canada's size, ensuring every member of the soccer community was pulling in the same direction would be a challenge. Given its history of poor results, the men's national team was not seen as the final beacon of success the way men's national teams around the world were for national governing bodies. In Canada, provincial organizations constantly disagreed about the best model for player development. And the lack of faith provincial organizations had in the CSA only compounded existing difficulties and threatened the ability of the country's best players to actually progress into national team programs.

"Football in Canada was constantly a fight," said Findlay, a sentiment not his alone. "We were using organization and bureaucracy, and we forgot we needed that innate motivation of the player just to fucking play."

• • •

Just as they had done a decade earlier, the CSA returned to their own back-yard when looking for the person they believed could take the men's team to the World Cup.

On September 2, 2003, less than two months after Canada crashed out of the Gold Cup group stage with a 2–0 loss to Cuba, Holger Osieck handed in his surprise resignation, citing personal reasons. His contract had been extended the previous year into the 2006 World Cup.

Though his work to establish national training centres across the country is perhaps an overlooked element of Osieck's history, the acrimony between him and his players could be ignored no longer.

Many players had begun quietly threatening to stop accepting invitations to Canadian training camps under Osieck, and the CSA needed both a more sympathetic face and gentler tone.

Desperate to find a coach who could not only connect with players, but one who might have some connections with Major League Soccer, which had not yet expanded to Canada, the CSA pushed hard for Frank Yallop.

After two brief assistant coaching stints in MLS, Yallop had taken over the bench for MLS's San Jose Earthquakes in 2001. The team had finished in last place in 2000. Yallop's management, and the addition of American soccer prodigy Landon Donovan on loan from Germany's Bayer Leverkusen, helped propel the Earthquakes to MLS Cups in 2001 and 2003.

Yallop immediately learned that the hurdles for the men's national team to reach another World Cup included not only a lack of resources from the CSA but also a lack of interest from players. During his first few calls to his player pool to gauge their interest in playing for the men's team, he'd regularly hang up the phone after being told "I can't play, I've got a big game on that weekend."

Years of mistrust from veteran players toward the CSA, and younger players who didn't feel much pull to be part of the national team, meant that the 2006 World Cup qualifying cycle was what Yallop calls an "in-between time" for the men's program.

"It was a team that didn't think it was going to win," said then national team forward Josh Simpson. "It was guys that were all pretty much just happy to be there."

Yallop did his best to instill positivity in team talks, and the players themselves connected with him on a personal level easily enough, but Yallop couldn't change the inherent belief, or lack thereof, in their World Cup chances as they entered the third round in a group with Costa Rica, Guatemala, and Honduras, looking once again for a berth in The Hex.

Canada's starting eleven for their first game of the third round, a demoralizing 2–0 loss at home to Guatemala, was a motley crew, including veteran holdovers from the 2000 Gold Cup–winning squad. There was a lack of coordination on the pitch. Cliques had quickly developed as players stuck to those they knew. When players did branch out in team dinners, they found themselves chatting with teammates they'd never met before, hearing stories about leagues in different parts of the world they were equally unfamiliar with.

"It was a culture of everybody coming from their own way," said Simpson. "You didn't know who was playing for their club team, who wasn't."

Yallop tried to turn his team into a group that would embody the defensively peskier Canadian teams of the past. He'd seen how a relentless work ethic could bring success.

"The spirit of the team is, until the last ball is kicked, we're going to keep fighting for everything we can get," he said in the middle of the qualifying run.

However, the lack of cohesion on the pitch continued to be evident. Despite some convincing individual performances at times, a few calls that didn't go their way, and one game in particular, a draw in Honduras on the fourth matchday, in which they outplayed the home squad, Canada were never a safe bet to go through.

They finished last in their group.

"When you get into the national team, you have to believe you're confident," said Simpson, "but the truth is, we were not. It was almost laughable. And then you've got everybody else [at their respective clubs] telling you 'You're no good.' That combination, that's exactly what we were."

Yallop resigned days before the 2006 World Cup kicked off and would eventually corroborate how the players felt.

"I needed to have a vision with the national team," he told the *Globe and Mail* in a rare moment of negativity shortly after he resigned. His frustration stemmed from the fact that while the countries that qualified for the World Cup had federations that made their men's national team the priority, the CSA did not. "I felt that I was living day-to-day with the team, and we never had a long-term plan for the country."

Frustrations with the CSA were shared by fans. That Toronto's BMO Field was less than half full for a September 2007 friendly against Costa Rica was concerning, but not nearly as concerning as how many of those fans wore black T-shirts proclaiming "Support Our National Teams: Sack the CSA." The shirts were being sold for just five dollars outside the stadium.

Frustration over the lack of results in World Cup qualification campaigns had reached a boiling point with fans, especially after Colin Linford had resigned as president of the CSA weeks earlier. Linford had suggested to the media that the CSA board of directors did not agree to a proposal that would have brought in respected Brazilian coach René Simões as the man to lead the men's national team forward. The admission highlighted the infighting and lack of professionalism within the organization.

So, these fans knew that the strife, mismanagement, reliance on volunteers, and lack of foresight toward the men's national team at the CSA would continue to prevent any serious progress.

"I think it's great that the fans have a say," said Canadian forward Tomasz

Radzinski after the match, and after he donned a black shirt as well. "I think it's the right direction and the guys feel it, but it's still a long way."

"If I'm in the stands next time I'm going to wear a black shirt as well," he added. "We've been trying to change things over the last five or six years."

Glimmers of hope that the success of the men's national team would finally be prioritized eventually came more than two years later during a CSA general meeting. At the behest of players, some of whom were in attendance at the meeting, and many other fans, a massive and long-overdue reform package of the board of directors was finally agreed to. The reforms meant that provincial representatives would carry less weight with the board, and long-time bureaucrats would be ousted. Players and professionals would have far more of a voice.

· · ·

The true meaning of the phrase *MLS 2.0* is, like so much in Canadian soccer, up for argument. But it's fair to assert the nascent league entered the second phase in its evolution in the mid-2000s, when it began expanding beyond the original ten teams the league started with in 1996, a.k.a. "MLS 1.0." Expansion itself signalled the next stage in the league's growth, but Toronto FC's inaugural season in 2007 itself was still a key turning point in "MLS 2.0."

"We had not yet embraced the hard-core supporter-driven soccer culture. We had not yet figured out the value of building accessible downtown stadiums. We had not yet figured out that in order to capture the value of being part of the world's game, we needed to have teams that were outside of the United States. And what better place to do that than [in] one of the most important cities in North America, the city of Toronto?" said MLS Commissioner Don Garber in *Come on You Reds*.

Twisting the telescope even more, perhaps the specific point when MLS ascended beyond its homely roots was on May 12, 2007, when Toronto FC finally, after going goalless in their first four MLS matches, scored their first-ever goal. Seconds after the goal, in an act of jubilation, thousands of fans leapt up to throw sponsored seat cushions handed out to spectators before the game onto the field, a moment that drew attention throughout the soccer world. "MLS 2.0" may have begun when TFC rallied its multicultural population into a fervent, European- or South American–type fanbase unlike anything MLS had seen.

"It signalled a new era for soccer in Canada and MLS," said former vice president of business operations at TFC, Paul Beirne in *Come on You Reds*. "From a cultural perspective, MLS had arrived."

Despite an early lack of on-field success, developing a dedicated fanbase in Toronto's crowded sports landscape inspired other Canadian expansion sides.

"[TFC] really changed Canadian soccer," said Yallop. "And they wanted to."

In 2011, the Vancouver Whitecaps officially joined the league. The team had a developed soccer infrastructure with a youth residency program. One year later, the Montreal Impact, who had also been playing in lower-tier leagues, rounded out Canada's MLS contingent.

MLS was on solid financial footing after some turbulent early years, which allowed clubs to invest in their own local academies and provide a pipeline for local teenaged players to progress and earn professional contracts. The advent of the designated player rule meant teams could lure high-profile stars such as David Beckham from abroad, but their exorbitant salaries would fall outside the team's salary cap.

And so, even if Beckham raised the profile of the league abroad, MLS's successful expansion into Canada had an irrevocable impact on the Canadian men's national team. Young Canadian players finally had a pathway to professional soccer and regular playing opportunities, not in a fledging league like the CSL, but a standard-setting one.

After retiring, former national team midfielder Nick Dasovic immediately immersed himself in the coaching world, working with Canada's U-20 team as well as serving as head coach for Toronto FC's academy side in 2008.

Even if MLS was not a truly Canadian domestic league, Dasovic saw first-hand how young, talented players from Canada's three largest urban centres had a connection to professional teams in a way his generation of players had not.

"It got [young players] to go to different showcases to get exposure," said Dasovic.

One such pivotal showcase came in September 2010, after Dasovic had taken over as interim head coach of TFC after Predrag "Preki" Radosavlijevic was fired.

In a Concacaf Champions League group-stage match against Panamanian champions Árabe Unido, Dasovic fielded a lineup with national team stars Julian de Guzman and Dwayne De Rosario, supplemented by four teenage players. He wanted to encourage academy players with valuable first-team minutes, but also to remind others of the talent that existed throughout the Greater Toronto Area. Two of the four players were recent graduates of TFC's academy and had signed professional deals: defender Doneil Henry, seventeen, and Nicholas Lindsay, eighteen. Midfielder Oscar Cordon, seventeen, and defender Ashtone Morgan, nineteen, were both playing out of the academy.

This is not out of my reach, the soft-spoken Morgan remembers telling himself, hunched over amid the clatter of studs on the floor of the cramped BMO Field dressing room leading up to the match.

And in the 1–0 win, it was Morgan's fearlessness on the pitch that nullified his inexperience. His spirited play stood out.

"I know for sure I wasn't that good when I was that age," said TFC defender Nana Attakora after the game.

Morgan had joined the academy at sixteen after bouncing around local soccer associations.

"It was the best thing for a young Canadian," Morgan recalled of TFC, again hunched over, laying his hands out in explanation.

Dasovic would eventually take over as Canada's U-20 national team head coach, leading the team into the 2011 Concacaf U-20 championship quarterfinals before losing to eventual champions Mexico. Seven players on that team would ultimately make their senior team debut, and four of those seven players were coming to the U-20 team from an MLS academy.

Six months after the 2011 Concacaf U-20 championship, Morgan committed to Canada's national team, though he was also eligible to play for Guyana. He made his national team debut against Saint Lucia in a 2014 World Cup qualifying match. Head coach Stephen Hart was impressed by how consistently Morgan had been playing for TFC, which only reinforced the importance of a pipeline from an academy to the first team.

"His game shows a maturity where he potentially could step into the team," Hart said of the twenty-year-old Morgan.

Here was a young Canadian player whose career hadn't been derailed the way those of hundreds of players, without a path to professional soccer in their home, had been. Morgan didn't have to rely on a tenuous connection abroad and separate from his family and friends in the fleeting hope of chasing professional soccer experience anywhere it was offered.

In becoming the first MLS academy player to play for the men's national team, Morgan had simply followed the same path players for the world's most-established soccer nations had long been walking.

This alone makes MLS expanding into Canada arguably the most critical step in the Canadian men's national team's evolution. Alphonso Davies, Sam Adekugbe, Jonathan Osorio, Liam Fraser, and Doneil Henry all played vital roles in qualifying for the 2022 World Cup and all earned experience playing in MLS academies.

"That's the reason," said Yallop of the Canadian MLS teams, "you're seeing a real difference in our player pool, and our results. There was a path for [Canadian players]."

Disagreements throughout Canadian soccer organizations undoubtedly continued, but there was now more evidence of the talent littered throughout Canada. And, accordingly, more of an understanding that co-operation between every splintered faction in the country can lead to sustained success if the continued improvement of players remains the sole priority.

"But out of all of those fights still came a group of players who came out of club football, provincial programming, MLS academies, private academies, National Youth teams, spotty development programs," said Findlay. "It still produced the basis and the foundation for the vast majority of the players on the 2022 World Cup team."

CHAPTER 8

"Change Was Inevitable": How Stephen Hart Utilized a Country's Growing Multiculturalism to Transform the National Team

STEPHEN HART WAS BORN CURIOUS.

Raised in the city of San Fernando, Trinidad and Tobago, Hart would walk the shores of the Gulf of Paria to the west of the city, which separates the small island nation from the mainland of soccer-mad South America, and wonder about what forms of life existed below, in the water.

And it was curiosity about living in another country that inspired Hart to leave his burgeoning career playing for the San Fernando Hurricanes to fly to a city with a far less hospitable climate, but still connected to the water: in Halifax, Nova Scotia, the teenaged Hart enrolled at St. Mary's University, where he majored in marine biology and played for the Huskies.

"Well," said Hart of his thought process behind the move, slowly drawing out the final part of the word as he often does to begin a sentence. He speaks at a leisurely pace, careful not to bowl listeners over with the knowledge he's attained from experience, though he could if he wanted to.

"I went to continue playing some soccer, but to experience it in a different culture, another way of life," Hart said, as if the life-altering decision came easy to him as a young man.

He had opportunities to study elsewhere, but he knew of a small community of Trinidadians who already lived in Halifax, a city he admittedly didn't know much else about at all, and thought that might help him integrate into Canada.

Even after finding that community, his curiosity was piqued by the dozens of other communities he found while walking the streets of Halifax and, of course, how the different walks of life brought their different styles of soccer to the city's pitches. He saw this first-hand when he joined the semi-professional side with one of the most tantalizing names in the history of Canadian soccer: King of Donair.

The team was sponsored by and named after the wildly popular local takeout restaurant, created years earlier by a Greek immigrant, which has helped to make pitas stuffed with beef shawarma and a unique sweet garlic sauce made from condensed milk an inimitable part of the city's cultural landscape.

But it wasn't the postgame meals that Hart remembers from his years playing for, and then coaching, King of Donair: it was the thirteen different nationalities that made up the squad.

"So, man-managing that scenario was very different, as you can imagine," Hart says with a sense of pride about the makeup of the team.

Players came from Libya, Croatia, Portugal, Egypt, Scotland, Greece, Cyprus, and of course, Trinidad and Tobago.

"You name it," said Hart.

Difficult to deliver a rousing pregame speech for every player to understand? Perhaps.

But what wasn't difficult was Hart's efforts to move away from the rigid style of play that had long been Canadian soccer's hallmark.

"It was a largely British set-up. The coaching staff was British and the style of play at the time suited the type of players that were available. A very direct style, a 'Let's-compete-for-second-balls' type of team," said Hart, emphasizing the word *British* with slight derision in a still-thick Trini accent.

Roughshod pitches in his hometown were a place for players to express themselves, and Hart came to believe the game should be a vehicle for self-expression. Heightened standards of training and coaching were in their infancy in Trinidad and Tobago, meaning the best players were the creative ones, who could invoke trickery and deception and move the ball without breaking a sweat.

That vision of the game, played with lightning-fast pace, came to fruition with King of Donair. He encouraged his players to use combinations of short passes and show their imagination and "flair" within the game. His suspicion that many other countries would appreciate that same creativity he had grown up with was confirmed.

"It was easier to project some ideas of how we wanted to play with those type of players," said Hart. "Things were changing culturally. [Canada] was becoming more multicultural and multi-ethnic."

Moving away from the physical style of play that had been long preached in Canada also came from a belief that by introducing more of the technical side of the game, Hart might interest more young players.

From his Halifax home, he saw his adopted national team play in their first World Cup with courage but without technical quality in attack.

His curiosity led him to wonder: With so many different players from different soccer backgrounds coming to Canada, was there not an opportunity to utilize those divergent styles of play? Could he not create a standard that was heavy on players' expressing themselves by relying on their natural instincts and creativity through dribbling and quick passing in the final third of the pitch, and bring the influences of different ingrained styles of play from different countries? Would that not be more representative of the changing face of Canada itself?

In his downtime, on a tiny television set, Hart devoured videotapes of games from around the world, including Spain's La Liga, and saw how playing the game didn't mean running away from flair and expression.

"Some cultures saw that flair as a luxury that was not really accepted. Even when you listen to the commentary at the time of certain nations' breaking into the World Cup, when one country made a mistake, they'd say, 'They're naive,' but when other countries that didn't play with flair made a mistake, it was just a mistake," said Hart.

He had his own raw material at King of Donair for testing his theories: if a player was raised to play the game with creativity, Hart didn't suppress those instincts.

"You pick a player for your team because they have a certain ability to bring, and you want them to bring that ability within the framework of the team, of course. That's important, but the game was changing," he said.

Domestic leagues throughout Europe were once bastions solely for players from that same nation. But the Bosman ruling of 1995 led to a lifting of restrictions on foreign European Union players within European leagues, while also allowing players to move to a different club at the end of their contracts without their new team being forced to pay transfer fees. High-profile players moved across borders to different leagues, bringing with them styles of play ingrained for generations. More opportunities for players across Europe led to greater investment in talent development, with smaller clubs seeing opportunities to develop players and then sell them for a profit.

European soccer had very quickly become a melting pot of different playing styles, and the product itself was garnering more international eyeballs as a result.

"Too many times you heard, 'If you're not playing in a certain way, you're not going to play, and you're not going to make it,'" said Hart. "Myself, and a couple of other coaches, wanted to change that narrative."

• • •

Hart's teams eventually garnered enough attention that he was named Technical Director of Soccer Nova Scotia in 1993. He took over a Nova Scotia team on short notice that won bronze at the Canada Games. Holger Osieck eventually asked him to join Canada's U-17 team as an assistant coach, while also running the Atlantic national training centre.

Hart and Osieck agreed that many Canadian players wilted in unfamiliar environments, such as Central America. Developing players who were eager to move abroad and embrace change might create a culture of adaptability within the organization.

"You drive around the United States, you see familiar sights and smells. But when you go into certain hotels in Jamaica, Honduras, and El Salvador, you have to eat a different type of food, transportation is what it is, and you're looking around and you see people live in a certain life and it's quite a cultural shock. But I think it's important to understand where your opposition was coming from and the environments that they were coming from," said Hart.

Hart's tranquil attitude and approach to talent identification began to resonate within local soccer communities in Canada. Club coaches born abroad could see that Hart spoke their language and had visions of an inclusive national team program more representative of the way the country looked at the turn of the twenty-first century.

"I had the help of a lot of ethnic coaches all over the country that felt a little more comfortable coming to speak to me then, about taking a look at certain kids," said Hart. "I'm not the scariest person to come and talk to."

Hart ran with the vision, coupled with his easygoing attitude: find players who can play exciting soccer, no matter where they come from.

After all, he'd had experience on a local level, scouting players in his free time throughout Halifax and encouraging them to bring the soccer knowledge they already had to the table.

On a national level, as he moved from coaching the Under-17 team to the Under-23 team, Hart's experience came in handy to broaden the scope of what a Canadian soccer player could be. Hart, after all, was one of them: a player who had come from abroad because of his interest in what Canada could offer him, who still wanted to hold on to what he cherished about his home.

"I beat the bushes all over," said Hart. "There were some instances where I found kids and brought them to the [national team program] and it ruffled the feathers of some provincial technical directors, because those youngsters weren't involved in the provincial programs. But as far as I was concerned, the only criteria that you needed to meet to play for a national youth team were: are you good, and do you have a Canadian passport?"

Hart remembers provincial programs being pitched to children as the "pinnacle" of youth soccer. Yet continually rising and sometimes cost-prohibitive registration fees bothered him. They prevented many players from progressing.

"All sorts of red-tape regulations. In some instances, after I picked players for the national team, then they ended up playing for their provincial team," said Hart, illustrating how the pay-to-play mentality that had become commonplace in Canadian youth sports may have limited the growth of the game as a whole.

He saw waves of players from Africa, with a particular wave of immigrants moving from Algeria to Quebec, as well as other immigrants coming from Caribbean and Central American backgrounds throughout Canada.

"Change was inevitable," said Hart, of how Canadian national teams should play.

In 2005, Hart got the opportunity to inject that sort of change into the national team itself. He was named assistant coach under Frank Yallop and would take over for Yallop as interim head coach after the team failed to qualify for the 2006 World Cup.

Hart became just the second men's national team head coach since 1977 who had not been born in either Canada or Great Britain.

"When Stephen Hart took over, everything started to turn," said stoutly built former national team forward Iain Hume. "We started playing proper football. We didn't rely on our athleticism and our physique to compete."

Hart was never truly in contention for the permanent head coach's role, however. The May 2007 appointment of Dale Mitchell as head coach meant his focus was the 2010 World Cup qualifying campaign. Hart would coach the team during the 2007 Gold Cup and Mitchell would take over afterward.

Mitchell was presented as a coach very much in the mould of Lenarduzzi: one who had played for Canada at the 1986 World Cup and could beat the patriotic drum to stir up fervour among players and the organization.

Critics questioned why, yet again, Canada opted to stick with a domestic coach despite the failed qualifying campaigns of domestic coaches previously. Few could doubt Mitchell's experience, since he had helped develop some of Canada's best players, including Atiba Hutchinson, soon to ascend to Canadian soccer royalty, during his six-year tenure as Under-20 national team head coach. But to many, it still stank of a loyalty to the past, not-so covert jingoism, and a lack of progressive thinking in the CSA.

"I think the best always hire their own," Mitchell said at his introductory press conference. "When you hire your own people, you keep your identity. And I think that that's important."

But when Hart took over as interim head coach, players noticed a vast difference from previous coaches.

"There was an abundance of playing with freedom under Stephen. He was loving, encouraging, all-encompassing," said Josh Simpson, who Hart named to his first starting eleven as interim head coach for a friendly against Jamaica in September 2006.

In the camp leading up to the match, it was easy to imagine the chorus from Monty Python's "Always Look on the Bright Side of Life," booming through loudspeakers.

Hart would move around players in training session drills, encouraging them to bring the feints and slick passes they might have shown only in practice into a game. Two of his trademark calls to his players became so commonplace in those first sessions that players would attempt their own Caribbean accents at dinners afterward, mimicking their new coach with adoration.

"Move my ball," Hart would say, and his players would too.

"Express yourselves," were perhaps the most common two words that came out of Hart's mouth, with the final syllables elongated both for dramatic effect and encouragement.

"He brought that just Caribbean style of life, that mindset where you should not take life so seriously," said Nik Ledgerwood.

Hart would pull players aside to engage in conversation about their families and friends in a way previous managers never did, working in playful barbs before returning to genuine questions about a player's life at their club side.

Many of his team talks would end the same way: with a smile on his face, providing consistent reminders about how fortunate players were to be playing soccer for a living. By doing so, he wanted to motivate players to perform well.

"He had a good staff around him that preached the same thing: let's try to take the best out of what we're doing, and not worry too much about the negatives," said Nik Ledgerwood.

Hart knew his time with players would be limited and heavy instruction wasn't an option. So why not allow them to bring their experience and qualities, and structure his team around those qualities, even if the team itself didn't play like Canadian squads of the past?

"There was an understanding: if he could bring them in, keep them happy, they'll perform at their best as an individual for me, and that'll pay off for the team," said Ledgerwood. "Tactically, there weren't a lot of restrictions to it. Everybody was relaxed."

Hart understood a lack of professionalism had hindered the national team in the past. But he believed that by boosting morale among the team and leaving players to their own devices, heightened accountability among the squad would follow.

"Players felt refreshed, being back in the national team, and having that freedom, they would perform," said Ledgerwood of Hart's tenure.

• • •

Hart knew full well he wasn't going to be head coach after the 2007 Gold Cup and never shied away from promoting an offensive, creative style of play.

"So why not give it a try?" said Hart. "That's how it was going to be: encouraging players to play to their abilities, their strengths."

He trusted players, which meant giving chances to players who had been out of the program, such as goalkeeper Pat Onstad. Onstad had last played for the national team in 2004, and in one of his last games, he gave up a goal on a corner kick that he'd yet to get over.

Entering the training camp for the 2007 Gold Cup, players were taken aback by how clearly Hart explained why specific drills were meant to benefit players in games. But they were also impressed by his knowledge of the best club and international sides around the world. The "interim coach" tag didn't seem to apply as he implored players to abandon the traditional line of thinking in Canadian international soccer, in which physicality and set pieces were expected to be the keys to success. In video sessions, Hart would show clips of how players on the world's best club sides would attack with purpose and tactical fluidity, and then empower various members of the Canadian squad to take up those same roles on the pitch.

"It was a transition to world football," said Hume.

The incredibly talented midfield of Atiba Hutchinson, Julian de Guzman, and Dwayne De Rosario felt empowered by Hart's insistence that, to borrow his phrase, "the ball doesn't sweat." The ball moved with speed and creativity in a way it never had before for the national team.

In their tournament-opening 2–1 win against Costa Rica, who were fresh off having qualified for the previous summer's World Cup, when the Canadian midfield didn't see an option they liked in possession, they circled the ball throughout the middle of the park, showcasing newfound patience. Back-heel and no-look one-two touch passes became commonplace as de Guzman scored two goals.

"We passed Costa Rica off the park," said Hume.

Walking off the field after the win, Onstad put his arm around Hart.

"You have no idea how much this means to me," said Onstad.

"No," Hart replied, "you have no idea how much it means to be able to coach someone like you."

Even after a surprise loss to Guadeloupe, Canada rebounded with two goals from De Rosario in one of his best performances for the national team and a resounding 2–0 over Haiti in the final group-stage game.

After not making it out of the group stage in the previous two Gold Cups, Hart's focus on attacking flair had the Canadians in the quarterfinals.

De Guzman has played more games for the national team than all but Hutchinson and doesn't hesitate to call that Gold Cup team one of the "best teams that's ever existed in the history of Canadian soccer."

Never was that more evident than in the quarterfinal against Guatemala, when defender Richard Hastings found himself tracking back into his own half to recover a loose ball while under pressure from a Guatemalan player.

Hart's efforts came to life. Instead of firing the ball back to goalkeeper Pat Onstad, Hastings quickly turned and passed the ball in one motion into the midfield for Martin Nash who, even with uncontested space in front of him, took just two touches before sending a crisp pass to De Rosario on the wing. As De Rosario made his first touch, multiple Canadian players made darting runs around him. He followed suit, sending a quick pass on his second touch into Hutchinson near the top of the box. Guatemala scrambled to recover as Hutchinson played a one-touch pass to de Guzman, mid-stride on his run into the box. He put a one-touch square ball to forward Ali Gerba, who had separated himself from his defender. Fourteen seconds, nine uncontested touches, more than half the length of the park and, at the end, what de Guzman argues is the greatest goal he's ever seen Canada score.

Hart flew out of his seat in the coach's dugout to throw multiple punches into the midsection of no one in particular.

"That is world-class from Canada," colour commentator Craig Forrest said on the broadcast. "You don't see that very often, certainly not in the past."

Whatever Canada's national team thought they could be in the past was essentially an afterthought under Hart. Cliques evaporated off the pitch as the style of play they showcased on the pitch presented a newfound cohesion.

All of which meant that the team felt buoyed heading into the semifinal against the United States.

"We were as good as anybody at that Gold Cup," said Hume.

And for most of the match, they kept the United States on their toes by fighting for second balls, being aggressive in tackles, and seeing a free kick bounce off the post to the left of American goalkeeper Kasey Keller in the first half.

As much as they attacked with precision, their defending left something to be desired, especially on the United States' first goal. But the second goal was essentially out of their hands: though they were caught slightly out of position when a through-ball put DaMarcus Beasley in close to goal, Beasley's leap in the air after Onstad came out to challenge him caused referee Benito Archundia to call a penalty against Onstad. Onstad threw his hands together to mimic a diving motion. But then he himself dove the wrong way as Landon Donovan converted the penalty.

After the United States continued to press, Hume found the back of the net with an impressive turn thirteen minutes after coming on as a substitute.

Hume's sense of dramatics came into play three minutes later when he stopped a sure goal by clearing a Clint Dempsey header off the line with the back of his foot.

In added time, Canada pressed forward for one last shot, and got it after a long ball into the box deflected off American defender Oguchi Onyewu and fell to Hutchinson, who at the very least appeared level with the last American defenders. His shot past Keller was clean, but the play was whistled offside before Hutchinson could celebrate.

The normally placid Hutchinson charged to the ref and stopped him dead in his tracks with his arms.

"How?" he screamed, echoing the frustration of the thousands watching in Canada.

Very quickly, some players' minds went back to a World Cup qualifying match in 2004 when the same referee, Benito Archundia, had called late fouls against Canada, awarded Honduras a questionable late penalty kick that tied the match, and then, almost inexplicably, called off a Canadian goal in the eighty-ninth minute after a Honduran defender made a meal of some incidental contact.

"It was cheating," Hume said of Hutchinson's disallowed goal. "There was something so fundamentally wrong about that decision and everything around it."

Canadian players believed they had been "Concacafed" once again, because of the Mexican national team.

"We all know the reasoning behind it," Hume said. "He didn't even ask his linesman. They did not want Canada in the finals against Mexico. You're not getting all the fans that way."

After the final whistle, players seethed, and stalking Archundia around the pitch to get a clearer answer on the disallowed goal proved fruitless. Kevan Pipe, former CSA chief of operations, who was then in charge of Soldier Field for the tournament, got between Morgan Quarry and Archundia. That not one of their own would get involved and plead their case only enraged players that much more.

Yet it was Hart who moved from player to player, easing them with the tone of his voice, as he had done countless times before.

"If it wasn't for Stephen Hart, we could've been in a lot of trouble," said Hume. "A lot of guys were ready to fight people."

In their dressing room, players continued complaining to no one in particular. Hart thanked each player for their service. The Gold Cup was over, as, essentially, was Hart's tenure as head coach, and there was nothing anyone could do about either now.

Back in their hotel rooms, once their anger had subsided, many players began looking at this team through a sober lens. They had surprised many with their style of play but had also done so by relying on younger players who had not yet hit their career peaks, from Hutchinson to Hume.

They had rarely appreciated playing for the national team as much as they had under Hart.

And so, the conversations continued among players and staff: Imagine if they'd made it to the Gold Cup final and showed fans at home they were not the Canada of old that sent long balls up like prayers into the box?

Could this team have transitioned away from the physical soccer of the past into a more modern approach in line with the best European countries? And could the entire program have benefitted with a dedication to modernity, younger players, attacking soccer and, crucially, enjoyment? Would that have convinced the CSA themselves that World Cup qualification could come with a coach who favoured this approach?

And, perhaps more quietly, but none less pertinently: imagine if the national team was always something every player wanted to be a part of?

Canada would not reach the Gold Cup semifinals again until 2021.

"It was a massive knock on our history," said Hume in reflection of the Gold Cup loss, "and what could have been a lot quicker transition."

CHAPTER 9

A Desperate Proposition, a Lack of Goals, and a Thousand Impediments: 2010–2018

JOSH SIMPSON FELT LIKE HE HAD REACHED A RESPECTABLE POINT in his career.

The self-assured and cheery twenty-four-year-old Canadian winger was starting to find the back of the net with regularity for FC Kaiserslautern, a historic German side playing in Germany's second division. Behind closed doors in their hotel rooms at national team training camps, Simpson had found common ground with his roommate and close friend Rob Friend, who was then a regular at Bundesliga side Borussia Mönchengladbach.

Yet when they'd leave the quiet of their hotel room and join their national teammates and staff members during camps ahead of friendlies in the lead-up to qualification for the 2010 World Cup, he didn't feel that same type of respect.

Simpson remembers being met by members of the Canadian national team's coaching staff at the time who did not properly remember which club Friend was playing for.

"To talk about professionalism, that stands out as what we were," said Simpson. "You don't even know where your players are playing?"

Because if there was one common thread that plagued the men's national team in their hopes to qualify for the World Cup as the decade turned, it was a lack of professionalism from the top of the federation down to some of its players.

And that attitude ended up making for a mostly dark, regrettable time for the team.

Despite one important box in the evolution of the national team being ticked — more and more Canadian national team members playing for respected teams in Europe — an unfortunate by-product of this growth had also occurred.

Between those players who had caught on in Europe and some playing in North America, the gap in training habits and standards of professionalism within the player pool had become far too wide. Some European-based players would arrive from their club teams and then stop in shock during national team training sessions, or in team meetings, to see teammates treating these camps and ensuing World Cup qualifying games as a vacation.

"Like they were just checking something off their list, because they're going to go to a nice resort, a nice hotel, and they'd get lucky if they even played a game," said midfielder Nik Ledgerwood.

Ledgerwood wanted to come to national team camps with the same hardened mindset that had been forcefully instilled in him in Germany's second division, but the slowly rising tide in the player pool had not yet lifted every boat.

"You would bring in some guys who had that serious professional calibre from Europe. And then you would mix it with some guys that were looking for a club, they probably weren't match fit or the sharpest. And some other guys coming from lower leagues were just happy to be involved," said Ledgerwood.

Ledgerwood's impressions were shared by other players. The national team was bolstered in 2007 by the addition of blond and oft-bearded left back Marcel de Jong. De Jong was born in Newmarket, Ontario, but had moved to the Netherlands, in part to advance his soccer career.

He'd spent eight years in the academy of well-regarded Dutch side PSV Eindhoven. It took an email from his mother to Stephen Hart to alert him to her son's interest in representing Canada, again highlighting how the networking capabilities within the program were still, to put it mildly, a work in progress.

De Jong was playing in the top Dutch division for Roda JC when he returned to North America for his first national team camps, less than a year before Canada's qualification campaign was set to begin.

"It was a culture shock for me, soccer-wise," said de Jong, as he observed a pervasive attitude that was night and day compared to what he had experienced in Europe. "After a loss players would go for drinks or go for dinner. After a game you lose, there's no way that you can go out and explore the city. These things are unheard of in Europe."

Different rules also applied in that some older players were not held accountable for their actions.

"A party atmosphere," said Simpson.

It meant that, under Mitchell, a sense of apathy had taken over the team in 2008 heading into the third round of qualifying for the 2010 World Cup. Canada had been put into a difficult group with Mexico, Honduras, and Jamaica. To players, Mitchell felt like more of the same after Yallop: another Canadian from yesteryear who couldn't always challenge players used to playing in Europe, from a tactical perspective. He lacked the stern approach of some of his predecessors and struggled to manage the egos of some players.

Mitchell had been given the national team duties partly because the Canadian Under-20 team he coached had gone on a surprising run into the quarterfinals of the 2003 FIFA Youth Championship.

That rare bright spot for Canadian soccer had led many to believe that better days were just ahead; though at the same tournament four years later, hosted in Canada, no less, Mitchell's team lost all three matches and was the only one of the twenty-four teams not to score a goal.

Even if many within the CSA felt rewarding Mitchell with the men's national team job seemed logical after his success in 2003, the players believed they would be better off sticking with Hart after the 2007 Gold Cup.

"It was hard for Dale. We were happy with Stephen," said de Guzman. "There was momentum that we felt Stephen could have continued."

But to the coaching staff, it was hard to completely motivate a team when de Guzman, the crafty midfielder and the first ever Canadian to play in Spain's La Liga, therefore one of their shining lights, wasn't holding up his end of the bargain. When the call from the national team came, de Guzman's mind raced with thoughts of travel and a break from the exhaustion of playing in a demanding club league.

"It was my dream to play for the national team, but when you showed up in those camps, it felt like a vacation, an escape to get away from your club," admitted de Guzman.

He would arrive late for team meals on a few hours' sleep and feel the piercing looks from teammates or skip meals altogether.

"And what's going to stop me? Because no one in Canada is talking about this team. You can get away with those things. In Europe, you cannot get away with those things," said de Guzman. "You just knew there was going to be some good parties, fun nights. We were able to do things that just weren't labelled professional."

The third round of qualifying began with a 1–1 draw at BMO Field in Toronto against Jamaica that saw large pockets of yellow jerseys in the stands.

"Essentially a home game for the visiting team," said journalist John Molinaro.

"Right there, you could sense in the mood that this was just not enough," said de Guzman.

Two weeks later in Montreal, their fortunes didn't turn. Though de Guzman himself called the game a "do or die" beforehand, a 2–1 loss to Honduras had them tied for last place, with just one point in two home games, with the top two teams advancing to the final round of qualifying.

"We all have to show what we're made of," Mitchell said after the game.

"I'd already given up, pretty much," said de Guzman, looking back. "I already had a party planned."

A loss on the road to Mexico followed. Their chances to progress were hindered ahead of their next match against Honduras, when the players' frustration with Mitchell turned into full-on dissent.

Defender Jim Brennan, who had logged forty-nine caps for the national team, told the media in October 2008 he wouldn't return to the national team "while the current manager is in place."

Dwayne De Rosario told the *Globe and Mail* ahead of the match against Honduras that he didn't know "how someone who coached the Under-20s to not score a goal in the World Cup was put in charge of the national team."

Predictably, a 3–1 loss meant Canada were officially eliminated from World Cup contention. The same group that had looked so promising one year earlier would end up logging just two points in six games, their worst total ever in a four-team group stage of qualifying.

Those who argued the difficulty of Canada's group was their downfall received some validation as Mexico and Honduras would both go on the make it out of The Hex and travel to South Africa for the World Cup.

In an interview for this book, Mitchell offered his thoughts on why his team didn't qualify for the World Cup: "We didn't get the job done. We didn't get the results, and that's it."

Years later, when he looks back at the opportunity missed, de Guzman can't overcome the regret he feels.

"That was obviously the downfall and the reason our country didn't make it, if it's not taken seriously," said de Guzman. "But that was just the state of soccer in our country. If we didn't qualify for a World Cup, it didn't matter."

Mitchell was eventually fired more than five months after the national team was eliminated. But the lack of professionalism, lack of faith in the CSA, and a lack of unity and progressive thinking throughout the entire organization was more pungent than the poor results.

CSA general secretary Peter Montopoli said at the time that while the results were part of Mitchell's termination, "the other part was maybe the way the program was moving forward, in terms of people buying into the program, the program progressing, whether it was or not."

Hart was an easy choice for the CSA to take over a team with a talented, but slightly aging, midfield. If they were going to qualify for a World Cup by getting the most out of the trio of Hutchinson, de Guzman, and De Rosario, it was going to have to be in 2014 in Brazil or bust.

Midway through the third round of the 2014 World Cup qualifying campaign, in a group with Honduras, Panama, and Cuba, Canada picked up where they'd left off with Hart: they sat at the top of the table and looked set to finally return to The Hex. Another win over Panama, who sat in second place, on the road, would surely do the job.

The Canadian contingent were booked into a hotel next to a bustling street in Panama City. At check-in, the hotel staff informed them that every room facing away from the street was booked and that the team, despite their protests, would be placed in rooms with windows facing the street.

"Sure enough, two in the morning, what happens? Cars pull up on the street, they start playing loud music, they start screeching motorbikes. [Panamanians] want every advantage and edge in the game," said Ledgerwood.

Along with teammate Kevin McKenna, he stormed down to the front desk in the middle of the night. They were met by a security guard who, despite their furious protests, flashed a wry smile and refused to move from his post.

"They know how big it is for their country," said Ledgerwood.

Perhaps not surprisingly, Canada crumbled in a 2–0 loss, made worse by the loss of De Rosario to a serious injury.

A win at home, this time against lowly Cuba, meant Canada were level with Panama on ten points at the top of the table heading into the final matchday. On that day, a draw on the road against Honduras would be enough for Canada to return to The Hex for the first time in four qualifying campaigns and would keep their World Cup hopes alive.

• • •

Stephen Hart sat up from his hotel bed in San Pedro Sula, Honduras, on the morning of October 16, 2012, with a sinking feeling in his stomach.

He hadn't gotten the most restful sleep the previous night. The flight the CSA had chartered into the city had endured mechanical issues and ended up landing far later than desired, before this crucial away match. To ensure his players didn't cramp up after the flight, he had dragged them to the rooftop of their hotel for some group stretching.

But then, he realized some players were battling food poisoning. Some, such as captain and centre-back Kevin McKenna, would struggle to be at their best. Others, like Ante Jazic, Hart's first choice left back, wouldn't be able to play at all.

Michael Klukowski, who had played just one competitive match for Canada in the previous year, came into the lineup. He would never play for Canada again.

Hart was battling his own issues as well: his contract with the CSA had ended in the middle of the qualification games, and the CSA were reluctant to even discuss renewing it. He was taking his professional career in his own hands with a game just hours away.

"But of course, you can't project that," said Hart. "You have to be very positive."

The bus waiting for the Canadian team outside their hotel immediately encountered traffic, thanks to an extended national holiday that had revellers filling the streets, draped in blue and white flags. Players quietly stared out the window.

"Myself and my staff," said Hart, "we knew we were in a bit of trouble."

The Canadians arrived at Estadio Olímpico Metropolitano to ecstatic crowds and soldiers milling with weapons at the ready. Nerves began to creep in as it became evident to the Canadian team just how much a win for Honduras would mean to the players, and the tens of thousands gathered around the stadium.

"It was a scary environment before the whistle had even blown," said de Guzman.

In the hours leading up to the game, rumours had started to circulate through the Canadian team that some Honduran players were being offered land or homes by their federation should they pull off the win and advance to The Hex.

Perhaps as would be expected, this rumour only heightened the nerves of some within the CSA, leading to a decision that aptly summarized the program's lack of professionalism, and how CSA officials failed to understand the magnitude of the task ahead of the team.

A CSA representative entered the overcrowded dressing room as players were putting the finishing touches on their pregame preparations and the tension was rising in the humidity.

To incentivize the players, the representative said they would be offered iPads and iPods if they won.

The room largely went silent.

Here sat well over a dozen players earning the kind of salaries that could see them afford multiple iPads every week, many of whom were about to play the most pivotal game in their international careers. Their silence spoke to how aghast they were that these electronics were being viewed by some in the federation as a proper price for a historic win. And the Honduran players were rumoured to have been offered life-changing rewards.

Players quickly cast around the room and began gossiping about the latest stumble from the federation they were representing.

"Were we just offered iPads as a reward?"

Their focus had been pulled in the wrong direction, with the sound of the crowd now easily audible from within the dressing room itself.

"That particular game had a different feel to it, that's for sure," said Hart.

Before the players walked out into the fray, Hart imparted one last message: attack the game early, silence the crowd, and put the opposition under pressure.

Hart felt like his message had been the right one in the second minute, when Ledgerwood sent a perfect cross into forward Tosaint Ricketts. He couldn't get a solid shot off inside the box, but it seemed the Canadians might be able to take the crowd out of the equation.

Yet, in the seventh minute, with eight Canadian defenders near a ball bouncing high in the air, two Honduras forwards were able to easily stride by the Canadians, and Honduran forward Jerry Bengston finished the attack with an easy tap-in.

Four minutes later, Canadian forward Simeon Jackson hit the post on a shot of his own. That would be the last sign of life from those in red.

In the seventeenth minute, the Hondurans, once again, easily picked the Canadian defenders apart with some quick passing and Bengston found the back of the net a second time, equalling the number of goals Canada had conceded in all five previous games.

Three Canadian defenders nearby raised their hands in protest, calling for offside.

They might as well have been raising white flags. The crowd hit levels of ferocity many players had never experienced.

"You can't even hear yourself think," said Ledgerwood.

In the crowd sat a seventeen-year-old José Escalante, who would eventually join Ledgerwood in the midfield for Cavalry FC seven years later. When he did, Escalante was quick to regale Ledgerwood with what he witnessed that day, standing alongside his father.

The Honduran government had made the day a holiday, and scheduled the game for 2:00 p.m. The price of tickets was purposefully made lower than normal. Furthermore, the federation ensured that a coupon for a free McDonald's Happy Meal would be included on the back of the ticket. The Honduran federation hoped the most rabid of fans could attend the game.

"That's the mindset of a Central American country that's on the cusp of qualifying, not for the World Cup, but just The Hex," said Ledgerwood. "That's a prime example of the difference between a Central American country and Canada. In Canada, when Central American teams come, we roll out the red carpet for them. 'Hey, I hope you guys got everything you need, good accommodation, we won't ruin your sleep at night, we'll let in all your fans to come watch the games, not a problem.' We're too naive in that aspect."

Canada's naïveté continued to show as Honduras knocked in two more goals before the half.

"It's all about damage limitation right now," McKenna admitted to Sportsnet's Arash Madani at halftime, all but admitting defeat. "It's pretty sad."

Allowing another goal just three minutes after half only exacerbated just how sad the state of things truly was for the Canadian team. Hart looked up and down his bench for substitutes eager to bring a spark to the game, but many slunk back in their seats in the hopes of not being seen. Some even went so far as to proclaim they didn't want to take part in the game.

Iain Hume answered the call, though, and knocked in a free-kick goal in the seventy-seventh minute. It was barely a consolation prize, as Canada had given up yet another goal just before that. Honduras would eventually knock in two more for an 8–1 final.

"Everything," said Hart, "just fell apart."

The loss eliminated Canada from World Cup contention. Just one goal off the most lopsided loss in the program's history, it served as a very public indictment of the men's program. And even if the loss was what stung, that this talented team couldn't get through a relatively easy third round of qualifying spoke volumes about the improvements needed in the player pool as well.

Hart didn't address his team after the game.

"There's nothing to say," he said.

A handful of players sought him out to personally apologize for their performance. He received calls from notable coaches to commiserate, including one who offered him a spot on his team in South America.

On a stopover during their flight home, TVs near the Canadian team's boarding gate showed highlights of the game. Broadcasters were taking digs at the Canadian side.

"Just miserable," said de Jong. "One of those days that haunted Canada for a very long time."

Many players argued this sort of devastating loss was needed to increase accountability.

"You're still able to walk the streets. No problem. No one's going to bother you. In the back of our heads, we knew that," said de Guzman. "But if that was Honduras, there's no way you could lose a game like that and expect to come back to a safe environment."

Hart offered his resignation to the CSA less than forty-eight hours after the loss, against the wishes of many players.

"I'm always going to be remembered for that one game," said Hart.

Once the shock of the loss wore off for some players, though others will argue it never has, a belief that more desperation in the team's play, and in the program's entire approach to the national team, was needed.

"It was a buildup of a lot of things that happened over the years, including how serious the sport was being taken. And it lacked it," said de Guzman. "This was the call-out match that put us in the spotlight. That game had to have happened. There needed to be a wake-up call."

• • •

The hangover from the loss to Honduras didn't just present immediate, penetrating pain. It created a crippling spell that lingered for far longer than anticipated, causing its victim to wander aimlessly through tasks, void of joy.

A rotation of interim managers led to a lack of stability in the national team and the program overall and, perhaps unsurprisingly, to a lack of genuine enthusiasm.

"There was uncertainty about which direction we were going. No real identity of who we were," said de Jong.

Two lifeless January friendlies in the United States saw Canada fail to find the back of the net. A 4–0 loss to Denmark, a team not heading to the 2014 World Cup, was marred by three goals from the Danes in the opening thirty-five minutes. Long-time players missed Hart's guidance and believed they could have made more progress had he not taken the fall for the loss in Honduras. Those players wondered: what does this team, and by extension the entire men's national team program, stand for? The women's side were coming off an inspiring run to the bronze medal at the 2012 Olympics by playing attacking soccer on the front foot and having a sense of passion about their purpose: winning games and increasing the profile of women's soccer around Canada.

In the months after winning that bronze medal, members of the women's national team held multiple clinics in cities like Halifax to hundreds of children, all of which quickly sold out.

In the shadow of the women's team's success, quietly, people within the men's side wondered if they were wandering toward a cliff too insurmountable to climb back up. That Canada had scored one goal in its previous three matches brought out its most glaring problem: Canada's six goals in six matches in that previous round of qualifying was tied for eighth among the twelve teams.

The identity that had long been the backbone of the national team, built on sturdy, organized defensive units, had run its course in the international game.

Canadian teams were in a different universe of expectations, yes. Nevertheless, it was hard to watch the Spanish national teams that won the Euros in 2008 and 2012 and the World Cup in 2014 strut through mazes with their passing and pick apart teams with their technical skills, and the German national teams that threw off the shackles of slow build-up play and ran teams into the ground with their counterattacking, en route to consistently strong finishes in tournaments at that time and not wonder out loud: Is there any way at all this Canadian team can learn from the advances in modern soccer? And if so, how far away is this program from at least trying to catch up?

More competitions and more television money being available to successful national team programs meant more coaching education

131

worldwide, and more access to a variety of matches and leagues worldwide led to a reduction in the effectiveness of physical, but technically lacking players.

Yet for Canada, three straight losses to Japan, Belarus, and Costa Rica in friendlies followed the January losses, with just one goal scored.

Fans of the team still following along for that summer's 2013 Gold Cup were likely wearing their masochism as a badge of honour: Canada was the only team in the tournament, including lowly Belize, to not score a goal throughout. Martinique, who had not qualified for the four previous Gold Cups, bested Canada 1–0 in the tournament opener. A predictable 2–0 loss to Mexico followed, and Canada couldn't flee the tournament soon enough after a meagre 0–0 draw to Panama.

Would another Canadian team ever embody modern soccer the way Hart's team had, and go after games in possession of the ball?

"We were going through the motions," said de Jong.

In 2013, the men's national team fell to their lowest-ever FIFA ranking to that point: 114th in the world.

One consistent problem the men's team faced was how they would go, according to Michael Findlay, "dormant" after World Cup qualifying cycles. The delay before playing again after qualifying matches while the world's best were engulfed in World Cup preparations would increase apathy within the players. Months on end without games would lead to a lack of development and progress with their tactical goals.

Yet many within the organization would argue back: the money to put on games that were, in the eyes of some, meaningless, just wasn't there.

"We would say, 'No, we need to play in every window, anywhere,'" said Findlay. "Because in between, you need to develop your team and your program. At that time, [the CSA] struggled to see that."

For federations around the world, the men's national team was almost always viewed as their most valuable property. The criticism from within and outside of the CSA was that Canada's men's team was not being treated as such. The lack of investment in the team, both financially and culturally, was part of the reason the seminal 2009 book *Soccernomics* named Canada as the most underachieving country in international men's soccer, considering population size and national income.

Former Canada men's national team coaches Carl Valentine (left) and Tony Waiters.

Canada lines up ahead of their game against France at the 1986 World Cup.

Craig Forrest celebrates at the 2000 Gold Cup.

Left to right: Jim Brennan, Richard Hastings, and Martin Nash at the 2000 Gold Cup.

Canada wins the 2000 Gold Gup.

Former men's national team head coach Stephen Hart runs a training session.

Former men's national team forward Alex Bunbury during a game.

Former men's national team midfielder Julian de Guzman during a training session.

Former men's national team midfielder Nik Ledgerwood (centre) during a training session.

Men's national team forward Cyle Larin (centre) during a 2015 game.

Canadian men's national team forward Cyle Larin (left) and defender Richie Laryea during 2022 World Cup qualifying.

Left to right: Canadian men's national team forwards Cyle Larin and Jonathan David, and midfielder Atiba Hutchinson during 2022 World Cup qualifying.

Canadian men's national team goalkeeper Milan Borjan makes a save that leads to a 2–0 win over the USA during 2022 World Cup qualifying.

Canadian men's national team defender Sam Adekugbe celebrates a goal during 2022 World Cup qualifying.

Canadian men's national team forward Junior Hoilett (right) during a 2022 World Cup qualifying match against Jamaica.

Canadian men's national team goalkeeper Milan Borjan (front left) and head coach John Herdman during 2022 World Cup qualifying.

Canadian men's national team head coach John Herdman (left) being interviewed by Kristian Jack after Canada qualified for the 2022 World Cup.

Left to right: Canadian men's national team defender Doneil Henry, goal-keeper Dayne St. Clair, and defender Kamal Miller after Canada secured qualification for the 2022 World Cup.

Canadian men's national team midfielder Jonathan Osorio during 2022
World Cup qualifying.

Canadian men's national team head coach John Herdman during 2022 World Cup qualifying.

Morgan Quarry remembers travelling with the team to Vienna for a March 2006 friendly against Austria, a team then comparable to Canada; at least by FIFA's rankings system. It was a World Cup year, and it was one of only five games for the national team that year, making it the leanest year of the decade for the squad.

Canada won 2–0, but when Quarry returned to the federation offices, multiple people approached him with the same question: "Where have you been?"

"The people there didn't care about soccer that much," Quarry said of the CSA that decade, highlighting how many important CSA jobs were stocked with volunteers. "There weren't enough soccer people."

Yet just months before Canada's humbling loss in Honduras, many had seen reason for optimism when Victor Montagliani was elected as new CSA president in May 2012. Those who knew Montagliani had faith, not just in his ability to deliver messages in a forceful way with short, purposeful sentences in lower tones, but also to create a player-focused federation instead of one that would consistently drown in its own bureaucracy.

"Victor," said Findlay, "has a football brain."

Montagliani had served as CSA vice-president for three terms, after being the president of the British Columbia Soccer Association. Even with his background at the provincial level, Montagliani was in favour of eliminating provincial and territorial presidents from the CSA and replacing them with national directors who would protect the interests of the federation. He wanted to advance the national teams, as opposed to simply looking out for specific provincial agendas. He immediately turned CSA board meetings, which previously were two-day affairs, into efficient, ninety-minute meetings. CSA employees got the message: it was time to start acting with a little more urgency in their day-to-day tasks.

"Too many of our structures have a 'legal' mentality, sort of like government," Montagliani said when he was named president. "That doesn't translate well in terms of international football and how decisions have to be made."

He wanted the organization to become more "entrepreneurial" and promote the national team with more professionalized promotions and marketing.

The association was too dependent on both volunteer directors to make crucial decisions about the direction of the men's national team and on amateur registration fees to keep the organization afloat. By utilizing his background in corporate management in the insurance business and his persuasive nature, Montagliani tried to ensure CSA took more financial risks, especially with sponsorship opportunities, to increase financial resources.

"That's something I always wanted to change; our attitude needed to be more from a commercial perspective and a corporate perspective," Montagliani told MLSsoccer.com toward the end of his term in 2016.

Montagliani was forthright in his belief that the men's team needed to qualify for a World Cup for the entire Canadian soccer ecosystem to benefit financially. An early step was to prioritize World Cup qualifying performances, which meant allocating resources toward improving travel conditions and accommodations for players so they could feel at their peak going into games.

Montagliani's attitude and background as a player resonated with current players.

"He was able to connect with the players and the staff in a way others couldn't," said Morgan Quarry. "He spoke their language. There was a sense that he was really fighting for national teams that we didn't always feel prior to that."

"Players' biggest frustration was that the country didn't seem to be turned on," said Montagliani.

What Montagliani saw was an organization, especially at the board level, too focused on growing the game in Canada at the grassroots level, and less focused on setting the national teams up for success.

"It's not a negative, in a sense," said Montagliani. "I just thought they didn't understand what the game meant outside the country."

For generations, central CSA figures had lacked foresight regarding the men's national team. Without a progressive mindset and planning for the future, history had repeated itself time and time again with disappointing World Cup qualifying campaigns. Immediate steps under Montagliani included the CSA's trying to allot more tickets to national-team fan clubs, which, hopefully, would prevent those not supporting the national team from getting tickets, and the CSA's no longer helping visiting teams to book hotels, security, and transportation.

"I remember being told, 'Hey, what happened to you nice Canadians?' I said, 'We're still nice, but this is World Cup qualifying,'" said Montagliani.

Investing in the men's team wouldn't be enough, though. To ensure repeated success in future qualifying campaigns, Montagliani was one of the earliest and strongest advocates of Canada's finally developing its own domestic league to complement the three Canadian teams playing in the American-based MLS.

Canada remained one of the few countries in FIFA without their own domestic league, which limited professional opportunities for young players. The CSA's *2014–18 Strategic Plan* clearly stated the need for a Canadian domestic league: "Our National Team coaches do not have the benefit of selecting players who regularly compete in an elite level domestic league. The world's top national teams draw from their domestic leagues. The development of a home-grown system in which our best players can compete is of paramount importance."

Montagliani put his belief into action by meeting with some of the country's wealthy sports executives. To avoid the pitfalls of the CSL, any new Canadian league needed to start on far more financially stable footing.

Montagliani also recognized just how much the perception of soccer had changed, even with the men's team's lack of success. The rise of the FIFA video-game brand among young adults, the continued popularity of the game's biggest stars, viewing international soccer tournaments in Canada and, finally, the attention the three Canadian MLS sides were getting was all proof: soccer was no longer a fringe sport. But with Canada's men's national team having dropped to 122nd in the FIFA rankings in 2014, a new low, Montagliani knew the survival of the team and by extension, domestic soccer in Canada, depended on better soccer infrastructure.

That was part of the message Montagliani delivered to Scott Mitchell, CEO of the CFL's Hamilton Tiger-Cats, during a lunch at a Vancouver sushi restaurant in 2014.

Montagliani all but dared Mitchell to get on board with a nascent Canadian league he was dreaming up. In a 2019 interview with the Athletic, Mitchell remembered a tenacious Montagliani saying to him "Anybody can tell me why this won't work. Why don't you tell me why it should work?"

What Montagliani did differently from some of his predecessors was make people like Mitchell understand that with an inventive business model, there could be financial incentives for early backers.

Hamilton became ground zero for the league. The Tiger-Cats ownership group became the first to be granted rights by the CSA to establish a team to play in their new stadium, Tim Hortons Field, and also one of the first to buy into the newfound Canadian Soccer Business, an enterprise launched in 2018 that represented commercial assets and inventory for marquee soccer properties in Canada.

Mitchell became CEO of CSB, and the set-up ensured that owners of any teams in this domestic league were also required to be investors in the CSB and therefore to support the growth of the sport and the men's national team in Canada.

Less than five years after that initial meeting between Montagliani and Mitchell, and propelled by the healthy relations built by former vice president of business operations at TFC and the league's first employee, Paul Beirne, the Canadian Premier League held its first game at Tim Hortons Field.

Seven teams made up the league in its first season, stretching, quite literally, from coast to coast: Vancouver Island, Edmonton, Calgary, Winnipeg, Hamilton, the York Region, and Halifax, with the league expanding to Ottawa the following year. Most importantly, the league mandated that each team had to dole out a healthy number of minutes to Canadian players under the age of twenty-one, both to increase professional playing time available for young players who wouldn't have otherwise gotten time, but also to showcase young players to the soccer world.

In 2019, goalkeeper Marco Carducci became the first CPL player to be called into the men's national team. The league slowly inched into the Canadian soccer consciousness, just a few years after Montagliani made it clear that was imperative for the sport's success in Canada.

"That," Mitchell reflected of the lunch with Montagliani, "was the turning point."

. . .

In May 2013, even as the CSA had gone seven months without naming a successor to Stephen Hart, Montagliani told the CBC that they did not see "any urgency" in naming a coach.

With Montagliani leading the charge, priority was placed on finding a coach with a strong tactical acumen and international experience. The extensive search saw the organization travel around the planet conducting interviews.

Among the names they coveted was Roberto Donadoni, who had previously coached the Italian national team in the 2008 Euros.

But the name they settled upon was one that ticked many of their boxes, and he was also the only person the CSA offered the job to: Spanish coach Benito Floro, known to some as "The Professor" for his obsession with tactics and for his ability to keep his players, his students, in line.

"I felt the national team was a country club," said Montagliani about why he pursued a personality like Floro's as head coach. "We needed a cultural shift."

The pensive, grey-haired Floro had a lengthy resume, having coached at Spanish clubs including Real Madrid and Villarreal and, having coached at Mexico's Monterrey, an understanding of coaching in North and Central America.

What he didn't have was any experience coaching international soccer.

"I love real projects," Floro said, with limited English, in his introductory press conference on July 5, 2013.

Montagliani believed Floro would usher in a new, ambitious era of thinking about Canadian soccer and waved away questions about whether Floro would understand things are "different" in Canadian soccer.

"Why are we different? We enjoy mediocrity? We enjoy parochialism?" asked Montagliani as Floro was unveiled. "I think it's time we wake up and say, 'What do we have to do to compete at the international standard?' And I don't think we've really done that. We've always been safe, inside the box, more within our comfort level."

Floro's early mission was to meet as many people within Canadian soccer as possible. That included Findlay, at the time director of football development at B.C. Soccer.

"His English was poor," said Findlay. "My Spanish was just as poor."

Near a fireplace inside the Sutton Place hotel restaurant in Vancouver, Floro quizzed Findlay on his tactical knowledge to attain an understanding of how soccer was played throughout the country. Questions were fed into the translation app on his phone, but when that proved unsuccessful and without a shared language to fall back on, Floro and Findlay used packets of sugar on the table in front of them to illustrate how they each preferred a team to move the ball in build-up play, and where players should move in transition. Floro's eyes grew wide while he waved his hands, talking tactics.

"Benito was a different cat," said Findlay. "But it showed me how universal football could be."

Floro would never hide his intellectual approach to the game as the men's team headed into an astounding period of tactical reorganization. As thought-provoking as he was in meetings and video sessions with his staff, his training sessions were far too heavy on tactical instruction, which didn't always inspire players to bring their competitive best. Structures on throw-ins would be practiced in alarming detail and length. Floro's preference for early morning sessions was a product of his own upbringing to ensure players avoided oppressive heat, but ahead of those morning sessions, Floro would only allow players limited snacks instead of the full meals they were used to.

Floro would ask his staff to catalogue hundreds of player movements, but when it came time to impart what he'd observed, player interest would sometimes wane as Floro became fully immersed in the minutiae of a lesson.

"It's like, 'The players have been here for an hour, we can't have them here any longer,'" Findlay remembers saying.

What he was trying to portray was actually quite simple: this Canadian team would be successful with rigid defensive structure.

"The first couple of camps, we all said, 'Woah, what's happening right now,'" de Jong said of player reaction to Floro. "He showed a lot of footage of his coaching career, which was funny, because some of those films were still black and white. When he came there, he put a stamp on it: this is how we play. Take it or leave it. That kind of coach was what we needed at that point."

Floro's changes caused friction during Canada's first four friendly matches to round out 2013, all of which did not yield a win. The team went winless in all twelve of their matches in 2013, the first time they'd gone winless in a calendar year in a generation. Even if losses were nothing new, Canada's first five games under Floro were alarming in how strictly they dropped deep when not in possession, while not scoring a single goal.

But many could still see Floro's mind for the game. In the pre-scout meeting ahead of a friendly against the Czech Republic that Canada lost 2–0, Floro promised the only way the Czechs would score was on a specific set play free kick.

"And sure enough, they did. It was hard to then not buy into what he was saying, because a lot of it came true," said Ledgerwood. "As a player, you think, either this guy's a little bit crazy, or he's ahead of so many other coaches in what we've been taught."

Not every player bought in.

"Players were not really always standing behind the coach," said de Jong, which flew in the face of Floro's belief that players should defend as a collective. "It only works if everybody does it. You cannot have eight players on the field doing it and then three players not doing it. Then the whole system crumbles."

De Jong remembers Floro insisting that while defending, players never look away from the ball.

"If you're a defender, you can't look to your right, even if the ball is left. And you can't really look to your teammates, if you're on the same line defending you always have to know where they are," said de Jong. "He would stop practices if a player was looking to the other side. He would go bananas and get really emotional if players did those things."

Canada lost just one of their five friendlies in 2014, allowing only three goals throughout, but Floro sometimes struggled to convince the media of his rationale.

Take his exclusion of then twenty-three-year-old Jonathan Osorio from the squad once the third round of 2018 World Cup qualification rolled around in 2015. Osorio was coming into his own as a poised midfielder for Toronto FC who could dictate the tempo of play and pick apart defences with intelligent passes, but Floro believed Osorio's tendency to slow the game down didn't gel with his approach and could leave Canada exposed to counterattacks. He instead defended his decision by touting the experience of the midfielders he did bring into the squad, such as Will Johnson and Atiba Hutchinson, while still bringing in a midfielder similar to Osorio's ilk in Kyle Bekker, who had logged limited MLS time in 2015.

Osorio had risen through the TFC academy and was logging regular minutes for a good side, making him a poster boy for a still-developing player pathway.

The decision spoke to a disconnect between what Floro was trying to achieve with the men's national team and what many within Canadian soccer wanted from the national team. There were few players who burned to play for Canada like Osorio, after all.

Findlay remembers coaching a nineteen-year-old Osorio at the 2011 Concacaf Under-20 championship, who at that point was playing for Uruguayan side Nacional's youth academy. Osorio was told he wouldn't start a match.

"He came to me in my hotel room in Guatemala and sat on the edge of the bed. And he cried his eyes out and said, 'I want to play, I can play, I know I can play, I'm going to help this team.' If you are identifying a player who appreciates sacrifice, and appreciates hard work, and is completely committed, it's Jonathan Osorio. I said to him in the hotel room 'Oso, you're gonna play, be patient, you will play,'" said Findlay.

Yet for his sometimes questionable lineup choices on the pitch, Floro was making in-roads off of it. Findlay remembers Floro making it imperative his staff "cast the net far and wide" in the hopes of finding players to bolster the player pool.

Findlay led the naturalization process to find players with other international options, confirm their eligibility to play for Canada under FIFA regulations, and then help dual nationals become Canadian citizens.

"My pitch to them always was: 'We're never going to beg you to play for Canada,'" said Findlay. "But what we told them was, 'This is a period of change in Canada. This is an opportunity to play international football. This is an opportunity to contribute to something not just about football, but the culture.'"

The coaching staff under Floro understood the motivating factors behind player decisions and offered them what other countries couldn't: playing time.

Take the case of forward Tesho Akindele, who was called into a United States camp in 2015 but did not play any matches. Akindele eventually joined the Canadian national team for World Cup qualifying matches and made the most of his immediate playing time, scoring in his second appearance for Canada.

"That's one of the motivating factors of playing international football for many players," Findlay said of playing time. "It changes your reputation and your contractual dynamic."

When John Herdman later took over the national team, he too made it a priority to convince dual nationals to play for Canada. But the groundwork was truly laid under Montagliani, whose efforts in his four-year tenure with the CSA saw him soon become voted president of Concacaf and therefore a vice president of FIFA, and Floro.

Montagliani made multiple trips to London nearly every month for a year to meet with Junior Hoilett to ensure the talented attacker would play for Canada and not Jamaica.

"At the end of the day, they've got to see it in your eyes, that you believe in what you're selling: that this player can make a difference for this country," said Montagliani.

Hoilett wasn't the only player. Influential dual national players for the 2022 World Cup qualifying cycle that would make their debuts under Floro included Sam Adekugbe, Steven Vitória, and Scott Arfield.

"A moment of change," said Findlay.

• • •

The goal for the men's national team in 2015 and 2016, as it had been for every World Cup cycle since 1998, was to at the very least qualify for The Hex.

Being in a fourth-round group with Mexico, Honduras, and El Salvador presented a serious challenge for qualifying for the 2018 World Cup in Russia. That was evident through the first five matchdays as Canada could only muster one win, one draw, and three losses, and a lowly two goals scored. While there was concern from within the organization about what kind of crowds their home matches at BC Place in Vancouver would garner, the 54,798 fans that attended Mexico's 3–0 win over Canada set a national team attendance record. Interest in the team, evidenced by the exuberant pregame and midgame atmosphere, appeared to be growing, though that interest wasn't always matched by the national team's performances.

"Perfunctory," said journalist John Molinaro of their play through this cycle. "It wasn't exactly playing to win."

Nevertheless, a win on their final matchday at home against El Salvador combined with a Mexico win at home over Honduras would have been enough to send Canada to The Hex.

Canada did their part with a rousing 3–1 victory at BC Place in Vancouver, but Mexico and Honduras drawing sent those teams through instead. As is custom, the wondering about what could have been had Mexico won at the Azteca, where they had won their previous five matches, grew to a sour taste throughout Canadian soccer.

By this point, with multiple trips to top European continental club competitions under his belt, then thirty-three-year-old Atiba Hutchinson had become the most appreciated player in men's team history. Yet the whispers about whether another failed World Cup qualification campaign would mean the end of his time in the program grew louder.

After all, the five goals scored in six games of the fourth round were ninth among the twelve teams.

Many who believed the CSA got their head turned with the appointment of Floro because he was Spanish and coached Real Madrid argued the federation got what they deserved.

"They didn't quite understand what they were getting," said Molinaro. "Yes, he was Spanish, but he didn't exactly preach tiki-taka [playing short, rapid passes with constant player movement], a brand of football that was very much en vogue at the time and with good reason."

As Canada was eliminated, Floro compared the country's plight to other Concacaf nations and echoed the consistent concern about a lack of training camps.

"With our team, it's impossible to do [have constant training camps]. Impossible, because there is no league, Canadian league," he said, adding that with just a handful of days to train as a group, "it's not enough to progress more or faster."

Eight days after Canada was eliminated from World Cup contention, it was announced Floro would not return as head coach.

But before he left, Floro offered a final, stern assessment of the state of Canadian soccer that summed up more than just his tenure with the program.

"It is very difficult for us because Canada always has more impediments than the other teams," he said, underscoring the consistent infighting and the need for more continued progressive thinking that plagued both the CSA and the Canadian soccer community as a whole. "A thousand impediments."

CHAPTER 10

"Sometimes There's a Reason Things Happen": Atiba Hutchinson Forged a Career Unlike Any Other Canadian

WHEN THE TEMPERATURE DIPPED IN VAXJO, SWEDEN, IN 2003, ATIBA Hutchinson would step out of his apartment building to walk the town's narrow, cobblestoned streets alone. His gaze would be lit only by the rare glow of a shop still open in the evening.

The chilly temperatures didn't catch the then twenty-year-old Brampton-born midfielder off guard the way some of the cultural differences did, though perhaps a layer of thermal underwear would've helped protect his astoundingly skinny legs.

Without much in the way of skills in the kitchen, he'd pull a toque over an early receding hairline and wander in search of dinner. It wasn't long after arriving in Sweden for the first time in his life that he came to realize how much earlier restaurants and grocery stores closed compared to his hometown, forcing him to camp out at the local McDonald's far too often.

What he longed for was some of his mother Myrtle's homemade lasagna. Myrtle sent him uncooked pasta sheets and tried to deliver instructions via phone on cobbling together his own lasagna, but it was a fruitless endeavour.

When Myrtle visited her son, she'd sometimes find nothing more than sour milk in his fridge.

So, as he snacked on fry after fry, the first year full-time professional for Osters IF continually wondered, *Is this the way professional soccer players are supposed to behave?*

After sitting alone in booths of faceless fast-food joints, he'd pop into a convenience store. Without a command of the Swedish language, he'd try to choose from the vast array of calling cards and find a payphone to call home, eager to catch his mom while she prepared dinner. For most of his career abroad, the quick communication apps like FaceTime had yet to appear.

"I was *really* homesick," said Hutchinson, rubbing the bald head that ended up becoming synonymous with the Canadian men's team for a generation.

Yet as he'd walk back to his apartment alone, he'd repeat a mantra over and over to himself: *This is what I've got to do. Things will turn around; I'll get used to it.*

"I never thought I'd miss my family and friends so much that I'd have to leave," said Hutchinson.

Hutchinson is not the type to reach out for help. He listens more than he speaks. And when he does speak, his lightly tinged Caribbean accent rarely veers into negatives. Instead, his ability to stay the course in the hopes of achieving something greater was evident from the beginning of his career.

"I left everything behind and took my chance," said Hutchinson. "I was just too focused on what I really wanted to do."

That attitude is why he'd barely had a drop of alcohol and would often turn down opportunities to be around his friends in Brampton as a teenager. Instead, he went on trials with German and Italian clubs and signed as a nineteen-year-old with the Toronto Lynx of what was then called the A-League.

And it's why he left the comforts of home in January 2003 for a small Swedish city he'd never visited before. He took a chance with an unorthodox one-year contract with Osters that could be terminated after six months if he didn't meet the team's standards.

On the pitch, he was built in a way no other Canadian male player ever had been, capable of using his spindly legs to win balls in physical duels in the midfield, spraying passes with remarkable accuracy to his teammates, and outlasting the opposition when tracking back to recover defensively.

He outlasted off the pitch as well: from being away from his home for nearly twenty years, only to return to a national team program that achieved little success, the story of Hutchinson's career is one of sacrifice. His experience in Europe turned him into the beacon of professionalism for a national team that sorely needed it, becoming not only their all-time games-played leader, but arguably the best player in the program's history.

And quite possibly, the greatest Canadian athlete most Canadians never heard of during his prime.

"I don't think people realize how tough it is," said Hutchinson's former coach Frank Yallop, of Hutchinson's efforts to continue with a struggling national team. "But Atiba did it."

. . .

Hutchinson continued to live a life unlike his peers' when, after he proved he could hack it with Osters, he earned a transfer to Swedish side Helsingborg. With it came the opportunity to live in a larger city and, for the first time, to visit a nightclub — as a twenty-three-year-old.

"And even going to the club, I was worried about going there," said Hutchinson.

Yet when he did reconnect with old teammates, whether or not Hutchinson himself could sense it, the reserved, sometimes cautious Hutchinson's confidence had bloomed in Sweden.

Never was that more evident than during the 2003 FIFA World Youth Championship as part of what then assistant coach Nick Dasovic called "the best team I've ever been around." The team had grown close, with their core meeting eight times in 2003 across different age groups and training camps leading up to the December tournament in the United Arab Emirates.

"That team just epitomized Canada as a nation: fighters and battlers," said Dasovic. "But also: technical skills."

Central to that was Hutchinson's resourceful, inventive play. His versatility made then men's team head coach Holger Osieck break from his stern persona to heap praise on the young midfielder.

"I am actually convinced — and you know that I'm always pretty cautious in my predictions — that he has the tools to play first division football in Europe," said Osieck, of Hutchinson at the time.

The Under-20 team would primarily play with three central defenders, but against stiffer competition they transitioned to four defenders. The coaching staff could make these changes because Hutchinson, who began with the Under-20 team in 2001 as an eighteen-year-old, could be shuffled from playing as a centre-back, on the right or left side of three central defenders, as a central midfielder, or even as an attacking midfielder. Hutchinson had learned from his father Dalton to always stay active on the field: *You don't have to play the game with the ball all the time*, Hutchinson was told.

"He never questioned anything," said Dasovic. "You put him anywhere, he just looked at you and said, 'OK boss, let's do this.'"

Yet it was Hutchinson who was the proverbial boss of a young team that always appeared to Dasovic to be "really jacked up" before games.

Dasovic tried to respect the locker room as a sanctuary for players. But he couldn't resist putting a finger on why his team's emotions boiled over leading up to kickoff. He snuck through a back door into the cramped dressing room and was asked by one of his players to film what was about to take place on a handheld camcorder. Dasovic then stood on a chair to witness the birth of Atiba Hutchinson, the leader.

Hutchinson would demand his teammates circle around him in the minutes before the game. He'd step into the middle and start an intense call-and-response chant, first with the raunchy lyrics in the chorus to the Ruff Ryders rap anthem "Down Bottom," before a more PG-rated call.

"It's for the North," Hutchinson would sing, while his teammates would quickly chime in "Hey," then Hutchinson would call for the South, East, and West, with the "Hey" call growing louder each time. The primal hollering reminded Dasovic of New Zealand's All Blacks rugby team performing their legendary haka.

"I thought, 'If you can ever build a team, build it around that type of passion, that group mentality, that warrior spirit,'" said Dasovic.

"An incredible experience," said teammate Josh Simpson.

Hutchinson would then flip a switch and adopt a remarkably composed demeanour when he'd take the pitch, reminding those on the inside of how much of Hutchinson's influence is rarely seen by the public.

Though Canada lost their first two games against more established soccer nations, Brazil and Australia, a gutsy win against the Czech Republic thanks to a late Iain Hume goal in their final game sent them through to the round of sixteen. Hutchinson saved his best performances for when they were needed most. He continually broke down Burkina Faso in a win to put them further into the tournament than they'd ever been.

Canada's best effort came in the quarterfinals, in which they pushed a talented Spanish side complete with one of the greatest midfielders of all time, Andres Iniesta, to extra time. The golden goal rule was in effect, and Canada was sunk in the ninety-seventh minute.

Still, as Hutchinson left Dubai, it was clear he could lead a squad in a way few of his peers could.

"Sometimes," said Dasovic of Hutchinson's role and the Canadian result, "there's a reason things happen."

．．．

Hutchinson was fast-tracked to the men's team, first under Osieck and later under then head coach Frank Yallop. In their first few camps working together, Yallop honed in on Hutchinson's poise with the ball and thought, *Why isn't he logging first-team minutes with a top European side?*

That soon came, as FC Copenhagen's incoming manager Stale Solbakken made Hutchinson the first signing of his tenure, beginning in 2006.

In Copenhagen, Hutchinson took one of the most important steps of his career: into the UEFA Champions League. He was one of just a handful of Canadians at the time to have competed in Europe's top club competition.

Facing such a high level of play, Hutchinson learned to play the ball quicker than he ever had before; Solbakken trusted him to play as a defensive midfielder in one game against Manchester United, and then as a forward in the return leg weeks later, almost always in an advanced midfield role when Copenhagen dominated on the ball domestically. Solbakken also noticed that, coupled with his tactical know-how, Hutchinson socialized with every type of character in the Copenhagen dressing room with typical warmth.

In annual European competitions and four league titles, Hutchinson's preparation meant Solbakken would leave him out of the Danish league squad only six times in five seasons.

"He played like he was a little bit older," recalled Solbakken of Hutchinson. "He has respect for the opposition, but he is not afraid of anything. And that's a good mix."

Yet Hutchinson's experience in Copenhagen was contrasted on the other side of the Atlantic Ocean with Canadian teams not living up to their potential. By the time Hutchinson was named Canadian male soccer player of the year for the first time, in 2010, he'd been part of two failed World Cup qualifying campaigns. The height of his success with the national team to that point was a peak still associated with failure: the 2007 Gold Cup semifinal loss against the United States on a team plagued with a self-inflicted lack of professionalism.

Referring to the Canadian soccer infrastructure, Stephen Hart, head coach of the 2007 Gold Cup team, said that Hutchinson's success occurred "in spite of it." Listing other national team players such as Kevin McKenna and Paul Stalteri as well, he went on to say that "they went to Europe fairly late by certain players' standards, but still made a good living from the game at a very high standard."

To further improve that standard, Hutchinson made the kind of changes off the pitch that most of his teammates did not.

"There's a huge mindset that needs to shift, if you want to be that professional and continue your career," said former teammate Nik Ledgerwood. "I don't think a lot of guys have that in them."

Ledgerwood and Hutchinson would often enjoy a glass of red wine together when they met at national team camps early in their careers. But as his star rose, Hutchinson would wave away waiters offering the restaurant wine list. Ledgerwood was surprised when Hutchinson told him he needed to cut out anything slowing his recovery. Because with lingering groin injuries, Hutchinson was learning to spot the warning signs of how his career might be altered.

He moved to a gluten-free diet to keep himself limber during training sessions and games; all the more difficult, given the wealth of breads and pastries available in Europe. Hutchinson paid thousands of dollars out of his own pocket for a physio trainer to increase his mobility. Almost every day, even after long hours spent training or travelling, Hutchinson would put his three children to bed, then quietly nip out to a local gym and complete a session tailored to his needs.

"If he is the most underrated Canadian athlete ever, it's because of that professionalism and mindset of wanting to show up and prove to everybody that he's the best," said Ledgerwood.

As he moved from Copenhagen and continued to play European competitions with PSV Eindhoven in the Netherlands in 2010, the example Hutchinson wanted to set for his young Canadian teammates was all the more evident.

Former Canadian teammate Marcel de Jong remembers new players trying to take liberties or embarrass other young players with the way they played in national team training sessions.

Hutchinson didn't speak up often, but he stressed that if the men's team was going to succeed, players would need to show continuous respect toward each other on the pitch.

"That's one of the reasons why players like Atiba are at their level," said de Jong. "They never take [playing soccer for a living] for granted."

Hutchinson would arrive early for every team meal, meeting, and training session, flash his toothy grin to teammates, shake a hand and stretch out his razor-thin legs, just as he would have with his club sides.

Through the grind of playing for Copenhagen and PSV, and appearing in the UEFA Champions League or Europa League, and in national team camps when he'd see his teammates' professionalism fall by the wayside, his mind would run back to those nights he spent alone, stranded from family or friends, in Sweden. He'd already sacrificed plenty to become the professional. Why do anything to jeopardize the career he'd built?

"Just try to lead by example," he said of his approach. "I don't want things to be taken away from me."

The dejection in his face before he buried his head in his shirt after the 8–1 loss against Honduras in 2012 spoke to what he'd had taken away from him.

He resisted the urge to blame those teammates who didn't always match the effort he put into the national team, though — not his style.

"Maybe, at times, we could have been better at figuring out ways to get the team more involved," said Hutchinson, choosing his words carefully and moving his head side-to-side. He rubs his long fingers across his chin, looking back, and then looks skyward while contemplating what could have been. "But it's a process."

Hutchinson's modus operandi actually ended up turning his career into a paradox: he constantly went about his business quietly, free of the drama that sometimes leads to teams of egotistical athletes. But that he kept his head down might have also meant he stayed far out of sight and out of mind in the greater Canadian public consciousness.

At a time when the women's national team could boast one of the greatest players in the world in Christine Sinclair, the men didn't possess the same kind of easily recognizable face of the team.

Hutchinson bet on himself in the summer of 2013, allowing his contract at PSV Eindhoven to run out so he would become a free agent. His desire was to challenge himself in the Premier League. Despite interest, the contract offers were lacking for a player of his quality. Perhaps if this move to the Premier League had materialized it would have boosted his profile.

Instead, he signed for Beşiktaş, one of Istanbul's legendary clubs but one that had only one top-three league finish over the previous four seasons.

Almost immediately, many within the Premier League saw what they'd missed. After an August 2014 UEFA Champions League playoff match between Beşiktaş and Arsenal, during which Hutchinson fought his way out of difficult situations with the ball on his feet, widely celebrated Arsenal manager Arsene Wenger was asked which opponent stuck out to him: "The best player on Beşiktaş?" he answered. "I was impressed by Hutchinson."

The complimentary words from Wenger probably struck home with more people in Canada than his play could. Turkish games were not widely available on television the way Premier League games were.

Hutchinson became a fan favourite in Istanbul. He was dubbed "*Ahtapot*," the Turkish word for octopus, by the Beşiktaş faithful because of his long legs and his ability to connect long passes to his teammates as if he were playing with tentacles. As a regular starter, he guided Beşiktaş to back-to-back Turkish Süper Lig championships in 2016 and 2017, their first back-to-back league titles in over twenty years. He'd leave his house at odd hours to avoid being mobbed by adoring fans while walking city streets, but when he did stop to shake hands, he would do so with a smile.

Yet away from a country where fervent fanbases worship their stars, Hutchinson, to his own wonderment, could walk the same types of streets in Canada unrecognized. Despite his position among the greatest male Canadian soccer players being unquestioned, Hutchinson's name was not among the finalists for the Lou Marsh Award, voted on by a collection of Canada's sports journalists for the top Canadian athlete of the year.

"Why isn't Atiba Hutchinson a household name in Canada?" read the headline of a 2016 Sportsnet article.

"Atiba Hutchinson is the best Canadian soccer player you've never heard of," went a headline in the *Toronto Star* in 2018.

Ultimately, the lack of men's team success at the peak of his career, coupled with the lack of exposure on Canadian screens as he played with Beşiktaş, led to the prime of his career being spent in anonymity.

"Two different worlds," said Hutchinson.

When he did return to Canadian camps, his lack of recognition would be a talking point among his teammates, including the towering and balding goalkeeper Milan Borjan. Hutchinson and Borjan were bona fide leaders in the group. Borjan had become a starter in the UEFA Champions League, first with Bulgarian side Ludogorets Razgrad and then with perennial Serbian contenders Red Star Belgrade, so both were stepping away from playing against some of the world's best in Europe and into a more depressing soccer environment with Canada.

Borjan and other players would press Canadian soccer officials on whether enough was being done to promote Hutchinson.

Hutchinson's anonymity in Canada never frustrated him, but it did lead to the same thoughts often creeping into his head.

It would creep in, for instance, when his legs were cramped into an airplane seat for twelve hours straight, from Istanbul to Toronto, on a lengthier return to Canada than many of his teammates.

And the thought would only emerge with more regularity when he'd walk out onto a pitch to see Canadian stadiums sometimes half full, and sometimes filled with more jerseys of the visiting team. Hutchinson craved

the slightest bit of pressure from fans. But, instead, he arrived at a sad conclusion: *Canada is not a footballing country.*

"It was demoralizing," said Hutchinson. "You're playing for your country, but they're not really there behind you."

He'd had his first child, Noah, in 2015, the same year qualifying for the
2018 World Cup began.

Something had to give. Hutchinson would ask himself how he could
continue to endure the travel, which was doing harm on his body, and continually spend time away from his children, to play for Canada. His next
son, Naya, was born in 2016 and his third son, Ayo Siyah, followed in 2017.

There were worrisome whispers around the national team when
Hutchinson began to drop hints in the press that this qualifying campaign
could be his last. Those whispers took on a graver tone when Hutchinson
and teammate David Edgar exchanged whispers themselves on the BC Place
pitch in Vancouver in late 2016, after Canada was eliminated from 2018
World Cup contention even with a 3–1 win over El Salvador.

Hutchinson had been named to Canada's all-time Best XI in 2012 as
part of the Canadian Soccer Association's centennial celebrations, he and
Dwayne De Rosario being the only active players to make the list. He was a
four-time winner of the Canadian male player of the year to that point, with
two more titles soon to come.

But after that loss in Vancouver, Hutchinson took a step back from the
national team, not appearing in any of the team's six friendlies leading up
to the 2017 Gold Cup.

After former assistant coach Michael Findlay had taken over as an interim head coach, the CSA (which would eventually rebrand to Canada
Soccer) hired Ecuadorian Octavio Zambrano to take over the men's team
in March 2017. His heavy figure made him one of the most physically imposing coaches in recent men's team history, but his slow and sometimes soft
manner of speaking provided a juxtaposition that many in the federation
believed would be the right fit to connect with young players. His thick eyebrows would furrow as he spoke in great detail about the changes needed to
build a program from the ground up. After multiple coaching stints in MLS
and with club sides in Ecuador, it was thought, he could understand young
Canadian players and the challenges they'd face playing in hostile locales.

Zambrano wanted players to free themselves from the defensive approach of his predecessor Benito Floro and play with aggressiveness. There was some evidence of that during the 2017 Gold Cup. Canada made it out of the group stage for the first time in three tournaments before losing in the quarterfinals to Jamaica.

But Zambrano butted heads with far too many people within the organization, demanding administrative and structural changes, including the way the federation scouted young players, but without always providing detailed explanations for those changes. He irked some in Canada Soccer for his lack of participation at Canada Soccer's 2017 Annual Meeting of the Members. Relationships between Zambrano and others in the organization soon became abrasive, even as Zambrano worked to bring players with dual nationalities into the fold.

"I didn't want to play politics," Zambrano told TFC Republic in 2021. "There was a lot of it in Canada."

Before he was fired in January 2018, Zambrano had managed just seven matches for Canada, giving him the dubious distinction of being the first Canadian head coach in a generation not to even get a crack at World Cup qualifying.

In the wake of Zambrano's firing, some people in leadership positions within Canada Soccer were forced to admit that they hadn't used as much foresight in hiring Zambrano as perhaps they should have. Hutchinson had opted not to play in the 2017 Gold Cup, meaning he'd played just one match during Zambrano's tenure. This led to a more despondent question: had Hutchinson's best years in a Canadian shirt been wasted?

"You never had that feeling that people are really behind you and supporting you," Hutchinson recalled of his time with the men's team to that point, "because regardless of what you do, nobody really cares."

• • •

John Molinaro awoke in his downtown Toronto apartment on the morning of January 8, 2018, expecting a day of relaxation. The unassuming journalist rubbed his constant grey stubble, eager for a rare holiday after covering Toronto FC's storybook run to their first-ever MLS Cup championship a month before. Very few Canadian soccer journalists wrote with the regularity that Molinaro had since he started covering the sport in 2001.

And so, with a mountain of books on his coffee table to get through, Molinaro prepared for some solitude ahead of a dinnertime plate of *aglio e olio* linguine.

Molinaro put down his book when his phone vibrated. It was a text message from a reliable source: "You'll never guess what!"

Molinaro rubbed his eyes, partly out of slumber but also with astonishment over the text that followed. It would end up seriously altering not just Molinaro's planned vacation day, but the Canadian soccer landscape itself: "I'm hearing John Herdman is going to be named the head coach of the men's national team."

This can't be right, Molinaro thought to himself.

John Herdman was the Englishman who had two Olympic bronze medals on his resume after rejuvenating the Canadian women's national team in seven years as head coach. But still, Octavio Zambrano had been head coach of the men's team for less than a year. The general public knew of nothing he had done to warrant a surprise firing.

After a few more hours of chasing down sources, Molinaro realized his story had legs. The problem? The majority of the women's national team players hadn't been told about their coach's move. It wasn't to be announced for another month.

A call from Canada Soccer followed. They implored Molinaro to hold off on publishing his story until they had arranged a conference call with the women's team. Molinaro was told the women's national team would be "devastated" if they heard the news from someone other than Herdman. He was offered President Steven Reed and Herdman himself for exclusive interviews. Reed would tell Molinaro that Herdman was chosen with the program's "long-term philosophy" in mind.

Molinaro scored his scoop, Zambrano's sacking on short notice became public, and Herdman's tenure began.

The quick start meant Herdman could get to work on an early order of business: interrupting a much-needed vacation Hutchinson and his family were enjoying on the Thai island of Ko Samui.

After working with Christine Sinclair, the very picture of professionalism and dedication to Canadian soccer, Herdman had heard Hutchinson was cut from the same cloth.

"The one person that I *really* wanted to work with on the men's side was Atiba Hutchinson," said Herdman.

Hutchinson's feet tucked into white sand and his mind was about as far away from half-empty stadiums in Canada as it could be when his phone delivered a text from Herdman, asking for a few minutes of his time.

"You're going to try to bring me back, aren't you?" a hardly credulous Hutchinson replied, as he shuffled his feet in the sand and felt the soreness in his ankle, very recently operated on.

Hutchinson had told himself and his wife Sarah he was done with the national team.

Herdman knew he had a mostly young core who could grow as a group, but he didn't have a hardened veteran who could guide them.

Hutchinson pushed back, telling Herdman that after his surgery he wasn't sure he'd ever play the game at the same level again.

In the back of Herdman's mind was a well-circulated photo of Hutchinson at the end of the 8–1 loss against Honduras in 2012, where his head was buried in his shirt. It reminded Herdman of a photo of a dejected Christine Sinclair sitting on the pitch in tears after a loss to France eliminated Canada from the 2011 World Cup. When Herdman took over the women's national team in 2011, he continually put that photo up for the entire team to see — to frustrate them and, hopefully, to motivate them.

And so he refuted Hutchinson's claim, insisting that he hadn't hit his potential yet as a player, and the only way to do that was in a Canadian jersey. Hutchinson replied with a torrent of memories about the difficulties of playing for Canada, from the lack of attention from the Canadian public, and the arduous travel, to the continual heartbreaks.

At once, Herdman dialed back his offensive, and Hutchinson discovered he had found a coach who would actually listen to his concerns.

"I didn't expect it," said Herdman. "A lot of these male pro players have managed to build such a thick skin. They wear a very strong mask. But he took [the mask] off."

Herdman avoided clichés, instead outlining clear plans for where he thought Hutchinson fit both tactically and from a leadership perspective. He insisted this young group was going to be driven by up-and-coming and otherworldly talented prospects such as seventeen-year-old Alphonso Davies, who had the potential to usurp Hutchinson as the best Canadian men's player of all time; but for any of Canada's young players to have success, the team needed Hutchinson.

That meant Hutchinson would be pushing himself to become one of the oldest players in men's team history and potentially the all-time games-played leader. Herdman believed that when athletes like Hutchinson have experienced the lowest lows, "they'll push certain limits and levels to put it right."

Herdman's attitude impressed Hutchinson after so many people in Canada had taken his quality for granted. At thirty-five and coming off surgery, Hutchinson recognized that many coaches wouldn't even have made the phone call. But Herdman told Hutchinson that he could prioritize his health and return on his own terms to have one more opportunity to cement his legacy in Canadian sports history.

It was the vote of confidence a wounded Hutchinson needed. He agreed to wear the captain's armband in Concacaf Nations League qualification games, a new tournament meant to eliminate friendly matches. The men's national team had to win every one of their matches to prove they deserved to be playing games against the region's best, not its minnows.

For the qualification games, Hutchinson agreed to another multi-stop day of travel in the middle of his Turkish Süper Lig season, this time to Warner Park in the seaside town of Basseterre to play Saint Kitts and Nevis. The dried-out pitch, with its short fences of chain and wood separating it from a few thousand spectators, was a far cry from some of the pitches Hutchinson had walked onto during his Champions League runs.

Canada had preceded this game with two dominant wins, against the U.S. Virgin Islands and Dominica, by a combined score of 13–0. Still, ahead of this game, Hutchinson broke from his normally quiet pregame approach and addressed the team, reminding them not to take any opponent lightly.

Minutes before halftime, Canada were at risk of embarrassing themselves, as they had so many times over the past decade, in a 0–0 stalemate against a host side intent on pressing them.

But, just as they had too many times to count, the thirty-five-year-old Hutchinson's legs kicked into gear. He strode untouched nearly the length of the entire opposition half. He leapt at least two feet in the air and connected on a header for the lone goal.

Crisis averted. Hutchinson's seventh goal for Canada in his eightieth appearance sealed a 1–0 win and kept the program moving forward.

"No one else was making that type of run," said Herdman, "to make sure he got the job done."

And Herdman reminded his group of that fact after the game. The men's national team had yet to prove themselves as an elite team in Concacaf.

But as the team members went their separate ways and Hutchinson made yet another trip from obscurity in Canada to celebrity abroad, there was a growing recognition within the national program that for any serious steps forward, Hutchinson would need to lead the way.

CHAPTER 11

A Brotherhood, Running Red Lights, and Running a New Program: 2018–2021

IN ONE OF THE LARGEST STADIUMS IN PROBABLY THE MOST FER-
vent soccer country on the planet, a coach closed his eyes, grinned, and
began swinging his arms back and forth as if he'd been possessed by a super-
natural force.

John Herdman had never shied away from showing emotion pitch-side.
Part of what endeared him to fans was his proclivity to yell intense, direct
commands to his players in his distinguishable Geordie accent. A Twitter
account appropriately called "John Herdman Yelling" had been created
in 2013 to log those commands, so easily heard on television. "GET SET
SINCY" had been tweeted on it days earlier.

This show of emotion was different, though. Sincy, known to the masses
as Christine Sinclair, had just finished some gutsy build-up play from the
Canadian women's side to send them up 2–0 against Brazil, to cries of shock
from nearly forty thousand fans clad in yellow inside Arena Corinthians in
Sao Paulo.

Herdman could be forgiven for his out-of-body experience, because with
that goal, he knew what others did, too: the Canadian women's national

team were likely to win a bronze medal for the second Olympics in a row. They'd become the only country to medal in both the 2012 and 2016 summer Olympics women's soccer tournaments.

That this latest bronze medal win came against the hosts of the Olympics was even further evidence Herdman could get his team to achieve success against the odds.

It was also proof, to Herdman, at least for now, that he had taken this program about as far as he could. He now knew he would soon have to push himself into another new experience.

His unfettered charisma was no longer a state secret. Nor was his ability to transform how players believed in their capabilities and to transform an entire program. With his infectious charm and obsessive planning, he had become the face of the women's national team when Canada hosted the 2015 World Cup. He won over nearly every skeptic in the country with thoughtful, passionate diatribes that came to life in a wonderfully amiable accent many mistook for Scottish.

At a time when the men's program was an afterthought in Canada, highlighted by Benito Floro's inability to speak completely fluent English and connect with the wider public, Herdman's tenure as women's team head coach represented what could happen when the country was galvanized by a forward-thinking and rousing persona.

In 2017, Herdman was awarded the Jack Donohue Coach of the Year Award by the Coaching Association of Canada. He was a deserving winner, but by that point, Herdman's celebrity in Canada meant he was "starting to drink [his] own Kool-Aid," as he told *Footy Prime: The Podcast* in 2021.

Herdman needed a new challenge. Calling bringing the men's national team back from the dead a challenge was an understatement, but it was about to become Herdman's next obsession.

• • •

John Herdman was never going to ply his trade as a professional soccer player. The then central midfielder didn't have the technical skills to progress past England's semi-professional Northern League, but had some of the necessary tools to keep him in soccer nonetheless: an exuberance toward the game, and in particular toward Newcastle United, that he had developed as a child growing up in the despondent northeastern English town of Consett. This would later manifest in his waxing poetic about the team and its grounds to any reporter who would listen.

Even though he was shorter than his peers, his gumption meant he wouldn't back down from a fight in a town that, hit with rampant unemployment with the 1980 closure of the steelworks, provided its fair share of scraps.

"People do have tough times here," Herdman told TSN in 2015 of Consett, "but the one thing that they all live for is Saturday afternoon. It's the saving grace."

Without the possibility of a career as a player, Herdman studied sports science and education and lectured at a university before returning to teach at his former elementary school, St. Patrick's. In 1999, as a twenty-four-year-old, he opened a Brazilian-focused soccer school out of St. Patrick's to expose the next generation of players to a more vibrant style of play. He encouraged expression through dribbling as opposed to the rough-and-tumble English style of play that was also being played by the Canadian men's national team at the time.

"English coaching is stagnant," Herdman told a local newspaper at the time, which perhaps spoke to his braggadocio and his interest in having his players push their boundaries, both of which would become hallmarks of his approach.

A job coaching at neighbouring Sunderland AFC's youth academy allowed him to truly showcase how well his studious approach to coaching could succeed. He presented detailed tactical plans for players to help them fulfill their roles, while also motivating them with his rousing speaking style. He'd whip his players up for games with slow, methodical sentences about player responsibilities before growing into a crescendo of fervent messaging about the battle ahead, meant to connect with players on a spiritual level. His players wanted to play for him — they believed he was genuinely interested in their own personal success.

Yet without a serious playing background his path ahead in England was full of roadblocks.

"At the time, it was not an industry for an academic who didn't have a strong playing background," Herdman told the Athletic in 2021.

His unorthodox jump to coaching in New Zealand, first in soccer development and then as head coach of the women's national team program for five years, prepared him in multiple ways.

The collaborative environment between all of New Zealand's sports programs meant Herdman was placed in accelerator programs and had access to the methods utilized by the legendary All Blacks, generally considered the best international rugby side in the world. The All Blacks would create a performance analytics program for Herdman's soccer teams that helped them to punch above their weight, and elements of that program remained in place years later when Herdman took over the Canadian men's side. Learning from the All Blacks helped Herdman better understand how to get a group to act as a collective and put personal agendas aside.

After his time in New Zealand came the job he'd make his name in: head coach of the Canadian women's national team, who'd fallen to their worst-ever FIFA ranking the year before his 2011 hiring.

Within a year, his dedication to high-performance systems developed athletes into more complete, aggressive, and energetic players, able to bring his high-tempo style of play to life. The way Herdman could connect with players, avoid generalities, stay up to date on what was happening in their careers outside of the national team, and provide specific feedback with organized tactical plans motivated players. They arrived at national team camps with more enthusiasm than ever. Because if a group of Hollywood script writers were to brainstorm a completely camera-ready coach, complete with his continually pitch-perfect and eloquent speeches and well-manicured short hair, they would arrive at Herdman.

A gold medal at the Pan-Am Games and the program's first Olympic medal didn't just make for some impressive additions to Herdman's CV in his first year. They served as warning to Canada Soccer: it wouldn't be long before other organizations would try to poach the emerging coach.

Herdman felt stagnant in his role come 2017, wondering if the women's team could progress without a domestic league that didn't have financial support at the time. The head coaching job of the England women's national team was available, and the England FA was interested in Herdman.

Canada Soccer scrambled. Losing him would be seen as yet another misstep for the organization, and some at the top wondered not only whether there might be enough of the magic dust he'd sprinkled on the women's program left in his bag for the men's side, but whether a Herdman power play could actually help them get out of their contract with Zambrano.

A united bid from Canada, Mexico, and the United States was the front-runner for hosting rights for the 2026 World Cup, which would be awarded later in 2018. Herdman was the kind of magnetic personality Canada Soccer could continually throw in front of the masses.

He was offered the job, even with Zambrano less than a year into his contract.

"I don't think that offer would have come if the England offer wasn't on the table," Herdman told the Athletic in 2021.

Herdman became men's EXCEL director, a fancy title giving him the autonomy he desired, overseeing every male national youth team from Under-14 up to the men's national team. A number of people within the organization were seen off as Herdman was given the freedom to do things his way. His near-obsessive approach meant, at least at first, he could be demanding of colleagues in his pursuit of success.

He had every right to do that considering how much he revolutionized the program from the beginning. *Alignment* was the term Herdman kept preaching in his early days. He backed that up by connecting with coaches throughout the youth levels to share his blueprint for how Canadian players should play. His thorough and wide-ranging document outlined exactly what roles and responsibilities he envisioned for all eleven positional players on the pitch, how they should act when in possession of the ball — off the ball and in transition. In doing so, every national team player clearly understood where they should position themselves to be their most effective and how their tactical focus needed to shift from their club sides. Players also understood which ball movement should trigger certain movement from them, which therefore increased their awareness of their teammates' responsibilities and helped the team act as a unit.

"That had never been done before," said someone familiar with how Herdman's blueprint impacted Canadian soccer.

And by trying to share his philosophy with youth club sides, Herdman's hope was to develop players in the style that mimicked Herdman himself:

relentless, and able to attack the goal, and capable of producing far more than was expected.

In one of his first days on the job, Herdman called Concacaf boss Victor Montagliani early in the morning, drove from his home outside of Vancouver to Montagliani's in the city, and spent more than six hours in Montagliani's kitchen. Herdman refused to sit in the living room for coffee, instead standing and grilling Montagliani on every facet of the struggling program. By the end of the impromptu meeting, Montagliani was reaching into the medicine cabinet in his kitchen for something to cure his headache.

"That guy," Montagliani told his wife after he finally closed the door behind Herdman, "is going to get us to Qatar."

. . .

On a brisk February afternoon in 2019, it was hard for some sitting in a conference room at BMO Field not to fall into a deserved mid-winter slumber as they were hit with a barrage of videos and corporate buzzwords.

Fresh off being awarded co-hosting rights to the 2026 World Cup, which presumably included automatic qualification, Canada Soccer wanted to capitalize on the momentum by trotting out their strategic plan for 2019 to 2021. They promised success was at hand, just as they had for, well, what felt like forever.

There was talk of cultural framework, of maximizing the opportunity to develop, govern, and grow the sport in Canada, and of reaching new heights. Given that the organization could sometimes drown in its own bureaucracy without serious results on the men's side, those whispering from the back of the room could be forgiven for whispering louder: *We've heard all this before.*

What those people hadn't heard before, however, was the kind of straight talk that the best soccer nations in the world ooze. John Herdman provided that as he slashed through the wall of corporate-speak with two sentences: "We're going to qualify for 2022, Qatar, and lay the foundation for 2026. So, if not now, then when?" said Herdman.

The whispers halted as Herdman stood alone. His daring promise for 2022 and beyond would either make him look like Nostadramus or have him laughed out of the job — as others before him had been.

Days earlier, the latest FIFA rankings placed Canada seventy-ninth in the world, between Belarus and Iraq and, more importantly, behind seven other Concacaf nations. What made Herdman think Canada could leapfrog those countries and grab one of the three guaranteed 2022 World Cup spots in the region?

In the men's team, he could see the raw young talent bubbling to the surface, but he also saw a collection of older players who had excuses for their lack of success falling out of their hip pockets. He worried that they were already preparing excuses for not qualifying for the 2022 World Cup.

If I don't believe it, Herdman thought to himself, of qualifying for the World Cup, *why would my players believe it?*

For months, Herdman had met with former players and coaches to understand what was plaguing this team. It wasn't a lack of talent; over the past few qualifying cycles, the men's team's players had plied their trade in competitive and relatively high-ranked leagues across Europe and in North and South America in ways that comparable Concacaf nations hadn't.

Herdman had heard how players treated Canadian national team camps as an escape. Yet, as detrimental as that might have been for team chemistry, he didn't run from that. Instead, he borrowed elements of it. From the calls he'd make to ensure a player was interested in joining the national team, to the player's arrival in team meetings, the message was uniform: Leave whatever is happening with your club side behind. Instead, embrace the people around you. Treat the national team as a sanctuary.

Intense tactical sessions to implement quicker ball movement toward the goal would have to wait. More important just now was preaching the necessity of this team acting as a brotherhood. Never was that more evident to Herdman than in his first training camp with the men's team in Murcia, Spain, in March 2018. Two fights broke out among Canadian teammates in two separate training sessions. Players told Herdman that this was common "in men's football." The subtle dig at Herdman's recent past as women's team head coach could have enraged Herdman, but he was more concerned with rebuilding the fractured team he'd taken over (he'd later call it "dysfunctional").

"I'll never see that again," he told players in a meeting afterward. He was adamant: when emotions boil over in training as players fight for lineup spots, Herdman wanted to eliminate threats inside the team, born out of the cliques he saw with players of different backgrounds grouping together.

But months later, ahead of Herdman's first competitive match, a Concacaf Nations League qualifier against the U.S. Virgin Islands, he noticed more of the same: players communicating only with teammates who perhaps spoke the same second language or had played with them on club sides.

Herdman whistled the training session dead.

"Unless you're willing to change this," he told his squad, "this team is going nowhere."

More time was spent off the field on team-building activities. Herdman continually stressed that there was enough collective talent among them, and that they were there for a common goal that would change all of their lives, and that they would change Canadian soccer forever, by playing in a World Cup.

The way he didn't dance around that possibility, but confronted it head-on, helped players buy into his methods. One of his common phrases became an easy get in any game of John Herdman Press Conference Bingo, "Play for the shirt": playing for the national team is a privilege, not a right.

Herdman would end up emphasizing these phrases so much that some media members would create over/unders ahead of time on how often he'd say them. Betting the under was never advisable. Behind closed doors, the players were hearing the exact same messaging, and just as often.

Herdman consciously worked to maintain the same persona with players and with the media. He knew more and more players were being exposed to better and better coaches. Their bullshit detectors were finely tuned. Trying to become someone he was not wouldn't work.

Conversely, the players' on-field personae were important to Herdman. Video sessions were run to analyze the players' body language on the field: were they emanating confidence in close quarters with the opposition? What could they do differently to intimidate opponents? When one of their teammates was involved in a scuffle, were nearby players quick to join the fight?

Herdman worked to bolster the squad's depth, too.

Former head coaches Benito Floro and Octavio Zambrano had taken important initial steps toward convincing dual nationals to play for Canada, and Herdman took up that cause with his typical relentlessness.

Midfielder Stephen Eustaquio could play with physicality and pull the strings from a deep-lying position in a way few Canadians except Atiba Hutchinson could. Born in Leamington, Ontario, to Portuguese parents, the moustached and tanned Eustaquio spent most of his life living in Portugal, developing in Nazarenos's professional academy and playing for various Portuguese youth national teams before moving to the Portuguese top division in 2018.

Eustaquio had kept an eye on the rising tide of Canadian talent, and noted that the World Cup would eventually be hosted in the country he was born in.

That was the foundation of Herdman's early calls to Eustaquio. But it was the frequency of the calls to gauge his interest, the detailed role Herdman presented to him as a possible successor to Hutchinson in the midfield, and Herdman's sincerity that Eustaquio ended up appreciating. Eustaquio had had enough of coaches playing mind games with him, making him question his own future at times.

Eustaquio came with a notebook full of questions for Herdman on every one of the dozen calls they had during 2018. Herdman's own preparation meant he had the answers. Eustaquio committed to Canada in February 2019, a month after he signed for top Mexican side Cruz Azul.

Eustaquio wasn't the only convert. Ayo Akinola, a powerful young striker, was born in the United States but spent nearly all of his life in Brampton, Ontario. The dreadlocked goal-scorer was a product of Toronto FC's academy. In 2020, with a breakout performance to start the MLS season, he fulfilled the club's vision of him as the heir apparent to club legend Jozy Altidore at the top of the pitch. Though he was eligible to play for Canada, many around Akinola wondered why Canada Soccer weren't aggressive in their pursuit of him as he came up through American youth national teams. There was a dearth of strikers in the U.S. player pool, meaning Akinola could be the heir apparent to Altidore on the U.S. national team as well. It was thought the door to Canada was closed when he scored for the U.S. national team in a December 2020 friendly against El Salvador.

Yet, given that he had only played in a friendly and not a competitive match, he was still available to switch national allegiances. The United States

Soccer Federation, perhaps to their detriment, didn't put in the time to make the young star feel like a part of their long-term vision.

Herdman did just that throughout 2020. While it was his tactical vision for him that had swayed Eustaquio, Herdman made Akinola feel valued as a person. Akinola turned away from a potential starting role as the United States' striker to join the Canadian ranks.

"He has the utmost care for his players," said Akinola. "And to be honest, as a player, that's all you want from a coach. You want a coach that shows passion, that shows the dedication, but also shows that he cares for you as a player and, outside of a soccer player, cares for your well-being. That's a huge factor in why he's been so persuasive."

Herdman's messaging began to pay off. Cliques evaporated.

"Everybody comes in with high spirits," said Canadian forward Junior Hoilett. "And that brotherhood culture pushes through games."

Herdman won all four of his first matches in charge through a light 2018 schedule focused on Nations League qualifying. These games allowed young players plenty of runway to adapt to national team play.

For some national teams, relying on teenagers was anathema: with so few games to play, only the most proven of players could be relied upon. But Herdman's results with the women's team and his compelling approach gave him rope. He opted for players who would be receptive to his messaging and who weren't burdened with past national team failures.

Six teenagers were used in a Nations League qualifying game. Alphonso Davies had been transferred to Bayern Munich months earlier, Alessandro Busti, Ballou Tabla, Liam Millar, and Zachary Brault-Guillard were all part of youth set-ups at highly respected European clubs, and Jonathan David had made his debut as an eighteen-year-old for top Belgian side Gent, less than a year after logging time with an Ottawa-based minor soccer association.

"I wanted to add that spirit, that fearlessness," said Herdman.

David bagged three goals in his first two games for Canada, looking like the potent finisher in the box Canada had long lacked. He'd emigrated to Canada from Haiti when he was six. French was his preferred language, but Herdman's efforts to pull him aside during and after training to better understand his desires as a player helped David develop confidence of his own.

"Right at the front of my mind is pushing human potential," said Herdman in 2018, "to places where they never thought they could go."

· · ·

The 2019 Gold Cup was supposed to be the men's team's coming-out party.

"The team have said we hit the quarterfinals last time and we want to ensure that we push further than that," said Herdman at the time, "and I think that's critical."

Lopsided group stage wins over Martinique and Cuba came as expected but, unfortunately, so too did a loss against Mexico, in which the Canadian side bunkered while playing in the Denver, Colorado, altitude. Anyone hoping for Herdman to take the reins off his young side in that game, even of playing Alphonso Davies in more of an attacking role, was disappointed.

By the time the quarterfinals came, though, Canada had played three games in nine days across three different time zones. They'd been buoyed by David's play, as he consistently strode through defenders with his back arched and chest puffed out, scoring five goals and just as consistently raised his valuation as a great striker in waiting.

Managing Haiti's athleticism in the quarterfinals would suggest this Canadian side was ready to contend with more than just the region's lightweights.

"It's just very clear," said Herdman before the game, "it's a must-win."

In the eighteenth minute, the reins looked to be off when Davies and David connected on a free-kick set play that saw them invoke some training ground trickery. Davies played a short pass away from the crowd and David roofed his uncontested shot into the Haitian goal. Herdman's desire to play quick soccer through the middle of the park manifested in a Lucas Cavallini goal that saw Canada head into the half up 2–0 with the semifinals, and perhaps respectability, in their sights.

But instead, the game, and the tournament, served as a stark reminder of how much fine-tuning Herdman needed to do with his young core.

A careless Marcus Godinho pass back to Milan Borjan in the fiftieth minute was a reminder of the Canada of old: it was soft enough that Haitian forward Duckens Nazon cut it off and poked it past Borjan, who could only turn and lambaste Godinho, miming what a hard pass should look like — undermining the culture of unity Herdman had worked to create. Another careless challenge from Godinho resulted in a converted Haiti penalty before the final dagger: Nazon targeted Davies, who had struggled with his defensive responsibilities at left back throughout the tournament, with a cross, and Davies was unable to contain Haitian winger Wilde-Donald Guerrier.

Davies slammed the most valuable left foot in Canadian soccer history against the post in anger after Guerrier's goal completed a stunning second-half comeback. The young Canadian side stood sunken shoulder to sunken shoulder with other disappointing teams of the past.

"We said that this would come down to a battle of wills and I just felt, at the end, we didn't have what it took," said Herdman postgame. "This was a good opportunity for our country to step forward. We've missed it."

* * *

The frequency of calls from Herdman to his assistant coaches and others within Canada Soccer, including the players, picked up after the Gold Cup debacle. Reflection was the order of the day: which players couldn't handle the demands Herdman placed on them, and which didn't offer the kind of quality required to qualify for a World Cup? Godinho would make just one more appearance for the men's team.

And Herdman asked his coaches: Were we brave enough in possession? How could we challenge players to push themselves to a World Cup berth if we weren't challenging ourselves?

Herdman wanted to avoid finger-pointing.

"Let's own the mistakes," Herdman told the team.

Brutal honesty was encouraged. Herdman came away realizing he had to build on the cultural changes he'd instilled. With detailed tactical plans, each player would be made to feel included in the culture of accountability and would understand where the team erred.

The chance to show that came a few months later when Herdman and Canada met the United States in Nations League play at BMO Field. Canada had not beaten the United States in a competitive match in thirty-four years.

An expanded coaching staff camped out for days in multiple BMO Field offices, breaking down video of the United States with a newfound collective behaviour, asking out loud: "Where are they vulnerable?"

Tactically, one constant represented a shift in Herdman's thinking: he and the coaching staff wanted to impose their own will on the game instead of being reactive, which the coaching staff had identified as a fault throughout the Gold Cup.

Herdman challenged his group to think outside the box.

That resulted in, ironically, a box itself: when the Canadian team learned they'd be deployed in an unorthodox 4-2-2-2 formation with a box midfield, requiring midfielders to play close together in a box shape, players exchanged quizzical glances throughout the meeting room.

"Changing the system against a big team in a big game, it was a shock," Canadian midfielder Samuel Piette said afterward.

Herdman keyed in on American midfielder Michael Bradley, long the engine of Toronto FC's midfield, as a player to hamper. Bradley liked to get on the ball and distribute it, but the men's team believed he didn't have the speed he used to. So Herdman asked Davies and David, two offensively minded players, to serve as the architects of his pressing system and make Bradley's life difficult when not in possession.

That demand resonated with the rest of the team: if Herdman could ask his two most talented offensive players to do some heavy lifting defensively, the rest of the team understood, they too had to buy in to their roles.

For this team to succeed, they had to think of themselves less as a collection of one-man shows.

"That week, he kept saying 'It doesn't have to be Phonzie [Emerging Canadian star Alphonso Davies]. Why not you?' to the group," said then twenty-two-year-old soft-spoken defender Kamal Miller, making just his third appearance for the national team. "And that stuck with me. I just kept telling myself it was going to be me. *I'm going to have a big game.*"

And Miller did, but so too did Davies, because his otherworldly speed and talent on the ball meant he clamoured for the biggest stages.

Canadian midfielder Scott Arfield followed Herdman's instructions and closed down on Bradley with his first touch, in the sixty-third minute, forcing a turnover. As a handful of Canadian attackers swarmed the play, thirteen seconds later Davies put an exclamation mark on a performance that cemented him as the face of the program, sneaking an Arfield cross into the American goal.

The goal itself was the embodiment of a performance that whipped up the BMO Field crowd into the kind of frenzy generally reserved for Toronto FC at their treble-winning best in 2017, not for the men's side.

They moved the ball with pace and verticality. They fought for second balls.

"They didn't have the urgency that we had," midfielder Jonathan Osorio said, of the American side.

By fighting for each other in physical scrums, Canada never looked afraid against a team that, for a generation, they would have been happy eking out a draw against. In the wee hours of the night, Atiba Hutchinson watched the game alone in his Istanbul home.

This team is really coming together, he thought to himself.

After forward Lucas Cavallini sank the Americans just after the ninety-minute mark with a well-intentioned half-volley, Borjan ran to the rapturous crowd behind him while pumping his fist. The memories of BMO Field being more stocked with fans of the visiting team was, for a moment, distant.

"I've been with this program for almost nine, ten years now and this emotion, I didn't feel it before," said Borjan.

Colour commentator and former men's national team midfielder Terry Dunfield's maniacal laugh after Cavallini's goal was not only an exaggerated version of Bob Lenarduzzi's laugh when Canada sank Mexico nineteen years earlier, it also spoke to the surprise felt across the entirety of Canadian soccer. Was this men's national team, actually, possibly, finally, for real?

"It's only one little drop in the ocean of what I'm hoping for this team," said Herdman after the match, of the win. "There's more to come."

* * *

Just like former head coach Stephen Hart almost ten years before, John Herdman woke up on the morning of June 12, 2021, in a central American locale with the sinking feeling that for all his planning, the fate of his team was out of his control.

The Covid-19 pandemic had not only restricted the men's team to just three January friendlies throughout all of 2020, it had shifted the entire 2022 World Cup qualifying outlook as well.

Canada's Gold Cup loss against Haiti had hampered their chances of moving into the region's top five teams in the FIFA rankings. According to new qualifying rules, Canada had only a glimmer of a hope to qualify for the 2022 World Cup. While the elite teams in the region received byes to the final round of qualifying, Canada had to start in the first round of qualifying. Inside Canada Soccer, some worried qualification was now too insurmountable a task for the men's team. But they toppled a group of Suriname, Bermuda, Aruba, and the Cayman Islands before a home-and-away series against Haiti in the second round. The winner would advance to the final round.

Leading up to the first-leg game in Port-au-Prince, political unrest in the Haitian capital was impossible to ignore. Widespread and violent protests demanded the resignation of President Jovenel Moïse, who would be assassinated a few weeks later. The Canadian government had already urged against all non-essential travel to Haiti.

A bus carrying the Belize national team had been stopped by armed gunmen in Haiti months earlier after a World Cup qualifier, requiring police to negotiate safe passage to their hotel.

And the U.S. Centers for Disease Control and Prevention had advised avoiding travel to Haiti, with the country in its highest level of Covid-19 warnings.

The complex situation had created internal challenges Herdman had never faced. Multiple players and staff members expressed vocal hesitation about making the trip, and other staff members refused outright to go, which only increased anxiety throughout the organization.

The team charter arrived later than usual, less than twenty-four hours before kickoff. It was greeted on the tarmac by armed personnel assigned to protect the Canadian side.

The normally chatty and upbeat young Canadian side could only stare out the windows of their team bus and take videos on their phones of other buses toppled over with their windows smashed, dilapidated houses, and scores of panhandlers. Many of the players reminded themselves of their own good fortune in being able to live in Canada. Their bus sped through every red light from Toussaint Louverture International Airport to their hotel. With a police escort in front of them, the directive to the team's bus driver was clear: should the team bus stop at a red light, it might be hijacked.

As the bus slowed in front of their hotel, waiting for a gate in a twelve-foot wall to open to allow entry, players held their breath.

"It was a moment where you're saying, 'What are we doing here? This is way beyond football,'" said Herdman.

The team had completed their required Covid-19 testing in the United States, which, they had been assured by the necessary regulatory bodies, would be acceptable in Haiti. But upon arriving, they were told by the local federation that more testing was required. It came as a shock to the entire Canadian side, as did the aggressiveness of the testing itself. Multiple testing swabs snapped when they were jammed further than normal up players' noses.

But none of this was nearly as shocking as when the test results were continually delayed. Just ninety minutes before kickoff, when any team would normally be settling into their pregame preparations inside the stadium, only thirteen players and staff had been cleared. Alphonso Davies, Jonathan David, and Herdman himself were among those whose tests had not yet come back.

"We felt that there was definitely something going on behind the scenes," said Herdman.

Unable to leave his hotel room, Herdman bounced off the walls as he was told who was and who wasn't available. Assistant coach Eric Tenllado was the only member of the coaching staff cleared to enter Stade Sylvio Cator. The team tried to put pressure on the Haitian Football Federation to release the results of the team's tests. Every fifteen minutes, another small handful of players was cleared, forcing Herdman to juggle his team's lineup just as frequently. Finally, Herdman's test came back negative and he was one of the last people to board the bus, which once again sped to the stadium.

Even inside the team's dressing room, the dark arts of Concacaf were at play. The team's bathrooms had been flooded, urinals sprayed water, the handles had been removed from the showers, and the temperature had been set to scalding hot. The temperature in their dressing room had been cranked to make it feel hotter than the nearly forty degrees it felt like on the pitch itself.

Haiti personified the chaos off the pitch with an equally aggressive approach on it, yet the Canadians found daylight when hulking forward Cyle Larin redirected a Jonathan Osorio cross into the net.

During the water break in the first half, players doused themselves in entire bottles of cold water while walking on their heels, eager to keep their toes off the oppressively hot pitch.

At halftime, players collapsed in their dressing room stalls and bent over to pull the bottom of their boots up to show them. The edges of the soles on the players' boots had melted on the turf.

In the fifty-fifth minute, Herdman winced on the sidelines. Both the heat and the emotions of the trip had led to a slow start for his team. He worried that all the ingrained excuses of the past might soon resurface.

Instead, though it was hardly the most appealing soccer, the players resisted the continued physical pressure from the Haiti side and a new image of the team emerged. This was a team that could grind out a result even in trying circumstances.

After the 1–0 win, team staff moved with pace to pack up the team belongings and get the Canadian side out of the stadium and out of the country. The sound of chaotic traffic outside of the team bus filled Herdman's postgame media conference as he held up a phone, taking questions on a choppy Zoom stream from reporters while his team sped once again through the streets, this time to an awaiting charter.

But his team's resolve had made the game one of his favourite experiences as Canadian head coach.

"For me, that was a real turning point," said Herdman.

Covid-19 restrictions in Canada forced them to play the return leg away from home. With their fate in their hands, the sound of Milan Borjan's voice hyping up his teammates echoed off the stands in an empty stadium in Chicago minutes before kickoff. Chance after chance came as Canada, led by Davies, attacked with continued speed and confidence.

Haiti eventually faltered when goalkeeper Josué Duverger's nerves overcame him and he whiffed on a soft back pass from a teammate, allowing the ball to slowly roll into the net as he lowered his head in shame. A clip of the embarrassing own goal went viral on Twitter.

It felt fitting to the thousands of loyal supporters watching back in Canada for a program wrought with embarrassing losses of their own to go through to the final round of qualifying on an equally embarrassing goal. When Larin pressed Haiti's back line on his own to force a second goal, and Junior Hoilett collected his own rebound to finish a chance in the eighty-ninth minute, many of those humiliating losses felt distant.

"Fuckin' right," Hoilett emphatically exclaimed on the pitch.

Canada was heading to the final round of World Cup qualifying for the first time in thirty-four years.

The enormity of the moment wasn't lost on Herdman.

"I think we're starting to give some hope," said Herdman after the match. "We haven't filled this country with trust. And with the amount of toxicity I've seen in the men's game, it's very fractured, side to side, front to back. A lot of people pulling in different directions. And I have to say that the men's team is the key to connecting this country together and giving it an anchor, a rally point."

He then thought of his players, the ones who, along with him, were standing on the cusp of history.

"For these young men, Alphonso Davies, Jonathan David," said Herdman, "these are life-changing experiences."

CHAPTER 12

"There Was Freedom of Expression": Alphonso Davies Represented a Generation of Change and Then Changed the Way People Looked at Canadian Players

SEAN FLEMING WAS NEARLY SHAKING. HE COULDN'T CONTAIN HIS excitement.

It was 2012 when the long-time, grey-haired coach had taken his hands away from his hips, where they so often rested, to hurry away from a patchy soccer field in Edmonton, indistinguishable from the thousands of others throughout Canada. He crossed a parking lot filled with parents encouraging their children, parents who secretly knew those children might not have a professional future in the sport.

He got into his car, and, finally alone, let out a wild scream.

"Yes!" he proclaimed, his voice reverberating off the windows.

Fleming had been invited by local soccer coach Nick Huoseh to watch a young player who Huoseh insisted was something special. This wasn't out of the ordinary. Few people were as intimately tapped into the development of young Canadian players. From 1996 to 2016 Fleming coached various youth national teams, including teams that went to Under-17 World Cups. Multiple senior national team players, including Atiba Hutchinson, were coached by Fleming.

And so he'd also seen his fair share of players oversold by coaches, or who couldn't handle more intense development with the national program. He knew the impediments facing young Canadian players and by extension, the men's national team: the level of professional coaching was coming along, but until 2019, there was no domestic professional league for players to graduate to.

Fleming believed that the growing interest in the game and changing face of the country would eventually have a wider impact. But to that point, Fleming, and Canada for that matter, just hadn't seen either the results of that change or a player with generational talent rise above the ranks.

All that had just changed when he saw Alphonso Davies on the ball for the first time. His hands came off his hips in shock as he watched Davies blow by his peers with brazen speed and score goals with wild creativity.

"Immediately," he said, looking back on his revelation, "I knew that he would be a national team player."

Davies, soon to become arguably the best player in the program's history, was the culmination of everything that had been building in Canadian soccer for a generation before him.

Policies of multiculturalism and open borders helped provide the Davies family with opportunities to maintain quality of life, and government-subsidized sports programs gave him opportunities he might not have received outside of Canada.

Canada having MLS teams meant there was a pathway to professional success for him where there hadn't been a generation earlier. Davies played the game with the kind of attacking flair first instituted by coaches like Stephen Hart. Eventually, onlookers understood how influential Davies's youthful exuberance could be.

And as the men's national team stepped forward into the final round of Concacaf World Cup qualifying in 2021, Davies represented everything the program could become.

• • •

Alphonso Davies had never even heard of the country that he would eventually help elevate to its greatest soccer heights when he first arrived in Canada as a five-year-old in 2006. Yet he could be forgiven for his lack of awareness.

Davies's parents, Debeah and Victoria, had fled from their home in Liberia during the country's second civil war. As Davies's star rose, they largely neglected to share details from their life in Liberia with the media. When they did, however, their voices would tremble as they described walking over dead bodies to find food.

"I don't like to talk about my country because it's so hard," Victoria said in a 2019 TSN documentary. "Sometimes you're in line and they take people. Some [people] are in front of you, they were killed there."

After fleeing to Buduburam, a refugee camp just west of Ghana's capital city, Accra, Victoria gave birth to Alphonso in 2000. His health as a baby seriously suffered and they wondered whether he would survive in the camp.

"Refugee life was like being put in a container and being locked up," Victoria said in a 2017 documentary made by the Vancouver Whitecaps. "There was no way to get out."

In 2002, the Canadian federal government implemented the *Immigration and Refugee Protection Act*, which saw more of a shift toward "protection rather than ability to successfully establish." Just as the country's doors were flung wide open by Pierre Trudeau decades earlier for immigrants to have their way of life welcomed in Canada, this act was meant to ensure families like the Davies family had proper protection in a country that had the financial means and the quality of life to provide it. Without any contacts in Canada, the family arrived first in Windsor, Ontario, before settling in Edmonton.

They told the Athletic in 2019 they came to Canada seeking "security, freedom, and opportunity for our kids." When Davies started playing soccer at the age of eight in an Edmonton-based program called "Free Footie" that gave marginalized children an opportunity to engage in sports, they realized they'd found the latter.

The program was free of charge for families who could not afford registration and equipment and relied, in part, on government assistance for funding.

Like Fleming, other parents would watch Davies in amazement. Dribbling past opponents came astoundingly naturally to him. Every chance he had to walk onto the field was a chance for onlookers to see a child who might have had no idea about the place he'd escaped to but was keen to embrace the new life in front of him.

Even if you took your eyes off the magic he created with his feet, you could not take your eyes off his constant smile.

"Life is too short to be frowning all the time, or angry," Davies told the CBC as a seventeen-year-old.

For four years, Davies continued to score goals for fun for the Edmonton Strikers and St. Nicholas junior high school, where head coach Marco Bossio called his control and progression "off the charts."

To challenge Davies, Bossio ensured he faced something new and different at every training session: working on his core and leg strength in the gym far earlier than others his age; forcing him to dribble and shoot with his right foot so he would not become too reliant on his left. Davies embraced every challenge.

Almost equally, Davies embraced being the centre of attention among his friends at St. Nicholas, especially in drama class, where Davies could confidently perform in front of groups. In one improvised Christmas performance he had the crowd in tears.

"Fearless," said Bossio of Davies's attitude as a child.

Edmonton fell under the Vancouver Whitecaps' scouting jurisdiction but Bossio, among others, had to continually pester them to give Davies a look. Some early viewings of Davies were because Whitecaps representatives were in town to see other players, not him.

In Davies's original trial for the club as a thirteen-year-old, his raw talent was evident, but so too was his lack of maturity and obvious hesitation over moving away from home.

A year later Davies appeared to be hitting his ceiling in Edmonton, scoring as many as six goals a game. Craig Dalrymple, who worked in player development and recruitment for the Whitecaps, returned to Edmonton to find a more mature Davies. He was armed with a bag full of Whitecaps merchandise to give to Davies once he signed a letter of commitment to play for the Whitecaps. Victoria stopped Dalrymple dead in his tracks.

"He'll take that when he deserves it," Dalrymple remembers her saying. "Right now, he's still in Edmonton."

Davies's parents were rightfully hesitant to see their son, who had not even been on Canadian soil for ten years yet, leave their close watch. But the club sold them on the structure and organizational support that wasn't available in Edmonton. Davies was still fourteen when he boarded a flight to join the Whitecaps' academy and residency program.

In Vancouver, Davies didn't cower. He had no reason to. The player pathway the Whitecaps had established benefitted him in the way it would have benefitted an outrageously talented player in Europe, even if Davies treated it as his own personal fast lane on the autobahn.

"We knew we had a talent on our hands," said Carl Robinson, Vancouver's then head coach and a former Wales midfielder. "But we didn't know how quickly he'd develop."

Davies's ability to twist opposition teams inside out within the academy, just as he did on the pitches in Edmonton, was enough for Robinson to invite him to the team's 2016 training camp when Davies was just fifteen. Their suspicions were confirmed: as a left midfielder, Davies could hold his own playing against men. He became the youngest player to ever sign a United Soccer League (USL) contract and play for the Whitecaps reserve side.

Off the pitch, Davies blossomed as the teenager who just would not stop beaming, forming immediate, and lifelong, bonds with his teammates.

The day after making his first-team debut, Davies returned to the academy, free of ego, after a full day of classes. All Davies wanted to do was train with his former Under-16 teammates that afternoon.

Dalrymple protested, telling Davies he needed his recovery from the game. But Davies protested back, albeit with a smile that softened Dalrymple.

"He never lost his sense of being a kid," said Dalrymple.

He had even less time to be around his friends when he signed a senior team contract with the Whitecaps as a sixteen-year-old, and made his MLS debut in July 2016, the second-youngest player to ever do so at the time. While Robinson made efforts to shield him from heightened media attention, that he didn't look out of place among men sometimes twice his age further solidified the hopes of Canadian soccer fans: Davies looked destined to become the attacking, youthful icon the country's men's soccer program had never had.

• • •

Davies had played for youth national teams under Fleming as a teenager. When it became clear Davies would qualify for Canadian citizenship and would play for Canada, men's team general manager Morgan Quarry got to work preparing the sixteen-year-old for his citizenship exam, paying special attention to ensure that he knew who John A. Macdonald was and could easily name all ten provinces and three territories in Canada.

Thankfully for the men's national team, Davies scored very well on his citizenship test in Vancouver, was sworn in as a Canadian citizen, received his passport, and met his new teammates in Montreal during a training camp ahead of a friendly against Curaçao — all within a day.

Davies's youthful swagger bolstered the mood in the camp. Even with the constant chatter from both inside and outside the camp questioning whether this generational talent could succeed on the international stage, Davies was blissfully unaffected.

"He had no fear," said Quarry, who remembers Davies taking on veterans just like he did in training. "And it wasn't about a lack of respect. It was just an incredible confidence in his ability to try things on the ball."

In the fifty-third minute against Curaçao, a linesman held up a sign with Davies's number twelve on it, signalling it was time for the youngest player in men's national team history to make his international debut.

"Like a small horse just being unleashed in the field, and going and doing whatever he wanted to," said Kristian Jack.

As he hit four shots, including three volleys, in a little over half an hour of play, all while terrorizing defenders on the left side of the pitch with his trickery on the ball, Davies looked far removed from a generation of players saddled with years of failure and a defensive mindset ground into them. He'd been prepared for his national debut in part because of the professional experience he'd already gained with the Whitecaps.

"There was freedom of expression," said Jack. "It was wonderful to see a young player not feeling the burden of putting on an international shirt and feeling like he can be whatever he wants."

After Canada's 2–1 win, Quarry and other members of Canada Soccer pulled Davies aside. There were dozens of media members waiting to speak with him. They gave him the same advice teammates had given Davies in the minutes before he stepped on the pitch: *Just be yourself. Don't overthink it.*

Davies stepped up to the encroaching cameras and microphones held out by people clamouring for a word from the ascendant to the throne.

As had been custom for the week, Davies smiled.

"Who do I look at?" Davies asked.

• • •

Davies would soon have to look at more and more people. Being named to the *Guardian*'s renowned "Next Generation" list of the sixty best young talents in the global game in 2017, which included one of the eventual best players of his generation in Norwegian striker Erling Braut Haaland, was more evidence that Davies would soon outgrow the Whitecaps. He was one of just four North American players named to the list and had done so by becoming a regular player as a teenager.

Even if he looked defensively adrift at times during the 2017 Gold Cup, his three goals in four appearances for Canada were enough to see him tied for most goals in the tournament and earned him the Young Player award. It was yet another box ticked: he could hang with the region's best in international competition.

"Do I see star quality in him? Yes, I do," then head coach Octavio Zambrano said in 2017. "Just by the way he manages to play without fear on the field. At a young age that's pretty unusual."

In 2018, Davies's progression predictably continued as a Whitecaps starter, and Manchester United was among his suitors. Still, what was lacking from many of these clubs was a true belief in Davies's immediate future. Some teams lowballed the Whitecaps with their transfer fee offers, citing what they perceived to be the low quality of MLS as a league, while others insinuated Davies would quickly be loaned out of their club.

But judging by the sheer number of Audis parked outside the offices of the Whitecaps for days on end, one club was more serious, and more organized, in their pursuit: Bayern Munich, the undisputed giants of Germany's Bundesliga.

"You could've punched me, I wouldn't have stopped smiling," Davies said in Amazon's 2021 documentary "FC Bayern: Behind the Legend," about when he first heard the club were interested in him.

Bayern's pitch differed in that they presented a detailed, multi-year plan on how they would develop Davies as a player in-house; offered nuanced tactical breakdowns of where they thought he could progress; and, finally, all but guaranteed opportunities to play in the UEFA Champions League.

It was enough for Davies to raise his pinky fingers and thumbs out wide in celebration, his braces unable to cover his grin as he posed for pictures in Philadelphia during a Bayern Munich U.S. tour. The $13.5-million transfer fee the German club paid was the highest in MLS history, with total compensation possibly reaching $22 million if performance targets were hit.

The transfer to Bayern Munich did leave a sour taste in Davies's camp as the Whitecaps asked Davies if they could withhold the 10 percent of the transfer fee that MLS players are generally paid. At the behest of Nick Huoseh, who had stayed with Davies to become his agent, Bayern Munich upped their original contract offer to Davies as a sign of good faith to cover the fee he lost.

Still, Davies's career may have foundered before it started without the coaching and training methods he'd received from the Whitecaps.

His development path at Bayern saw him eased into the hot waters of European soccer: he spent more time playing in Bayern's reserve side in the fourth tier of German soccer than he did in the Bundesliga but would sit with Bayern's legendary left back David Alaba in the club hot tub as Alaba preached patience. Davies made frequent mistakes in training, owing to the intensified pace of play and demands in Europe.

"The hunger is much stronger here," he said in February 2019, his voice strangely quiet as he was engulfed by the hordes of media members swarming some of Bayern's more renowned players around him for postgame interviews.

Just hours earlier, well before kickoff, a wide-eyed Davies had walked onto the pitch at Liverpool's Anfield stadium with some of his young teammates. The chances of Davies's getting into the game-day squad were limited, so he took a moment to stand in the middle of the pitch with his phone and take a 360-degree video of one of the world's most hallowed grounds.

Even with Davies's quality, it was fair to wonder how his career would pan out in Europe.

Less than a year later, though, a freak ACL injury early to teammate Niklas Süle led to lineup juggling and an open spot for Davies at left back.

Within a few games, Davies's warp speed allowed him to push forward in attack, showcasing all the qualities a modern fullback requires, while also recovering well defensively in a manner that overshadowed his relative inexperience. He'd earned the trust of head coach Hansi Flick and a place in Bundesliga and Champions League starting lineups.

Any doubt about whether he would fulfill his potential in Europe evaporated in his first Champions League knockout game against Chelsea with one-touch passes and the kind of precise movement he had lacked in early Bayern training sessions just a year before.

As he literally leapt over longstanding Chelsea and Denmark international centre-back Andreas Christensen and maintained possession of the ball on a counterattack, hundreds in Stamford Bridge rose to their feet. Davies cut inside, quickly turned his head to survey the situation in front of the goal and sent a perfect pass to Robert Lewandowski for the team's third goal, all but booking Bayern's ticket from the Round of Sixteen to the quarterfinals.

"The teenager, who is storming through his career, from Canada to Germany, and here in London, he is putting on a show," said famed broadcaster Martin Tyler on the air.

After the 3–0 win, as Davies celebrated with his teammates on the pitch, the collection of Bayern travelling fans began shouting "Phonzie!" repeatedly, in adoration of Alphonso "Phonzie" Davies. Davies tucked his head away before Lewandowski himself literally pushed Davies out of the fray and toward the fans.

Davies did what he'd always done: flashed a wide smile, this time for a far larger audience to see.

Even Owen Hargreaves, the talented Canadian player who had chosen to represent England instead of Canada years before, was impressed. "This is probably the beginning of what's going to be the potential to be anything," he told DAZN after the game.

As celebrations among players and staff went on late into the night in the garish gala room the club had rented in their London hotel, Bayern sporting director Hasan Salihamidžić and Davies's agent Huoseh camped out in a room of their own in London until the early morning, working to finalize a contract extension that would keep Davies in Munich until 2025.

Davies's magical season continued in the Champions League quarter-finals against Barcelona and Lionel Messi, arguably the best player in the history of the game. Davies collected the ball near half and dribbled past Messi himself before stopping in front of Portuguese international right back Nélson Semedo.

"Go, go!" shouted longstanding Bayern forward Thomas Müller.

In the Amazon documentary about Bayern's season, Davies described his thought process of wagging his left foot with swagger over the ball to trick Semedo very simply: "Let me try something."

After multiple feints on the ball, Davies left Semedo in his wake. Then, just as he had against Chelsea, he laid off another perfect pass, this time for Joshua Kimmich, in a highlight-reel assist that would quickly go viral. Lewandowski slapped Davies's face out of sheer shock at his audacity.

Early in the game Davies had agreed with Messi to swap shirts at the game's conclusion. But after Bayern had desecrated Barcelona with an 8–2 win and Davies was pulled into doping testing, none of his Bayern team-mates wanted to follow up with Messi about getting Davies his prize.

Davies would soon clinch a far greater prize, however, as he started in every one of Bayern's games en route to a Champions League win over Paris Saint-Germain. He became the first Canadian men's national team player to do so, and posed for photos after the win with a Canadian flag tied around his waist, having changed the way many in the soccer world viewed Canadian players.

"I'm happy that I was part of [winning trophies], to lift those trophies and carry the Canadian flag with pride," Davies said.

Soon enough, multiple young Canadians established themselves among Europe's elite, proving that a Canadian moving to the world's best clubs was no fluke.

"He's not following in anyone's footsteps," said former Whitecaps teammate Russell Teibert, of Davies, in 2019. "Maybe you learn from who's gone before you but he's leading in his own way."

Cyle Larin was transferred from MLS club Orlando City SC to top Turkish side Beşiktaş ahead of Davies's move to Bayern in 2018, and while he initially struggled to solidify himself in their lineup, he would finish tied for second in Turkish league scoring in the 2020–21 season. Less than three years after playing amateur soccer in Ottawa, Jonathan David had earned a €30 million transfer to top French side Lille OSC, the largest transfer fee paid for a Canadian, making him the most expensive player the club had ever transferred for. In 2021, less than three years after he was drafted by MLS's New England Revolution, Belgian first division champions Club Brugge paid seven million for winger Tajon Buchanan's services, a club-record fee.

When you add in the likes of Stephen Eustaquio, the midfielder who in January 2022 was loaned from Portuguese side Pacos de Ferreira to 2021–22 Portuguese first division champions Porto, it means that five teams who competed in the 2021–22 UEFA Champions League had Canadians on their rosters during that domestic season. That's the most in the Canadian men's team program's history.

This mattered to a Canadian soccer community desperate for young talent to showcase to the rest of the country as proof of concept, and it mattered to John Herdman. He wanted his players performing regularly in the most challenging club environments, believing it would harden them and the knock-on effect would benefit the national team program and their results.

And it mattered to young players who wanted to prove themselves abroad, representing Canada and taking them to new global soccer heights, as Davies was doing.

"[Canada] is the country that welcomed me," David said in 2019. "I owe it to the country to play for them and fight for them."

Davies became the focus of countless profiles, with many around the world wanting to know how it came about that a refugee from Liberia emerged in a country not necessarily known for producing world-class talent to become one of the best left backs in the world.

The feel-good story first and foremost should highlight just how singularly talented Davies himself is and how it is his effort that deserves the majority of the credit.

Davies himself recognized when he was just sixteen, ahead of his first men's national team game at BMO Field in Toronto, that the most important element of a player's progression is his mindset.

"If he thinks he can do it, he can do anything," said Davies, in 2017.

Perhaps it is a perfect coincidence that Davies being raised as a professional in Vancouver came when the Whitecaps began touting the tagline "It takes a village" as one of their marketing slogans, in reference to the Whitecaps team that won the 1979 NASL Soccer Bowl under Tony Waiters. Commentator Jim McKay had said during the ABC broadcast of the game that "Vancouver must be like the deserted village right now."

Because, as Morgan Quarry said, "Everyone thinks they discovered Alphonso Davies," and he said it not necessarily with derision, but in the realization that many different circumstances and just as many decisions, made by many different people, had to break in such a way as would benefit the player.

What if the better part of Canadian society hadn't long held an understanding of the importance of welcoming immigrants and refugees into the country, and official government policies hadn't recognized those beliefs? Surely Stephen Hart's diverse brand of soccer was just a start.

One of the most inspiring and important elements of the 2021 men's national team was its makeup: refugees, immigrants, and people of colour made up the roster, making it an accurate representation of the changing face of Canada. That young people in Canada of different races and backgrounds could see a diverse national team could very well inspire them too.

What if MLS had never expanded into Canada? Would players with the talent to separate themselves from the herd and inspire other young players have simply fallen by the wayside and given up on playing soccer?

What if Davies hadn't been raised to play with a liberated, attacking mindset, the likes of which Hart first instilled in men's team players when Davies himself was just a child?

What if John Herdman hadn't turned the keys to the program over to the country's young players, giving players like Davies continued confidence?

For all the right reasons, come 2020, Davies had firmly established himself as the face of a Golden Generation of men's players.

Of course, as the naysayers will note, a generation of players can only be labelled as "Golden" if they achieve enormous success.

That type of success was clearly in focus for Davies in September 2021 as he led Canada into the final round of Concacaf World Cup qualifying for the first time since 1997, a time before he had even been born.

Fourteen more qualifying games, the most ever in the final round of Concacaf World Cup qualifying, thanks to changes brought on by Covid-19, awaited Canada. Finishing in one of the top three spots would mean Canada would, after more than a generation, return to the World Cup.

Doing so would catapult Davies and his teammates both into global soccer consciousness on the sport's grandest stage, and, finally, into household names in Canada, as the faces of a sport and a men's team that had long disappointed but was now deserving of widescale domestic appreciation.

"When I was growing up, I felt like no one gave Canadians a chance. And now that they see that we have quality in Canada, they're coming on side," Davies said late in 2020, a smile once again breaking out, even amid the acknowledgement of a depressing past. "It's amazing to see."

CHAPTER 13

A Poem, a Sword, and an Impossible Dream: The Final Round of 2022 World Cup Qualifying

THE SOFT AFTERNOON SUN HIT BMO FIELD IN TORONTO ON AN UN-seasonably warm September 2021 day much in the way you'd hope it would on a quiet patio at the end of a long work week.

The men's team walked out onto the pitch in packs. Players squinted, then smiled at their fortune with one of the last unseasonably warm days of the year.

First came the goalkeepers. Milan Borjan turned out to the smattering of journalists gathered in the stands, found an impeccably dressed Terry Dunfield, and visibly mocked his tailored suit.

Other groups of players followed before finding balls at the side of the pitch and then continuing their conversations while firing quick, one-touch passes back and forth. When John Herdman hit the field, the sun radiated off his bright white Nike trainers. He too walked up and down the sideline, surveying which journalists were in attendance.

You'd be hard pressed to believe this relaxed-looking group was about to start their last training session ahead of the final round of World Cup qualifying for the first time in thirty-four years. The next day they would face Honduras, who had just arrived in Toronto. This was the same Honduras side that had topped Canada in their group in World Cup qualifying five years earlier.

"If we showed that we were nervous, that would be because we don't trust ourselves, and that we're not ready for the main goal," said midfielder Stephen Eustaquio.

Eustaquio shrugged his shoulders, wondering why this team would emanate anything other than tranquility.

"We know what we're doing," said Eustaquio.

Eustaquio's confidence was justified. He was part of a group of front-runners for a spot in Canada's starting eleven for the duration of the fourteen-game tournament. Eustaquio's smallish stature didn't affect the grand vision he had on the pitch. When Herdman wanted his team to deploy possession-based build-up play, the ball had to flow through Eustaquio just ahead of the centre-backs. He could pull the strings as well as any other midfielder in Concacaf.

After he made his first start for the national team earlier in 2021, that summer's Gold Cup had been his coming-out party. Canada had been without Alphonso Davies, Jonathan David, Milan Borjan, and Atiba Hutchinson because of either injury or need for a rest after a gruelling club season. Eustaquio, with his trademark thin moustache, was thrust into the spotlight.

His relentless motor and long-range passes had stood out. So did his three goals in four matches, including an impressive finish to seal a win against Costa Rica in the Gold Cup quarterfinals that Herdman would later call his most memorable win as a coach. It silenced some of the doubters who believed Herdman couldn't win without Davies and David.

Eustaquio wasn't alone in commanding a regular lineup place after the Gold Cup: Alistair Johnston, the scrawny, good-natured former hockey defenceman took up the role of enforcer in the back line. He was another newcomer who provided tactical awareness but never shied away from a scrap. Kamal Miller and Richie Laryea had also become trusted players in John Herdman's books after playing only a handful of national team games, providing consistent energy en route to the team's first Gold Cup semifinal appearance since 2007.

Two months earlier, in the July 2021 Gold Cup semifinal in Houston, Canada had attacked Mexico throughout the match, instead of sitting in more of a defensive block as they had done against the same team in the 2019 Gold Cup. This got under the skin of the Mexican players. Ugly fouls were persistent. But after Mexico went up 1–0, Tajon Buchanan, playing on his off wing on the left side, showed no hesitation in charging toward the Mexican goal. With a stepover and cut inside that was reminiscent of famed Dutch winger Arjen Robben, he levelled the score at 1–1.

The twenty-two-year-old daring and creative winger, whose frizzy brown hair shifted wildly every time he cut by defenders from the touchline, commanded eyeballs with every touch. He'd debuted for Canada only months earlier but had quickly become one of Canada's most dynamic attacking players and part of a group of game-breaking talent such as had never existed on a Canadian roster before.

A lengthy stoppage in play, after Mexico's fans used a homophobic chant, drew the game out. That Mexico required that break to regroup and score the winner well beyond the preset stoppage time was something Canadian players of the past were used to.

What few were used to, though, was Canada having every right to win in Concacaf. The confidence Canada gained from a strong Gold Cup performance was another important step in their evolution as a team.

But World Cup qualifying was different.

Matches would take place in hostile surroundings Canadian players had never played in. Every team's best players would be available against Canada. Though the men's team had been bolstered with more coaching, training, physio, and support staff than ever before, Herdman still didn't have access to the financial resources other similar organizations did. The team's goal was to land twenty-three points through fourteen games in the hopes of qualifying. In the hopes of raising funds to help bolster his coaching staff and provide his team with the proper resources, Herdman was not above trying to fundraise for the team's training camps himself by walking up and down Bay Street, in Toronto's financial district, hat in hand, to meet with financial power brokers.

Opposing teams were also laden with the experience Canada lacked.

That was never more clear than after Canada took to BMO Field against Honduras in September 2021. The hosts looked jittery in possession against an organized deep block. They had little answer for the visitors' time-wasting and chippy approach.

Down 1–0 at halftime, the Canadian players conferred in the home locker room, and many shared a similar feeling: *This might be harder than we thought.*

"*Holy shit* moments," Herdman called them.

"The fantasy was that we were going to get out there and it was going to be a tiki-taka evening and we were gonna score fifteen goals by halftime," said Herdman.

After Canada settled their nerves in the second half, Canadian forward Cyle Larin's converted penalty in the sixty-sixth minute was enough to force a draw.

It was Larin's nineteenth goal for Canada, which put him just three back of Dwayne De Rosario as the team's all-time top goal scorer.

Larin's three MLS seasons had provided the playing time and the springboard to greater opportunities that he, and his peers, needed. Now, he was proving to be a vital piece for Canada's World Cup hopes.

After the game, Milan Borjan shouted across the pitch to gather the entire Canadian staff in the centre of the park. Borjan crouched down low as the team crowded round. The veteran goalkeeper moved his head throughout the circle to make eye contact with his entire team. He slapped his goalkeeper gloves emphatically so his message would land, especially with the aforementioned new core: *It's only going to get more difficult from here on in. We've got to find another level in our game.*

Three days later at the Nissan Stadium in Nashville, the team's performance improved, as Canada effectively sat back to stifle the United States out of possession and hit the hosts on the counterattack, but the result didn't: a 1–1 draw put Canada in the murky middle ground in the standings with Honduras, the United States, and El Salvador, but already four points behind Mexico. Larin had again scored for Canada, but the goal was more the product of a daring run from Davies, who separated himself from his defender and played a perfect pass to his waiting forward.

The boos that rained down from the forty-three thousand in attendance were partly directed at the home team: even with the lion's share of possession, they were unable to convert their chances.

Canada had to own some of the vitriol too. They didn't attack as perhaps they could have, given how timid the Americans looked in possession. But their approach was also evidence of the versatility Herdman wanted from his group. Opponents would present different shapes and looks throughout the tournament. If Canada couldn't adapt beyond their freewheeling, electric style of play, they'd be easier to pigeonhole and defend against.

"We were tactically sound. We knew what our game plan was coming into the match," said defender Sam Adekugbe, expressing regret over not getting the win on American soil, with the kind of seriousness rarely heard from men's team players.

Herdman wanted his team to be impenetrable defensively, just as Canadian teams before them had been. He believed in the power of visualization, as evidenced by a mocked-up cover of the *Toronto Star* he had made that imagined what it would look like when Canada qualified for the World Cup, for players to be inspired by. He wanted his ideas to resonate in new ways and to keep the players committed. Herdman relied on the team's mental and cultural manager and former women's national team player, Robyn Gale, to ease every player's adjustment from their club teams to the national team. Herdman had learned that his rousing speeches didn't always land the way they had with past teams. In a 2018 training camp, he'd invited members of Canada's military to speak to his team about the code associated with military uniforms. He saw how players responded to the idea of going into battle for one another and kept that notion in the back of his mind.

And none of the players could have imagined how he'd bring that notion to life: by having a steel medieval-style shield made to symbolize his team's adherence to defensive responsibility.

Herdman wanted his players to see it and remember Canada's national anthem, and the idea that they should "stand on guard."

"Get your shield up for what's coming against you," he'd tell his players as they'd pass the shield around. The shield became as vital a piece of their travelling equipment as the team's uniforms. Preparing for battle merged from cliché into reality.

• • •

As the team boarded the flight from Nashville back to Toronto, for the game against El Salvador on September 8, their desire to show off the plethora of talent they had up and down the lineup bubbled to the surface. The maturity in the team's younger players was evident in that they understood Herdman's tactical demands and that going into a defensive block as they did against the Americans would help them get results in a long tournament.

Still, players wanted a performance to show Concacaf they were to be taken seriously.

If a full-scale attack was to happen, it would have to be done without Davies, who had left the game against the United States in the second half with an injury. Multiple reports from Germany had Davies already on a flight out of Canada, returning to his club side.

Ahead of the El Salvador match, the first question to Herdman was about the status of Davies. After telling reporters via his prematch Zoom press conference that Davies had not trained, he fired back his answer after being asked if Davies was indeed still with the team.

"Yeah, he's still with the team," said Herdman, not wanting to give an inch of rope to the El Salvador side in their preparations. Hours later, Canada Soccer officially ruled him out of the following day's match. The next day, Davies posted a photo on Instagram that showed him walking through a shopping centre, his head turned back, with the caption "They won't realize how big of a part you play, until you're not there to play it anymore" with a peace sign as well. The placeline on the post read "Munich."

The men's team's rise had been a feel-good story ever since their 2019 win over the United States, but the first stink of drama was wafting through the doors that Herdman wanted to keep airtight as he continued to preach team brotherhood.

Davies would later tweet that that caption was "just a caption."

"I fully support the national team and there are no issues," he wrote in the tweet.

The drama surrounding the team still hadn't dissipated closer to kickoff, though. It was evident in an elevator that slowly rose toward the third floor of BMO Field, carrying a family of four that wasn't where they probably should have been.

The elevator was meant for media and BMO Field staff. But on this day, it carried four natives of El Salvador decked out in blue jerseys, two of whom sported the blue and white El Salvador flag painted on their cheeks, just above their beaming grins. They were lost, sure, but that couldn't dampen their mood as their home team arrived in an away venue.

"Canada is our home now," said the father, "but El Salvador is the country we cheer for."

This family wasn't an outlier: throughout the stadium, blue and white flags were draped over the backs of a rambunctious fanbase. Canada was faced with a reality of yesteryear: even with their rise in talent and popularity, blue jerseys outnumbered the red ones in the stands at BMO Field.

Salvadorans make up the third-largest group of Latin American immigrants in Canada, more than six times that of Hondurans. More people of Salvadoran descent live in Ontario than in any other Canadian province, making it all the more possible for BMO Field to feel like an away game for the Canadians.

On social media, an angry tenor emerged among fans who wondered why these crucial games were being held in Toronto, with its history of feeling like an away venue for the national team, and not in Vancouver, for example, which has a lower population of Salvadorans. But BMO Field was always the preferred choice for this final round. It had the best facilities and playing surface in the country; it was closer to Europe, meaning shorter flight times for arriving players and fewer time zones for them to cross; and the large percentage of the players hailing from Toronto were motivated by being able to see family and friends for short periods during qualifying.

With those benefits, however, still came frustration inside the Canada locker room in the hour or so leading up to kickoff, as word of the high number of blue jerseys filtered in.

The staff prepared a message for the players, who were already brimming with excitability as they hoped to go in full tilt with offensive play: *If you want to change soccer culture in Canada, you can start changing things here tonight. Win, silence the crowd, and you can change the perception of what our games should look like in Toronto.*

Players clapped a little more vociferously at that message. And even after the El Salvador national anthem was sung far louder than many Canadian fans and national team employees would have liked, Canada backed up their own enthusiasm with two one-touch goals from Atiba Hutchinson and Jonathan David inside the first eleven minutes, the quickest two goals Canada would score after kickoff in the entire qualifying campaign.

Both Hutchinson and David peered knowingly into the stands in their celebratory runs after their goals. Herdman's glare remained venomous. Tajon Buchanan added one more goal in the second half, making for a smothering 3–0 win. Canada held El Salvador to a grand total of zero shots on target.

The team had answered questions about what they were capable of without Alphonso Davies, but still had questions of their own.

"We need Canada to wake up and to support this team because this team can go a long way," Borjan said emphatically after the game. "The World Cup is just right there. We have one foot inside. We just have to keep going and the stadium has to be full of red, not blue, green, or whatever. It has to be red."

• • •

John Herdman quickly blew a whistle in the middle of a training session in Mexico City, to the surprise of his players. Canada were just days away from their pivotal away leg against Mexico, but the session was prematurely finished for the time being.

Paranoia was running rampant throughout the Canadian contingent. Canada had lost their previous five games against Mexico. Getting a result at Estadio Azteca, one of the world's most celebrated soccer stadiums, would provide an immense boost to their World Cup hopes.

They'd have to get that result amid the continually prying eyes of the Mexican media and, by extension, those of the Mexican team themselves.

Herdman couldn't take his eyes off the massive cliff overlooking the training pitch used by famed Mexican side Pumas. Herdman regularly used drones to film his team's training sessions to review afterward. On this early October day, the drone served another purpose: to spot anyone who might be hiding out on that cliff, eager to gain exclusive insight on Canada's starting eleven and possible tactics.

And with good reason. The drone did indeed capture someone spying on Canada's training session, which was enough to make Herdman blow that whistle and close up shop, at least outdoors, for the day. The following day, although local media were informed this final day of training would be at the Azteca, the Canadian team instead returned to the Pumas' training ground. And Herdman rolled out a fake starting eleven for good measure, just in case.

Yet players tried not to get swept up in the prematch drama. It wasn't out of the ordinary for Herdman to set his team up inside a large hotel conference room as they would be positioned on the pitch, to continue tactical planning in a different and still enjoyable fashion. Players would pass a ball back and forth with their hands to mimic what kind of passing routes they wanted to follow in upcoming games. Those who weren't in the lineup as often could see how plays were meant to develop and where they would be expected to line up on the field to be at their most optimal.

Very few of the Canadian team had ever played in arguably the most impenetrable place for visiting teams to play in North America.

Mexico had not lost any of their previous fourteen games at the Azteca.

"Maybe we didn't overthink it," said veteran midfielder Samuel Piette, of how the team's mentality was driven by their young, somewhat inexperienced core.

But one player who had experienced personal success in front of the tens of thousands of ravenous fans at the Azteca was midfielder Jonathan Osorio. His goal against Club America in the 2018 Concacaf Champions League semifinal had helped push Toronto FC to the final, and he had celebrated it by goading the home fans as he ran toward them with his arms stretched out wide.

Now, three years later, Osorio showed just as much tranquility, even with Canada already down 1–0 in the first half. His smart run off the ball created enough space to collect a precise Alphonso Davies pass with one touch and score the tying goal with his second touch.

Once again, Osorio ran toward the Mexican fans with his arms wide. This time, he smacked the Canadian crest over his heart for dramatic effect and looked up at the crowd, stone-faced, before hollering as Davies jumped on his back.

It was Canada's first goal against Mexico in the Azteca in forty-one years, and enough to secure a valuable draw on the road.

As players gathered postgame ahead of the traditional huddle, opinion on the result was split. Long-time squad members who had played at the Azteca, including those who had been in the squad and humbled by Mexico at the hallowed ground in 2018 World Cup qualifying, felt lifted by escaping with a draw.

But for the young players who weren't burdened by the team's past failures, a draw felt almost like a loss.

"A draw is not our standard anymore," said one young player in the middle of the huddle.

Herdman sided with his young core.

"I think we'll walk away from this, looking at this in time, thinking we could have taken three points," he said.

The sense of disappointment leaving Mexico paled in comparison to the mood after a plodding 0–0 draw against Jamaica in an empty Kingston National Stadium three days later. On a bumpy, torn-up pitch, a pesky Jamaican side frustrated the hell out of the Canadians with foul after foul, allowing them little time and space on the ball. Canada's build-up play stuttered. Davies was left to do the heavy lifting on his own with darting runs.

Perhaps most concerning from the draw was how Jonathan David struggled to get meaningful touches on the ball for the second game in a row.

With just one win in five matches, expectations about Canada's World Cup hopes were rightly tempered leading up to their return to BMO Field on October 13 against Panama. Canada sat in fourth place, one point behind Panama, who had qualified for the 2018 World Cup.

Arriving crowds were scanned for proof of Covid-19 vaccination, which led to long queues.

Canadian expectations soured in the fifth minute when, with thousands of fans not even in their seats yet, Panama striker Rolando Blackburn finished a stunning combination of Panama passing for an uncontested goal.

Anxious fans in the queues outside the stadium heard the groan from inside and watched the goal replayed on their phones.

On the touchline, Herdman didn't bury his head, but instead flailed his arms in encouragement. Onlookers wondered if Herdman and his team would adopt a conservative mindset, to sit deeper and try to hit Panama on the counterattack in hopes of another draw. After all, that approach had been ingrained in the national team's DNA for so long.

But instead, in what would end up being arguably their most remarkable performance of the qualifying run, Canada and Davies kept their foot on the gas.

After some smart movement off the ball helped Canada force a turnover in Panama's half, Davies fed David with a perfect pass to put his friend in toward goal. No defenders were in front of him. But instead of shooting, David strangely sent the ball back to Davies. After the ball was cleared, Davies threw his hands toward the goal to emphasize the opportunity David missed.

"Keep your head up," Davies told him. "And next time, shoot the ball."

As he'd done before, Davies took Canada on his back.

His teammates kept feeding him the ball as he danced around any Panama defender who entered his airspace. Panama wilted and allowed an own goal off a forceful Davies corner kick.

In the sixty-sixth minute, David sent a long ball from his own half into a wide-open pocket of space in the Panama half. Starting from behind his friend on the pitch, Davies caught up to the ball as it slowed to a crawl by the touchline and went on a run that would raise his profile to as close to a household name in Canada as he'd ever been.

Panama centre-back Harold Cummings tried to protect the ball and see it off the field for a throw-in. But instead, Davies swept in, deftly corralling the ball midflight with his off foot to keep it in play as Cummings overran it. As Davies continued, he dragged every person in the east stands out of their seats with him.

With just one defender in front of him and Tajon Buchanan wide open, Davies played with the same freedom he had throughout his career, running directly at Panama centre-back Fidel Escobar, darting to his own left side, then firing a shot through Escobar's legs and into the Panama goal. He held a single finger up to his mouth, silencing anyone who doubted what he, and Canada, were capable of.

Buchanan got his opportunity minutes later when he jumped to finish an excellent Jonathan David cross with his head for his second goal of the campaign. The trio completed their euphoric second half as Davies sent a well-timed, floating cross through to David. David's calm finish not only sealed Canada's 4–1 win, but as Davies emphatically punched the air in front of him, sent a declarative message throughout Concacaf: this team could be more aggressive than they'd shown.

As the team walked off the pitch looking up at the 26,622 in attendance, then the largest-ever crowd for a men's national team game in the city, many players echoed the same message: they had never felt the self-belief, and the support from fans, ever, in a Canadian jersey.

"What you've seen tonight is Canada step forward," said Herdman.

A few hours after the final whistle, forward Liam Millar sat quietly by a side entrance at BMO Field, wearing an oversized track jacket that hid a Gucci T-shirt. His lips pursed as he continued to stare outside the stadium in hopes that the car he was waiting for would arrive soon. Surrounded by his young wife and friends, all of whom were ecstatic after an impressive win, all Millar could think about was the black SUV with tinted windows finally arriving to pick him up.

When it finally did come, Millar popped into his seat and began the short trip to famed Yorkville Italian restaurant Sotto Sotto.

Millar's anxiety paled in comparison to how he felt when the doors of the swanky restaurant opened later, and Drake strode through the door.

Perhaps it was inevitable that, given their rapid ascent, the national team would end up with the global hip-hop star, one of Toronto's most celebrated exports. But they hardly played it cool, however, perhaps speaking to how fresh the spotlight was for this young team.

When Drake began following Davies on Instagram after Davies's Champions League win, Davies celebrated with an elated, childlike Instagram video of his own.

Drake's music had been a constant in the men's national team locker room, which the men's team staff was all too aware of. Even if Drake's then recently released record *Certified Lover Boy* wasn't getting heavy rotation in John Herdman's car, he couldn't help but smile and shake his head in his postgame press conference when he told reporters that Davies had just received a text from Drake, who wanted to meet Davies.

"Hopefully, tonight, he's got a chance to take that off his bucket list," said Herdman.

Inside the locker room, Alistair Johnston was sitting on his own, scrolling through Twitter, where Herdman's revelation had hit the app like wildfire. Johnston's eyes widened. He was unaware of any Drake text, as were his teammates.

Just then, Davies walked into the locker room.

"Phonzie?" asked Johnston slyly, "Did you get a text from Drake?"

"What do you mean? Did Drake text me?" Davies said, his voice hitting the same high, excited tones it did when he found Drake had followed him on Instagram. Johnston showed him the series of tweets, and Davies, in a panic, opened multiple different apps on his phone.

"If he did, I can't believe I missed it," said Davies.

As Davies hit the roof, many of his teammates crowded around him wondering if their win had elevated their celebrity status.

Davies hadn't missed a text, though. Drake had made contact with someone close to the team after the game to see if Davies and a few teammates would be interested in meeting him. The players had yet to find out, but Herdman, having a sense of occasion, had dropped that nugget to the media knowing full well how quickly word of his team's brush with fame would go viral.

Eventually, Davies calmed when he was told that Drake had arranged for transportation for him and a select group of teammates to Sotto Sotto.

Drake was no stranger to Canadian sports, having been a fixture courtside for years at Toronto Raptors games, and a constant in their run to becoming 2019 NBA champions.

"It's a sign of how far we've come as a program that if Drake's taking notice, it means you're doing good things," Johnston said.

Drake gladly posed for photos with Millar and Buchanan at the restaurant, congratulating them on the win, but he himself lit up when Davies gave him his game-worn jersey.

While the group chatted, Davies's goal was being played repeatedly on television and phone screens across the country. Davies, and this team, were no longer an afterthought in the Canadian consciousness.

. . .

When the schedule for the final round of World Cup qualifying was announced, it was hard to overlook two games for Canada: in the middle of November, scheduled just days apart.

The fact that Canada was the only team to get both games at home in this third qualifying window presented a unique opportunity to set up a home base for a week. Rumours circulated: the mild weather in Vancouver and the fifty-four thousand available seats in closed-roof BC Place seemed appealing.

But with a nod to former men's team head coach Tony Waiters's line of thinking, Herdman and Canada Soccer announced the two World Cup qualifiers would be played in Edmonton, where winter would be in full force come November.

"We could have made things a lot easier and played in maybe different environments, but we wanted to make it difficult for the opponent," said Herdman. "We wanted to make them travel across time zones, play in a Canadian winter, and on a surface that they won't be happy with."

Making opponents uncomfortable was in line with how Concacaf teams regularly acted in World Cup qualifying. The two games would also serve as a homecoming for Alphonso Davies. He would play his first matches in his hometown as a professional.

Davies's face was omnipresent in banners across Edmonton. With the Edmonton Oilers on the road for the duration of Canada's games, he dominated local media coverage. In the community centre inside Commonwealth Stadium, children clamoured to get a glimpse of the city's favourite son. When they shared word of whether he might or might not be approaching, they missed established veterans like Atiba Hutchinson walking by them in plain sight. Hutchinson could only smile.

The games also presented an opportunity for Canada Soccer to show off the 56,302-seat Commonwealth Stadium to visitors from FIFA. The largest open-air stadium in Canada was a prospective host for 2026 World Cup matches.

But it was still a gamble. The idea that Canadian players were built for playing in colder climates was a myth. The reality was that nearly the entire team played regularly in far more temperate climates. With more comfortable surroundings available, failure to get results would see the organization's decision blow up in their collective faces.

"Minus-ten is not easy on anybody," Davies said quietly in Edmonton, when asked about the weather.

Players tried to make the most of it. As the sound of DJ Khaled's "All I Do is Win" echoed through the stadium ahead of a training session, goal-keeper Maxime Crepeau ran out of the tunnel as the first player on the training pitch. He hid behind a snowbank and began pelting his teammates with snowballs as they walked onto the pitch, with the temperature dipping below freezing.

The weather wasn't the only thing to surprise the Canadian side.

For six matchdays, the medieval shield the team had carried with them had inspired them. Thanks to their focus on defending as a collective unit and some game-saving moments from Milan Borjan, they'd allowed just four goals through those six games, tied with the United States for second-least in the group.

But to enter Concacaf's elite, they needed to embrace the attacking mindset that was such a strong part of the team's core.

And so, if the team's shield led to raised eyebrows, what John Herdman brought out next from his bag of tricks led to audible gasps: a thirty-four-inch-long medieval sword with the words *Qatar 2022* engraved on it, as well as *Nihil timendum est*, Latin for "Fear nothing."

Herdman wanted the sword to help his players adopt a new mindset — that they would not only defend their honour, but attack with pride as well. Toronto-based swordsmith Steve Karakostas received a vague email ahead of the qualifying campaign from someone looking to commission a one-of-a-kind sword for a group of men on what he was told was a "significant international quest."

"That's New Canada," Herdman would later say of the sword. "That's the swagger we want to play with."

Like the shield, the sword would travel with them to every stadium. The team had small swords added to the back of their jerseys, purposefully kept out of the view of social media photos. The sword would be planted into the pitch itself before each match to symbolize that, according to Herdman, "we'll own their ground."

· · ·

Alistair Johnston walked into a cavernous CFL dressing room, noting first how Canada Soccer had tried to combat the green and gold colours of the Edmonton Elks on the floor with red banners draped across the top of the room.

But something else stuck out from the corner of his eye. Every player's red kit had been laid out perfectly as normal — except for one.

Johnston rubbed his eyes. *Were those sweatpants?* he asked himself.

He walked closer to see an *18* had been pressed onto the kind of ratty, grey sweatpants Johnston might have pulled on after waking up alone in a cold apartment.

Then it dawned on Johnston: to combat the cold, goalkeeper Milan Borjan was going to take to the field in sweatpants.

"We're going to look like we're playing in Sunday league out here," he said to the rest of his smiling team.

Five years earlier, Hungarian national team goalkeeper Gábor Király, whose balding head and husky physique are reminiscent of Borjan himself, introduced his standard gameday attire of similar-looking ratty grey sweatpants to international soccer when he backstopped Hungary to a surprise place atop their group at Euro 2016. Borjan was hoping for some of the same magic, and when he walked into the dressing room and began pulling on the pants, Johnston threw down the gauntlet.

"You better keep a clean sheet," he said to Borjan and to anyone else listening, "or we're never going to hear the end of this."

Borjan did his part by using his reach and composure in goal to make the necessary saves when Costa Rica pressed forward. The visitors mostly employed stingy defensive tactics to limit Canada to a few moments of individual brilliance.

One of those moments came, not from the man of the hour, Davies, but from his close friend, Jonathan David.

David's wild ascension with the Canadian team had mirrored his rise within club soccer. His path to stardom had been unconventional: after emigrating to Canada from Haiti, David spent his entire career as a teenager, not in a Canadian MLS academy, nor abroad, but with two youth minor soccer organizations outside of Ottawa.

His innate talent for creating goals out of nothing meant Canadian MLS teams tried to court David to join their academies. But he wanted to go straight to Europe, without any stopovers. There was concern from within his camp that, though playing in MLS might have benefitted his development, playing time might have been limited, especially given how prone a team like TFC was to playing veterans. MLS teams generally dropped serious dollars on foreign attackers, limiting how domestic forwards like David would be used.

"Of course, every time an opportunity came, it was difficult to refuse," David said in 2020. "My mind was always set on Europe. I had to focus on that and stay on that."

While scoring two goals for Canada at the 2017 Concacaf Under-17 Championship, David formed an immediate bond with Alphonso Davies.

"They had a natural chemistry together," said then head coach Sean Fleming.

David's agent organized trials in Europe, including at VfB Stuttgart in Germany and Red Bull Salzburg in Austria. TFC offered David a professional contract, but David continued to bet on himself.

Travelling back and forth from Ottawa to Europe eventually paid off when he signed for Belgian side Gent's reserve team in January 2018. He rose to the first team, scoring five goals in his first four appearances with them, all off the bench. Days after that fifth goal, Gent extended his contract, recognizing that they had one of Europe's up-and-coming strikers on their hands.

In just two seasons in Belgium's first division, David notched twenty-six goals in fifty appearances, all before the age of twenty-one.

Only two years after he made his professional debut, historic French side Lille paid a then-club-record €30 million transfer fee for David. It was the most expensive transfer fee ever for a Canadian national team player.

In David's first season in France, he finished second on the team with thirteen goals, and helped guide Lille to their first French league championship in ten years. That finish guaranteed David would join Davies playing in club soccer's most celebrated tournament, the UEFA Champions League.

"What I'm most proud of is that I had the guts to wait and really go after what I wanted, which was to go play in Europe," David said in 2020.

Herdman would dub David the "Iceman," due both to his cold-hearted ability to poach goals but also because of his solemn, determined nature:

David put instruction into practice immediately, yet in a vote for the team's quietest player, David would win in a landslide.

Herdman believed in David when he gave him his debut in 2018, even though he was relatively unproven. They would connect briefly after training to share a few jokes, but also for Herdman to remind David that with continued effort off the ball, he could become one of the most clinical and impactful Canadian forwards to ever play the game.

"As a young player, sometimes you lack confidence. When a coach has that confidence in you," said David of Herdman in 2018, "it makes you play at that highest level. Because you're not really afraid to make a mistake. And that's when you play your best."

Like many strikers, David's goal-scoring could go hot and cold. But in the coldest of temperatures David made good on Herdman's faith after collecting a rebound with patience on ball and the same ruthlessness close to goal he had always had. His fifty-seventh-minute goal had been enough for Canada to secure a 1–0 win over Costa Rica and stay in third place in qualifying standings. It was David's eighteenth goal for Canada, in just his twenty-third game.

"It's [about] just keeping things simple for Jonathan," Herdman said of David postgame, his voice hoarse and weary.

But Herdman's low-key appreciation of David understated the fact that despite Canada's week in Edmonton being an opportunity to celebrate the career of their most famous soccer export, it was now inappropriate to mention Davies as the star driving Canada without mentioning David in the same breath.

• • •

In the days leading up to the anticipated game against Mexico, inclement weather seemed unavoidable. A few short hours before a training session at Commonwealth Stadium was supposed to start, a confused press corps were told that the training session was cancelled due to weather concerns. Not a single snowflake was falling.

After a flurry of suspicious texts, another update arrived: Canada would be training at the Edmonton Soccer Dome, usually reserved for recreational teams, thirty minutes south of the city, off a barren highway.

The inordinate number of black SUVs in the parking lot and security guards at the doors to the facility were just part of what made the training session look different: standing pitchside with his white shirtsleeves rolled up, watching the men's national team work through their training session, was Canadian prime minister Justin Trudeau.

Trudeau had been in Edmonton to announce a childcare deal with the Alberta government earlier in the day, but the team's foray into Canadian consciousness presented a photo opportunity too good to turn down.

"What a pleasure and an honour," Trudeau said as he shook hands with Herdman.

"We'd only stop a training session for Katy Perry or the prime minister," Herdman retorted.

Trudeau stood in front of the team, thanking them for inspiring Canadians, and "bringing us together."

After taking photos and receiving a signed jersey with "Trudeau 22" printed on the back, the prime minister stepped aside but remained on the pitch to chat with Canada Soccer officials. Herdman screamed "Let's go" as he tried to wave Trudeau to the sidelines so his team could have the full pitch to continue their preparations.

Herdman had the team's week planned down to the minute. Every advantage was necessary for Herdman if his team was to upset Mexico. It helped that the Mexican side weren't keen on leaving their Indianapolis base as Edmonton snow beckoned. They arrived in Edmonton less than twenty-four hours before kickoff. When they asked to use the Edmonton Soccer Dome to train in beforehand, they were told no: there were house league games to be played. Canada was pulling Concacaf shithousery on their own terms.

A sizable Mexican media contingent arrived days ahead of the team they were covering. After Mexico had lost 2–0 to the United States, shivering reporters wanted to know if Canadian players still saw Mexico as the giants of the region.

Canada showed resolve in their win over Costa Rica, but they were hardly dominant. Should Canada be considered among Concacaf's elite with Mexico?

"Definitely," said Davies ahead of the game. "There's a lot of people out there that, when we got into (the final round of qualifying), wrote Canada out of the competition. We're proving them wrong. And we're proving to ourselves that we can compete at this level."

. . .

In the moments before the Canadian players ran from their downtown hotel to their bus to avoid the snow and make the drive to Commonwealth Stadium, they were shown a video message from legendary Edmonton Oiler and the most famous Canadian athlete of all time, Wayne Gretzky, who encouraged the team to make their country proud.

They arrived to see tractors encircling the pitch, pushing snow into snowbanks even as fans, most of whom were dressed for a ski hill, entered the stadium. The Mexican team took their time coming out of their dressing room before the game and when they did, were dressed in as many layers as the team had brought on the trip. They wore miserable faces as the game kicked off at –9°C, the coldest temperature for a game in Mexican national team history. And they were given a rude welcome within a minute of kickoff when centre-back Doneil Henry flattened Mexican winger Hirving Lozano with a crushing tackle.

The beginning of the first half ended up being devoid of rhythm: Canada defended in numbers and Mexico fouled relentlessly.

Yet as the crowd of 44,212 grew into the game, so too did Canada, pressing Mexican players effectively on the ball, forcing turnovers, and constantly picking apart the Mexican backline in possession. Dressed in black, the Canadians had an extra hop in their step the Mexicans did not. Where Mexico ran, Canada didn't just follow, but overpowered the visitors.

In first-half injury time, Johnston read an unfolding play, stepped in to cut off a Mexican pass, and fired a shot from distance on goal. The shot surprised Mexican goalkeeper Guillermo Ochoa as he fell to make the save, but didn't surprise Larin, who was in the right place to bang home the rebound.

An erupting crowd caused snow from the Commonwealth Stadium rafters to fall onto them, and onto the snowbanks around the pitch. If Canada could hold on to their lead, they'd take over top spot in the qualifying standings.

Eustaquio, same as he hadn't ahead of Canada's first game, didn't much care for the word *could*.

His fifty-first-minute free kick from thirty yards out fell perfectly on the feet of Larin, who had charged past multiple Mexican defenders to tap in his second goal of the game.

As he ran toward the snowbanks in the northwest corner of the stadium, he was mobbed by his teammates and stopped short just before the snow. But Sam Adekugbe didn't want to stop.

With a feverish smile, as if in disbelief, he epitomized the Canadian fearlessness Herdman wanted and leapt into the snowbank.

His Fosbury flop was replayed across the soccer world in the days after Canada's 2–1 win.

That Mexico put up a late push and Canada required Borjan's heroics to clear a Mexico shot off the goal line didn't sour their party. If Davies's goal against Panama had showcased just what this team might be capable of, Adekugbe's celebration proved just how much fun they were having in the process.

For the first time in this qualifying campaign, Canada had all the answers against the region's elite. They showcased both the firepower they wanted to, and the defensive stability they had to. Borjan celebrated by grabbing a beer from someone in the crowd as he strutted across the pitch after the final whistle.

This team had bet they could get results in frigid conditions. Had they not, their entire qualifying campaign might have been derailed with persistent questions about whether they belonged in the conversation with Mexico.

As Davies waved a Canadian flag, leading his entire team as they walked around the stadium for the thousands of fans who refused to leave, there were no more such questions.

"We are a top team in Concacaf," Larin said declaratively postgame. "I believe that; the team believes it. And we think we can make the World Cup."

In a locker room meant for rosters far bigger than that of a national soccer team, players first sat far apart, then moved closer and closer. With no training session the next day and players set to depart on flights back to their club teams, the sound of beer cans being cracked was omnipresent. The conversation was uniform: each and every player believed that, having now beaten Mexico, they were manifesting their World Cup dreams in real time.

Hutchinson and Borjan embraced, united by past shortcomings, but also by their future: Canada had taken over top spot in the qualifying standings.

"This is it," Hutchinson told his close, and equally long-suffering friend. "We've been waiting for this a very long time."

• • •

Atiba Hutchinson was in the middle of the Estadio Olímpico Metropolitano pitch in San Pedro Sula, Honduras, on January 27, 2022, surrounded by his teammates, and needed to bring the exorcism that had just been performed to a close.

Their last five trips to a city that, until not long before, was known as one of the most murderous on the planet, had ended in harrowing fashion. The 8–1 drubbing in 2012 that Hutchinson himself had been on the pitch for led to questions surrounding this team heading into their trips to Honduras and El Salvador: could they win in countries that had traditionally been hostile to them?

But as Hutchinson tugged on his captain's armband after a 2–0 win, the ghosts of past losses in Honduras haunted him no longer.

"I fuckin' love this team!" screamed Hutchinson emphatically.

No longer did they haunt Borjan, another veteran of those losses.

"What a fucking game," said Borjan in the postgame huddle, to laughs from Herdman and raised eyebrows from teammates. "This is how you leave your heart for this shirt," he continued, patting his right hand over the Canada Soccer crest on his jersey.

"We stand together, as brothers, as one big family," he shouted, before his teammates swarmed him, smacking his bald head while he took cover.

Brotherhood was a term used so unfailingly by Herdman and his players that it threatened to become a hollow cliché as qualifying moved forward. Yet among the players, they took the notion of this group acting in the best faith of others to heart.

And in this qualifying window, they'd have to rely on that brotherhood in new ways.

Less than two weeks before the team travelled to Honduras, Bayern Munich had announced Alphonso Davies showed signs of mild myocarditis, an inflammation of the heart, after a bout with Covid-19. Rest and time away from the pitch would be the cure. Davies would miss the entirety of this crucial qualifying window, and the team would miss the player who had taken them on his back in the win against Panama.

"We've got a lot of players who are hungry to have that opportunity and to take that limelight," said Herdman.

Junior Hoilett showed well in the starting lineup in a left-wing role typically occupied by Davies after not playing in the last two windows, and then showed his excitement postgame.

"I fuckin' love everyone here," he said, before leading the postgame cheer of "Brothers" on a countdown to three.

He had plenty of reason to be excited. After Samuel Piette started just his second game of the window in a defensive midfield role, an injury meant Herdman had to bring on Liam Fraser in the thirty-ninth minute.

Fraser had warmed the bench for almost the entirety of the long qualifying campaign, logging just 115 minutes in the fourteen games leading up to his appearance.

But Herdman's insistence that players treat each other as equals gave Fraser the confidence to play with poise. In the seventy-third minute, Fraser had runway in front of him with the ball at his feet just outside his own six-yard box. But Fraser took one look far up field and sent a soaring, but precise, long pass to Jonathan David, who blew past the Honduras defenders.

Back in his Munich apartment, Davies couldn't miss out on the fun. Decked out in his white Canada jersey, he streamed himself watching the game on Twitch, a streaming app, with his father Debeah sitting nearby.

"What a ball from Liam Fraser," he said calmly on the stream.

David perfectly corralled the pass with his chest, nudged it forward with his head and then chipped the ball over Honduran goalkeeper Luis Lopez for what would end up being the second-most aesthetically pleasing goal of Canada's qualifying run.

Davies shot up out of his chair, flexed, and screamed, "What a golazo! Johnny!" in a sky-high pitch. Davies's ease in front of the camera helped turn clips of his live stream viral, only turning more heads onto the brotherhood those within the team had long known about.

In the eighty-first minute, hulking striker Lucas Cavallini was substituted in. It was just Cavallini's third appearance in the final round of qualifying. He had been a far more regular starter through earlier rounds of qualifying and the Gold Cup in 2021, but now, his role meant entering in the final minutes of a win to give a starting forward some rest.

Cavallini had made his Canadian national team debut as a promising nineteen-year-old while rising through the ranks with various clubs in Uruguay. But after his second appearance with Canada came in the dreadful 8–1 loss to Honduras in 2012, he refused call-ups, to the ire of some players who *did* play for Canada. He appeared for Canada just once between 2012 and 2017, though he continued to score with regularity in Uruguay. It took some convincing from then Canadian head coach Octavio Zambrano to bring him back into the fold.

Though Cavallini had developed a reputation as being reticent with the media, he was far more engaged with his teammates off the pitch, at least if the team's WhatsApp group chat is any indication. Even when regular playing time didn't come his way, Cavallini was one of the most active members on the team's chat, cracking a joke at every opportunity, but also congratulating players for scoring goals with their club sides.

By 2021, he had transferred to the Vancouver Whitecaps. Even if his form had slightly dipped, his importance to the national team hadn't. That a player who wasn't receiving regular playing time remained engaged and kept the mood light spoke to how players could put aside personal agendas and buy into this team's greater purpose.

And though there were dual nationals outside the program who were intriguing enough to warrant a call-up, to Herdman, brotherhood meant loyalty.

"The simplicity for me is that there's a group of men that have been committed since the beginning of this [final round of qualifying]," said Herdman. "There's a loyalty to people who've committed to the journey, there's a loyalty to those players that have showed up every window. And some, they may not have contributed massively on the pitch, but their contribution off the pitch. When people really understand how teams form and team spirit and culture, it's as much about what you do off the field."

Just over four years before, to the day, Herdman had taken over a team ranked ninety-fourth in the world by FIFA. Herdman's belief in the importance of a team acting as a unit to achieve a goal that would have seemed impossible previously had been fully instilled during his time in New Zealand. With the Canadian team's brotherhood seemingly never stronger and their momentum growing, achieving a berth in the World Cup was starting to look like more of a real possibility with every passing match day.

"If you've ever seen a team overperform, it'll always be factored on three key things," said Herdman. "Team spirit, and that team spirit is the level of trust that you build, and that level of trust is the shared purpose that every man is turning up to achieve the same thing."

. . .

Inside the Canadian bus that was forced to slow to a crawl on Melrose Avenue in Hamilton, players quickly pulled out their phones to take videos of the scene unfolding outside their windows.

Just outside of the entrance to Hamilton's Tim Hortons Field, the blinding red smoke set off to welcome the team to the stadium made it impossible to see your hand in front of your face, never mind the red and white streamers hung from nearby trees and the hundreds of fans clad in red.

The voracious welcome, organized in part by longstanding Canadian soccer fan club The Voyageurs, produced viral scenes that weren't unlike those produced by the most fervent fans in South America and Europe.

"We burned the fucking White House down," sang fans as the players and coaches walked off the bus ahead of Canada's game against the long-time aggressors of the region, the United States. It was a not-so-subtle nod to when the British army burned down the White House as retaliation after an American attack on the province of Upper Canada, then part of Great Britain.

"It was the first time I really felt like I'm living in a football country," said Herdman.

Amid the chanting, players walked with their backs arched straight up, their eyes focused ahead. Even if the Americans owned more possession and had more shots, Canada's confidence emanated in how they defended with aggression and quickly won fifty-fifty balls.

Canada looked like the bullies they'd always wanted to be.

Buchanan laid a hip check on American Sergiño Dest that would have been at home on the old Copps Coliseum ice in downtown Hamilton before filling his ear afterward. Dest cowered, walking backwards.

Canada then made the most of their chances in transition. Cyle Larin capitalized after some swift passing between Jonathan Osorio and Jonathan David in the seventh minute, and Sam Adekugbe finished off the Americans by blocking a shot from close range in the eighty-seventh minute, then storming down the field minutes afterward, untouched, to rapturous applause.

One team looked beaten down by the opposition's physical play. The other showed swagger for days.

"Our swagger comes from our brotherhood," said Adekugbe. "We have so much confidence in each other. We've all grown up together. We've all grown up in this last cycle through John Herdman."

The 2–0 win over the Americans might have been cemented forty-five minutes from its end when Borjan leapt high to swat away a sure Weston McKennie goal off a header. It felt like a foregone conclusion as he walked to the crowd to his left, and again slapped his thick gloves on the Canada Soccer emblem over his heart. Borjan, the emotional heartbeat of the team, was mobbed by teammates afterward. Those emotions were catapulting this team.

This game was a homecoming of sorts for Borjan. Born in what was then known as Yugoslavia, his family of ethnic Serbians fled from the Yugoslav wars. They found refuge in Canada, first living in a hotel provided by the federal government, then eventually settling in Hamilton.

After he played for two Hamilton youth soccer organizations, Borjan's career took him to Uruguay, Argentina, Turkey, Romania, Bulgaria, Poland, and eventually to Serbia's most popular club side, Red Star Belgrade.

Borjan could have played for either Croatia or Serbia but chose to represent Canada.

"Canada gave my family everything," Borjan said in 2022. "When somebody gives you that much love, you have to return it."

And he did just that throughout the qualifying campaign. Borjan allowed just four goals in his ten appearances. The underlying numbers suggested he should have allowed far more, but Herdman could count on him for at least one game-saving moment every appearance.

And off the pitch, Borjan's bombastic presence and curse-filled locker room speeches were the yin to the yang of fellow veteran Atiba Hutchinson, who was best known for his quiet confidence.

Borjan was sometimes the centre of team meals. One dramatic retelling of a story featured Borjan unjustly getting pulled over in Serbia and having to use his influence as the captain of Red Star Belgrade to rectify the matter. As young teammates were enraptured by the story, Hutchinson sat back in his chair. With a knowing grin, he incredulously prodded Borjan about what type of vehicle he was driving to warrant being pulled over.

"Well, a gold Range Rover," Borjan told the group.

An outpouring of laughter followed from the young players at the key detail Borjan had skipped but Hutchinson knew how to coax out.

By this point in the campaign, players would look forward to shaking their heads and laughing when Borjan tried to rally his team by counting to three but inevitably butchering his pronunciation of the final number: "Brothers, on *free.*"

"He's not afraid to be himself," said Johnston. "That's what's been so important about this entire group: everyone is just so comfortable around each other. No one's nervous."

And Borjan certainly did not look nervous as he sat with a Canadian flag draped over his back in his postmatch press conference.

"This," said Borjan, "is what Canada deserves."

· · ·

In the afternoon before Canada's final game of the window in El Salvador, Derryn Donaghey sat down at his desk to let the emotions bubbling up inside of him come to the surface.

As both a former board member with Canada Soccer and a security guard for the men's national team, he knew the struggle for recognition the men's team had endured.

Derryn's father Sam had been vice-president of the Canadian Soccer Football Association and had put his house in Edmonton up as collateral on a loan to finance bringing the Scotland men's national team to Canada to play a friendly. He'd eventually be named to the Order of Canada for his work on growing the game.

But in Sam's lifetime around the sport in Canada, he'd never seen a team like the one set to kick off against El Salvador. And that inspired the first line of a poem he wrote called "Herdman's Heroes." The opening stanza begins:

> Never before has Canada ever witnessed a men's side as strong as today
> Coach Herdman and his coaching team have mastered an effective style of play
> So, let's take a peek at the side that has awoken the world
> By surprising most everyone, as up the FIFA rankings they hurled!

The remainder of the poem lauded the entirety of the team and commended them on their journey.

Hopefully, he thought to himself as he hit Send on an email to Herdman with the poem enclosed, *this inspires the lads a little bit.*

Not long after Herdman received the email, his staff had set the poem to a video of the team, with an assistant coach reading out every line. Herdman gathered his team to show them the video before the match. Donaghey wrote:

> You have given this country something to make them unite
> In these times of uncertainty of fear and fright

Herdman looked out to see a few players with tears in their eyes.

Herdman told his players, these are the people that have long supported the men's national team, regardless of their results.

"These are the people we've been fighting for," he told his group.

With Canada on top of the Concacaf table to start 2022 and with the finish line starting to look like less and less of a mirage, Herdman wanted to keep his players fixated on the end goal.

The powers of the shield? Canada had not allowed more than one goal in any of their games.

The powers of the sword? Canada's thirteen goals after eight matchdays were tops in Concacaf.

Now it was time to narrow his team's attention.

No one in the team's dressing room was surprised when Herdman brought in the final piece of the medieval-themed puzzle: a helmet he had designed that allowed players to see only straight ahead.

"Regardless of the noise, regardless of what's on the side and what people are saying about Canada, good or bad, [the goal of the helmet] was to stay focused," said midfielder Mark-Anthony Kaye.

In the game, staying focused in the persistent humidity while growing fatigue set in proved to be difficult. The continuous travel players had had to endure to arrive in Florida for a training camp before heading to Honduras, flying back north to Hamilton and then again south to San Salvador, seemed to be having an impact. Neither team looked capable of breaking their plodding spells. A 0–0 draw, which at least on the surface would suit Canada just fine, seemed to be the most likely outcome.

That is, until the sixty-fifth minute, when Jonathan David had the ball in Canada's half and Atiba Hutchinson stood beside him. Cyle Larin was the only Canadian in El Salvador's half, and was surrounded by four El Salvador players, but David still sent him on a run with a lengthy pass that seemed to be, at best, a chance to kill some time off the clock.

Without a single option for a pass, Larin put his head down and continued his charging stride. But when he looked up again, Hutchinson, just days from his thirty-ninth birthday, had dusted off his tired legs and beat multiple El Salvador players with a determined fifty-yard run.

Larin's low cross inadvertently bounced off a falling Hutchinson, then off the post, before taking another odd bounce off Hutchinson's backside and over El Salvador goalkeeper Kevin Carabantes.

Confusion ensued as the ball barely crossed the line. But Hutchinson's widened eyes told the story: not only was it the strangest goal of his career, it was another moment where Hutchinson dragged his team across the finish line, just as he had nearly fifteen years earlier in the Gold Cup.

Borjan ensured the goal had its desired effect in added time, when, after coming far off his line, he stretched to prevent El Salvador midfielder Marvin Monterroza's shot from surely finding the back of the goal. Seconds later, with the entire El Salvador side pressing deep in Canada's half looking for a goal, Jonathan David corralled a pass and had the entire opposition half to himself. With his back arched confidently once again, he audaciously chipped the ball over Carabantes.

Eustaquio leapt off the bench, shoved Canada Soccer employees aside, lowered his hands in anticipation and then darted onto the field, as did the entire bench, to swarm David.

Defender Derek Cornelius wagged his finger at David as if he were a toddler, having broken the rules. By getting all nine available points in the window without their best player and doing so with lengthy travel, Canada were indeed breaking preconceived rules within this international window.

They were one win away from qualifying for the World Cup.

I know my dad was smiling down upon them, Donaghey thought to himself.

After the game, Hoilett strutted around the ballroom inside the team hotel, live streaming a party on Instagram. Many players offered simple, but tired, smiles and raised their glass of red wine in appreciation.

But when Hoilett turned to Borjan, the goalkeeper leaned back, smiled and said out loud what more and more of the soccer world was thinking.

"See you in Qatar!"

• • •

"¡Hasta el último minuto!"

The words were perhaps indecipherable to many of the Canadians who had arrived in San José, Costa Rica, ahead of what could be a historic day for the men's national team. But after seeing this phrase hung on signs outside Estadio Nacional de Costa Rica, printed on shirts worn both by members of the Costa Rican federation and Costa Rican fans and in the top corner of television screens as newscasters wore Costa Rican jerseys, its meaning was inescapable: "Until the last minute."

Canada had travelled to hostile Central American locales but had not yet been engulfed in this kind of urgency. Honduras and El Salvador had all but been eliminated from World Cup contention when Canada left both countries with wins. Having qualified for four of the previous five World

Cups, Costa Rica expected to go to Qatar. But ahead of matchday twelve, Costa Rica was one point back of Panama for fourth place in the table and had a lot breaking in their favour. The Costa Rican Football Federation shut down their top domestic league for two weeks to allow players extensive training ahead of this window. Two of their final three games would be at home in their 35,175-capacity stadium, expected to be full for the first time since the beginning of the Covid-19 pandemic.

The days leading up to the match painted a picture of how unifying a national team could be for a country, and perhaps showed the steps Canada Soccer and the growing fanbase would need to take to turn their own team into the same unifying force. You would have had to work hard not to stumble into Costa Rican national team jerseys for sale, including at the checkout of grocery stores for discounted prices, or people wearing those jerseys. That included most newscasters on Costa Rican television on the morning of the match.

Even though many Costa Rican fans' voices around the stadium the day before the match dropped when they said, "We fear Canada," with the sound of chaotic traffic behind them, it was the Canadian players who stepped off their bus at the Estadio Nacional de Costa Rica and into the wind with blank stares.

Some players hobbled, owing either to being cramped in the bus or to nagging injuries, the news of which had begun swirling. Steadfast centre-back Steven Vitória would not be fit enough to play.

The possibility of World Cup qualification the following day had brought the most sizable travelling media contingent to a Canadian away game in years.

"Good to see yas," Herdman said to the media standing by the bus, offering polite handshakes.

The players, however, looked far less enthused. Weary, even. This was the opportunity they'd bowled through the region to get. After training for three days in Miami to keep tactical plans far from prying eyes and chartering to San José that afternoon, the travel, or maybe their fate, meant their long faces didn't quite project the steely resolve they'd shown previously on the road.

Unbeknownst to the travelling media, the team's sword had been seized by Costa Rican customs officials, citing laws preventing possession of this type of weapon.

Many player's faces lit up only when they saw Julian de Guzman, working as an analyst for TSN. After a brief walk-through of the stadium, veterans implored de Guzman to abandon his post and get back on the pitch with them.

"I wish I had my boots with me," said a giddy de Guzman.

Twenty-four hours later, the bus bringing the Canadians circled Avenida de las Américas and, with two police motorcycles in front of it, slowly pulled into the stadium. Night had fallen, and the streetlights lit thousands of smiling Costa Rican fans swilling beer outside the stadium. Dozens of those fans welcomed the Canadian bus with middle fingers in the air.

Inside the stadium, the party continued. Fireworks were set off during the Canadian national anthem to get in the heads of the visitors, as they stood arm over arm. But that didn't stop midfielder Mark-Anthony Kaye from doing as he had done throughout the entirety of qualifying: he sang the anthem at the top of his lungs, squeezing his eyes tight as he belted out the final few lines.

"The way you sing the national anthem," said Kaye, "is going to let everyone know how serious you're taking this game, how serious you're taking the opportunity in front of you, and I think it gives us a little mental edge on our opponents."

After absorbing Costa Rican pressure, as was the plan, Kaye tried to exert a little more of that edge. But his studs-up tackle on Costa Rican defender Ronald Matarrita landed him a yellow card. After weathering the storm and trying to take the crowd out of the match for the first thirty minutes or so, Canada started to break through with a few attempts on goal.

But, as Herdman highlighted postgame, "Pressure does things to people."

Kaye had been jawing back-and-forth with Costa Rican forward Johan Venegas. Perhaps as a means to assert a physical presence, but also taking the bait at the same time, Kaye laid a shoulder into Venegas, who promptly dropped to the ground in the most dramatic of fashions.

Another yellow card for Kaye forced him off the pitch. With strands of grass in his hair, he crossed the touchline, briefly looked back, and seemed to wonder what this meant for Canada's World Cup hopes on the night.

Down to ten players, Canada spent the rest of the first half scrambling, playing some of their least convincing soccer in years. Unsurprisingly, Costa

Rica capitalized with a goal off of some shambolic Canadian efforts to clear the ball just before halftime.

Canada's response in the second half also wasn't surprising: they dictated the tempo of the game when they had the ball. Tajon Buchanan's header banged off the crossbar, and Jonathan David's redirected shot hit the post. With Panama, strangely, having drawn Honduras earlier in the evening, had one of those balls found its way past esteemed Costa Rican goalkeeper Keylor Navas and Canada managed a draw, they would have qualified for the World Cup.

Instead, the postgame huddle with Milan Borjan finished a little quicker than usual after a 1–0 loss. Borjan told his teammates how proud he was of their second-half performance.

Canada now needed a win or a draw in their next game, against Jamaica at BMO Field, to qualify for the World Cup.

"Maybe it's in the stars," Herdman offered postgame, "to qualify at home."

• • •

As soon as Liam Fraser heard the sound of Drake's voice in his 2017 hit "Passionfruit," he raised his eyelids and began bobbing his shoulders from side-to-side and singing along. The midfielder was the first player out of the tunnel ahead of Canada's final training session before their March 27 game against Jamaica, but his teammates soon joined in lip-synching.

Any lingering pain from what John Herdman dubbed the "gut punch" of the loss against Costa Rica had dissipated on their flight back to Toronto.

As had been custom under Herdman, the men's team welcomed a local teenaged team, an Under-19 League 1 Ontario reserve side, to help out with training. They jumped in to mimic the upcoming opposition when needed and marvelled at what the players in front of them could pull off.

"Osorio's one-touch passes in the middle of the park, woah," said one player to his teammates as he watched a player who had grown up in the same area as him now on the precipice of the promised land.

As much as Herdman tried to preach the importance of keeping "two feet on the ground," the sheer confidence that was evident ahead of their opening match more than six months earlier would only be exceeded that late Saturday evening in the driving wind.

During the training session, Craig Forrest had told friends he was prepared to streak through BMO Field not if, but *when* Canada won.

"We're gonna win," Stephen Eustaquio had told a group of reporters fighting for space with their microphones in a way they had not at previous Canadian training sessions.

"That's it," he added, before looking over at a Canada Soccer media representative and asking, "Are we good?" and ducking back into the tunnel to join his teammates.

Any suspicions that Jamaica, already eliminated from World Cup contention, were sitting ducks were confirmed some ninety minutes before kick-off on the day. Hundreds of delirious fans again set off flares and red smoke to welcome the Canadian bus to the stadium. First off the bus, Alistair Johnston threw his hands in the air. Herdman was one of the last off the bus and cut through two police officers to pump his fist with the gathered crowd.

Herdman implored his team to impose their will on Jamaica, just as they had done at home against Panama months earlier.

"This is your opportunity to write your story in Canadian history," he told them before the game, as he had before. To help them visualize doing that, they held their pregame meeting in the Toronto Raptors dressing room at Scotiabank Arena and watched videos of how the team's 2019 NBA championship had galvanized a country of fans.

They walked out into the kind of snow flurries that might have made for picturesque viewing at home but froze Jamaica in their tracks. Canada wasted little time penning their own final, thrilling chapter. Jonathan David cut through three Jamaican defenders on his own with the ball in the fourth minute, to the adoration of the 29,122 fans already in attendance, another record for the team in Toronto. BMO Field crowds were notorious for arriving late to their seats. But the stadium was all but full when Sam Adekugbe, having the game of his life, busted down the left wing in the thirteenth minute and overlapped Junior Hoilett, who played a stretching, square pass to a wide-open Eustaquio.

Cyle Larin watched the ball and held up a single finger to show Eustaquio where he wanted a pass. With one touch, he smashed home his sixth goal of the final round of qualifying, the most of any player.

"Let's go!" he screamed.

The 1.65 million viewers on Canadian television, the largest audience through the qualifying run and more people than had tuned in for a Toronto Maple Leafs–Montreal Canadiens game the preceding Saturday night, knew where Larin wanted to go. So too did the teammates in black winter jackets who swarmed him: straight to Qatar.

That the flurries let up and the sun emerged just as Atiba Hutchinson was subbed on in the sixty-second minute, to chants of "A-ti-ba!" had Canadian supporters holding their heads in shock.

Jamaican jerseys were nowhere to be seen. Instead, the long-time Canadian fans, much like the players, were seeing their dreams being realized in storybook fashion.

Larin's goal would have been enough to propel Canada past a hapless Jamaican side, but Canada still piled it on with an outlandish twenty shots, two of which found the back of the net: a close-range tuck-in from Tajon Buchanan that was followed by his trademark backflip, and a cheeky chip from Junior Hoilett from just outside Jamaica's six-yard box.

Adekugbe was then rewarded for his relentless work rate during the game when yet another darting run forced a Jamaica own goal.

After being mobbed by his fellow coaches during the previous three goals, Herdman could only turn around and hold his hands out in stunned surprise.

When the final whistle came, the flurries and wind had picked up again. Players fell to their knees.

"As time ticked down, I realized it was a dream come true," said Larin.

The first stage of qualifying for the World Cup was healthy pride. The Voyageurs sang "Ole! Ole! Ole!" to see Jamaica off the pitch with such voracity that the BMO Field press box was vibrating.

The second stage was disbelief: nearly all the players shook their heads when they embraced teammates.

"I've waited for this moment for a very long time," said Hutchinson. "I didn't think it would come, especially after the last cycle."

Alphonso Davies appeared on a large screen in BMO Field to provide a recorded message.

"Our brotherhood is unmatched, and it's an honour to be a part of this group of players," he said, with a smile, of course. "To the fans: thank you for all your incredible support throughout this entire journey. We wouldn't have been able to do this without you guys. Everything we do, is for you."

And that smile was quickly followed by the kind of jubilation not often seen from the Canadian men's national team.

Herdman clenched first his fists then his entire body as he walked by a group of reporters, some of whom might have doubted his ability to get this team to where it is now.

"Fucking come on!" he shouted.

He'd later grasp two reporters by the back of the head and look them square in the eyes.

"We're going to Qatar, eh?" he said. "We're going."

The final stage was one of reflection.

For years, former players had grown frustrated by the federation's lack of recognition of the sacrifices former players made to play for Canada.

Yet before the current team was recognized in full, some of the most important Canadian players of the past, including Paul Dolan, Lyndon Hooper, Julian de Guzman, and Dwayne De Rosario were called out onto BMO Field by the public address announcer to have their moments in the sun, and to recognize the path they'd paved.

Tears streamed down a fully clothed Craig Forrest's face as he hugged Atiba Hutchinson and refused to let go.

The disappointment Forrest and his teammates had endured for years had seemed to evaporate with every passing matchday through the incredible run Hutchinson and his teammates had delivered.

"Thank you," Forrest said to Hutchinson.

Once the bottles of champagne were popped and players threw on goggles to celebrate in the dressing room, only a select few visitors were allowed inside. Herdman implored Victor Montagliani, former president of Canada Soccer and current president of Concacaf, to come in. Immediately, Milan Borjan poured beer on Montagliani's head.

Herdman called for the music to be turned down and tried to introduce Montagliani by his many titles.

"Fuck that," Montagliani interrupted him. "I'm just a Canadian today."

Borjan poured even more beer on him to the cheers of the room.

Montagliani addressed the room, recalling how about half of the current team were on the national team during his tenure from 2012 to 2016.

"While Tajon was in kindergarten," shouted Hutchinson, to more cheers.

"Do you remember our passport discussions?" asked Montagliani.

Doneil Henry shouted in approval.

When Montagliani would meet with Canadian players, he'd always wave his own passport to show Canadian players that he was on their side.

"You, more than anybody, knows that the most difficult passport in global football is the Canadian one," said Montagliani.

"It's hard," he continued. "It's hard when we're abroad and it's hard when we're at home. Because we're all screaming at the top of our lungs, and nobody is listening to us."

Montagliani would always tell the players that they would be the ones to change that.

The room went quiet, though the sound of laughter, celebration, and pride from the team's family members outside the room could be heard.

"Today," said Montagliani, "you guys made this the best passport in the world."

The uproar was heard not only several rooms away, but back out on the field, where a few stragglers remained, eager to take photos and pull up a few blades of grass from the pitch to celebrate the occasion.

It was on that pitch where Jonathan Osorio had stood an hour earlier, his lips quivering in the frigid cold as he struggled to find the words to describe what it felt like to finally qualify for a World Cup. Dozens of friends and family members of the players had taken to the field to join in on the celebrations. Osorio looked past the reporters and into the crowd. His mind wandered back to the continued losses in 2013 when he debuted for the national team and their FIFA ranking had plunged to its lowest number ever.

"As a Canadian kid, to dream of something like this was impossible," he said.

Osorio had walked around the field holding Steven Vitória's son on his shoulders. Osorio knew there had been countless children who had watched this team play, just as the Under-19 side had twenty-four hours earlier. Even more would watch Canada play at the World Cup in eight months.

Their dreams of not just watching Canada at a World Cup, but of perhaps one day playing soccer for Canada on the greatest stage no longer seemed impossible.

The words came to Osorio much easier when he looked up at a stadium full in a way it never had been for this team, and when he thought of what he wanted those children watching at home to take away from what had unfolded.

"Believe," he said. "Believe in yourself. Because you can do it. As a Canadian kid, you can be whatever you want to be."

Epilogue

THE CELEBRATIONS FOLLOWING CANADA'S WORLD CUP BERTH
continued late into the night with, naturally, another meeting with Drake,
this time at a swanky downtown Toronto steakhouse. The men's team then
brought their tired smiles to the following night's Toronto Raptors game,
where they were welcomed as guests of honour.

It was perhaps expected that Canada would subsequently fall short in
the final game of their World Cup qualifying campaign in Panama. A win
would have secured enough points in FIFA's ranking system to move to Pot
3 of the four-pot World Cup draw and potentially more favourable opponents, at least on paper. Yet the 1–0 result wasn't a total loss; Canada still
earned first place in the table, earning five more points than they'd wanted.

Exhausted and emotionally spent the following morning, players said their
peaceful goodbyes, and returned to their club sides across North America and
Europe. Some would likely see each other again in June when Canada's Nations
League campaign began, but every player, coach, and staff member would be
united from afar less than forty-eight hours later for the World Cup draw.

They'd have to wait until the very last moments of the draw to learn
their fate. A white ball with Canada's name inside of it was the final one to
be pulled by legendary coach Bora Milutinović, who, coincidentally, had
brought the United States out of the group stage when they hosted the
World Cup in 1994.

Milutinović beamed, perhaps knowing what kind of challenge Canada was going to be up against. They were drawn into a group with the recently top-ranked team in international soccer, Belgium, 2018 World Cup finalists Croatia, and Morocco, a team on the rise that had mopped the floor with the Democratic Republic of Congo in their final qualifying round.

Over the course of thirty minutes or so, the draw revealed just how different the World Cup would be from everything they'd achieved over the previous year.

But there was little doubt the Canadian side would welcome the crash course they'd enrolled in, just as they'd welcomed previous challenges.

"We'll be at our best when we rely on our grit, our spirit, and to bring that [aspect of] 'no fear,'" said John Herdman, sitting in the TSN studios in Scarborough as the draw unfolded before his eyes live on television.

The Canadian team that would travel to Qatar possessed much of what the team that went to Mexico in 1986 lacked: attacking talent, diverse backgrounds, legitimate professional experience at the highest levels, and, finally, international recognition. The country itself was different: more multicultural, for the better. Across the world, media outlets scrambled to understand how a team that just years earlier had been an afterthought had so quickly ascended to the top of the region and, with a likeable, fun-loving group, promised to be one of the most-discussed teams at the World Cup.

But back in Toronto, Herdman instead channelled his inner Paul Dolan as he thought about what Canada could be capable of when they took the field for their first World Cup game in thirty-six years.

"We want that underdog story," said Herdman.

Herdman, the hundreds of players and coaches who had contributed to the team's evolution, and the countless fans who had followed the rise of men's soccer in Canada understood full well: while the men's national team had accomplished history in their own right, there were still so many higher peaks to climb.

Acknowledgements

THE FIRST WORDS OF *THE VOYAGEURS* WERE WRITTEN ON A WOBBLY side table set up in a bedroom closet as my family, like so many around the world, anxiously tried to figure out how to exist in a global pandemic.

Eventually, the rest of this book was constructed on kitchen tables, in basements, cafés, bars, hotel room desks, press boxes, flights, and even a hospital bed as my family and I tried to become, day by day, a little less anxious.

Writing this book felt like a solitary process at first, before more and more people began lending their hands, eyes, and ears in ways that I am truly grateful for.

I need to start with my good friend and brother, Adam Kesek, whose edits, direction, and encouragement kept me moving forward. It's rare to have a companion like him. This book would not exist as it does without him, nor would my life be as enjoyable as it is without his friendship.

Kwame Scott Fraser came to me not only with enthusiasm about another book, but also with the freedom for me to pursue this story as I thought it should be told. Thank you for believing in *The Voyageurs* as you did, Kwame.

Russell Smith's guidance throughout the writing process was always a tremendous help.

Thank you to the rest of the staff at Dundurn Press who worked toward any success this book might have.

There was no shortage of talented journalists who were either eager to share their insights and their own efforts for this book, or helped me understand World Cup qualifying and to look at the men's national team in different lights, or were tremendous companions on the road, Dan Robson, Sam Stejskal, Pablo Maurer, Matt Pentz, Paul Tenorio, John Molinaro, Oliver Platt, Kristian Jack, James Sharman, Laura Armstrong, and Chris Jones among them. All of you do your work with pride, and I am thankful for your sharing of your time.

James Grossi's transcriptions were a massive help along the way. Appreciate you, Jimmy.

My editors and colleagues at the Athletic allowed me to pursue this book but have also continually helped and pushed me to become a better writer. Ian Denomme, James Mirtle, Jonas Siegel, Craig Custance, Paul Fichtenbaum, Alex Abnos, and Brooks Peck, thank you for continually believing in me and trusting in the work I want to do.

Sincere thanks to every single person who agreed to be interviewed and to share their memories, perspective, and insight.

Richard Scott, Sandra Gage, and Brad Fougere have been helpful and accommodating to make Canada Soccer players and coaches available for interview.

John Matisz was one of the few people I spoke to about this book in its early stages, and, whether or not he wanted to hear it, I appreciated how he let me ramble on. See you at Buddy's, Johnny.

Dave Lucyk is one of the biggest soccer fans I know, and I'm sure he'll appreciate this book in a way no one else will.

To Rob Notenboom and The Voyageurs: thank you for your blessing on my using that title. I hope this book has done justice to your fandom.

Thank you to my good friend Marco Sauri for the help with Mexican national team questions and for literally giving me the jersey off your back!

And to every fan of the Canadian men's national team new and old: The history of this team is a long one, and there might have been moments I've missed. Hopefully, there's something in this book you enjoy. I admire anyone who can stick by a team in their darkest day. You have done that, and you deserve praise. Enjoy the World Cup.

Finally, to my wife, best friend, and partner, Jess: nothing good at all, including this book, happens without you. Your support and belief are endless, and they are endlessly appreciated.

About the Author

JOSHUA KLOKE IS A STAFF WRITER AT the Athletic, based in Hamilton, Ontario. He has been covering Canadian soccer and the Toronto Maple Leafs since 2015, and his work has been published by *Sports Illustrated*, ESPN, Sportsnet, the *Toronto Star*, and the *Globe and Mail*. He is also the author of *Come On You Reds: The Story of Toronto FC* and *Escape Is at Hand: Tales of a Boy and a Band*, a memoir about his twenty-year dedication to being a fan of The Tragically Hip. When he is not watching or writing about sports, he is likely hanging out with his wife and young son and eating entirely too much pizza.